The author in New Square, Lincoln's Inn

(photogragh by Kay Brennan)

Time Past Time Present

Other books by Sir William Dale and published by Butterworths

The Law of the Parish Church
(1932, sixth edition 1989)

'I cordially recommend it as a book to be acquired and used' – Lord Atkin, in his Foreword.

Legislative Drafting: A New Approach
(1977)

'Like a breath of fresh air' – Clive Schmitthoff in the *Journal of Business Law*

'To the lawyer and parliamentarian Sir William's views might seem revolutionary. To anyone else, they would appear to be sound commonsense' – Marcel Berlins, *The Times*

The Modern Commonwealth
(1983)

'This is a voice which combines experience, erudition, wisdom and tolerance' – Sir Bryan Roberts, in the *Journal of the Commonwealth Magistrates' Association*

'It is remarkable for its sense of history, its conciseness, its lucidity and its perception' – Sir Roy Marshall, in the *Commonwealth Law Bulletin*

'La lecture du livre . . . est passionnante au premier degré, et fascinante au second degré. Car il y a un premier et un second degrés' – P. Juillard, in *Revue Internationale de Droit Compare*

Time Past Time Present

An Autobiography

Sir William Dale KCMG

To Rosey and Peter
our special friends
with much affection
and thanks for help with 'Beirut'

William

Dec 1994

Butterworths
London, Dublin, Edinburgh
1994

United Kingdom — Butterworth & Co (Publishers) Ltd, Halsbury House, 35 Chancery Lane, LONDON WC2A 1EL and 4 Hill Street, EDINBURGH EH2 3JZ

Australia — Butterworths, SYDNEY, MELBOURNE, BRISBANE, ADELAIDE, PERTH, CANBERRA and HOBART

Canada — Butterworth Canada Ltd, TORONTO and VANCOUVER

Ireland — Butterworth (Ireland) Ltd, DUBLIN

Malaysia — Malayan Law Journal Sdn Bhd, KUALA LUMPUR

New Zealand — Butterworths of New Zealand Ltd, WELLINGTON and AUCKLAND

Puerto Rico — Butterworth of Puerto Rico Inc, San Juan

Singapore — Butterworths Asia, SINGAPORE

South Africa — Butterworth Publishers (Pty) Ltd, DURBAN

USA — Butterworth Legal Publishers, CARLSBAD, California and SALEM, New Hampshire

A CIP Catalogue record for this book is available from the British Library.

ISBN 0 406 05187 9

Typeset by Doyle & Co, Colchester
Printed and bound in Great Britain by Antony Rowe Ltd, Chippenham, Wilts

'Time present and time past
Are both perhaps present in time future,
And time future contained in time past.'

T. S. Eliot, *Four Quartets – Burnt Norton*

To Gloria and Rosemary

Contents

I The Pad 1

II Almost a Solicitor 14

III The Bar 24

IV The Double Bar – Palestine 36

V The Colonial Office 56

VI War 68

VII End of a Raj – Sarawak 81

VIII Standing up for the Empire 96

IX Rise of a Kingdom – Libya 110

X London in the Fifties 130

XI Diverse Pursuits 143

XII Commonwealth Relations 156

XIII An Unexpected Announcement 171

XIV Beirut 187

XV Time Present 200

Index 211

I

The Pad

NOT that my father, born in the year the Duke of Wellington died, would have called his rectory, with fourteen rooms, outhouses, acres of garden and glebe, a pad. I use the word to denote the platform from which I was launched. My Cape Carnaveral was the East Riding of Yorkshire, flat enough, most of it, to launch any number of rockets. My father christened me William after himself, and Leonard after my mother, that being her family name. There would be no champagne – but plenty of water. It appears that, peeping through the circle of Yorkshire aunts, uncles and surpliced clergymen round the font, were two Italian gentlemen. Who they were, and how they came to be there, is a mystery. They may have been acquaintances of my father; but this seems unlikely, as he had been abroad only once, and that was to Switzerland, on a reading party. Or they may have dropped in to the church to view the Gothic font; but this seems equally unlikely – Preston-in-Holderness was no tourist centre. It was my Aunt Emily, my godmother, who told me later about the Italians. It is possible, I suppose, that at the font she had a vision: if she did, it was *ben trovato*.

My father was one of ten children, all born and brought up on a stony farm on the North York Moors. After a year or two as a schoolmaster he went to the Theological College at Durham, and was ordained. Most of his brothers and sisters became, or married, farmers. They all worked on their farms: fathers, sons, and – as I came to learn – visiting nephews. The women worked as well, housekeeping and cooking, and making enormous cheeses; for the hired men, who lived on the farm, had to be fed as well as the family.

My mother too had been born and bred on a farm, The Grange, Marfleet, three or four miles from Preston. Rose was the second of four daughters: Aunt Emily was the eldest, the other two having died in early youth of tuberculosis. A son, Herbert, came in the middle. Their father, my grandfather Leonard, born in the year of Waterloo, traced his descent from the Huguenots ejected by Louis XIV. He never worked on his farm; and when people remarked on it his reply was that it was a poor farm that could not support one pair of idle hands. My Uncle Herbert thought the same way, making it two pairs. Seeing the land was clay, suitable for making bricks, he went in for that. He did well, and bought a motor-car, with solid tyres, a blue Ford Trojan. Where the clay had been dug the usual pond formed, growing almost into a lake. When the Trojan needed a wash, my uncle drove in into the pond. The farm belonged partly to St John's College, Cambridge; and what the College thought of these proceedings I do not know.

My parents' wedding was recorded on a silver salver which had been given to them by the parishioners, and stood on our hall table to enable the (non-existent) butler to bring in visiting cards. The date was 16 August 1905, and my birth followed on 17 June 1906, at 8 a.m. sharp. The day was a Sunday, as I learned from copies of the *Times* for the Saturday and Monday given to me to mark my eightieth birthday. This must have been awkward for my father, as 8 a.m. was the hour of his early Communion service. In any case he disapproved of Sunday labour.

I can remember my fifth birthday, when I was in bed with scarlet fever. The coronation of King George V was taking place about the same time. There were Union Jacks all over, and the two celebrations became a little confused. My father brought my brother Reggie, three-and-a-half years of age, under my window, and told him to wish me many happy returns of the day. A small voice came piping up: 'Happy and glorious, brother'.

June is obviously the best month of the year in which to have a birthday, because the days are longest then. In England they last 16 or 17 hours. I look back on these June birthdays with delight: the sun and the warmth, the early morning bird-song, the endless twilight. On my sixth birthday my mother gave me a Meccano set, and I sat in the sunshine for hours, taking my first steps in construction. They were quickly succeeded by first steps in destruction. After tea I wanted a change of occupation, and asked my father if, as a present to him, I could weed his pansy beds. He was pleased, and said I could. I wanted to do the job thoroughly, cleared the bed, and threw away the young plants. He was not pleased.

It must have been on my seventh birthday that my Aunt Emily gave me a red motor car, the sort that one sat in and pedalled about. But between these two birthdays something happened which had a more constructive bearing on my life than any number of Meccano sets. It must have been in July or August, because I remember the warmth, and the brilliant afternoon sun shining through the large kitchen window onto the table, scrubbed white. On the wall outside, a pear tree bore luscious, ripening Jargonelles. I was sitting on the table with my arms round the neck of one of our two maids. She had burning red hair, and I can see it now, against her pale skin, the black of her dress, and the white of her apron. It was a moment or two of great beauty, and I have no doubt of sensual enjoyment. But from the drive outside the open window, there came the sound of my father's bicycle bell. She whispered that we must stop, and I had to let her go, and get off the table. My father had not seen – it was a habit of his to ring his bell to tell us he was back from his visiting. But somehow or other he or my mother must have sensed danger, for the red-haired girl soon went.

As we grew older the three things which mainly occupied the time and attention of my father came to occupy the time, if not altogether the attention, of my brother and myself. My sister Hilda, three years younger than I, was not yet caught up. These three things were the bicycle, the church, and the garden.

My father's parish was large, and contained within it three outlying hamlets, and scattered farms. His only means of visiting was by bicycle. A horse and carriage, or just a horse, belonged almost to the past, though there was ample accommodation for them in our outbuildings. The rural dean went about on a horse; but he was a dignitary. He was also absent-minded. On one dark Sunday night, riding to a distant church against a head wind, he reversed his horse to enable him to light his pipe, forgot he had done so, and, on arriving at a church, found he was back at his own.

My father's bicycle was a prim-looking model with straight handlebars and a 'step', a short bar protruding from the back axle. A rupture – we did not know exactly what this was – disabled him from mounting in the usual way. Behind the machine, his left foot on the step, he hopped forward until he had gained sufficient momentum to project himself into the saddle. There was always an instant after he had left the ground when we feared he would not land safely; but I saw him come to grief only once, when a hen ran under his front wheel. Rain or fine, my father went everywhere on his bicycle. In winter he wore black leggings, coming up over his knees, like the things the 'well-greaved Achaeans' are depicted as wearing. One Sunday evening one of the leggings fell off as he was walking from the pulpit to the altar, and lay stranded in the middle of the chancel floor until after the blessing.

My brother and I soon had bicycles of our own, a size or two too large, like our suits. Clumsy blocks of wood were tied onto the pedals, to enable us to reach them; but naturally they caused the pedals to turn up their sides to us. A little later my sister joined us in the red motorcar, but that had to be tied by a rope to my father's rear carrier, and made mounting more hazardous for him. Sailing the countryside, which was like the surface of a pond, we must have looked like a family of young ducks taking to the water. My mother never learned to ride a bicycle. My father obtained a tricycle for her, and occasionally she brought up the rear. But the tricycle was too hard going for her; she got left behind, and we had to dismount now and then and wait for her. She gave it up, and visited the villagers by foot.

For longer distances we left my sister behind with my mother, and went to neighbouring vicarages, to garden fêtes, and even, later on, for days at the seaside, twelve miles away. My father had many friends amongst the country clergymen, some of whom, to use my mother's word, tended to be 'unusual'. One of them, who had children of about our age, was writing a book on the history of the Greek Church. When we were all sitting at a meal, he would suddenly rise from the table, very awkwardly because of a stiff leg, and limp off to his study. We felt very awed. It was only a matter of time before he went out of his mind, as did his wife: both had to be taken away – we imagined in a kind of removal van.

My father was sensible, level-headed. He had no fancy ways; and he kept to the Bible, the Prayer Book, the *Church Times*, and the *Yorkshire Post*. On Sundays no work was done, and only religious books could be read. In any case there was little time except for church-going: 9.45 a.m. Sunday school (the Collect for the day to be learned in advance); 10.30 morning service; 2 p.m. Sunday school or children's service; 6.30 evening service. Add to this – after confirmation – Holy Communion at 8 a.m. or midday. My mother taught in the Sunday school, and was at church as often as we were. My brother and I sang in the choir. My father had a musical, tenor voice, and would start off a hymn if there were no organist, or at an open-air service. He always carried in his waistcoat pocket a small, worn tin box containing what he called his 'droplets' (Nigroids, still obtainable). He would take one before the sermon, leaving the box behind for the men of the choir to pass along.

A way through this arduous church-going gradually opened out to me. From an early age I had strummed hymns on the piano in our cold drawing-room, and later taken piano lessons from our organist, who had some sort of diploma, and used to cycle out from Hull with his academic ribbons flying. When the war came my mother had to turn organist; and I climbed onto the bench myself, and began to play, and to practise, in an uninstructed way. In those days two great difficulties beset organists: the intense coldness of the churches in winter; and, at all seasons, the need of a blower. The instrument was supplied with wind, as a rule, by means of a pump; but for some reason our organ had been fitted with the more modern invention of the wheel. The organ blower, Ellis, had lost his left arm in some railway mishap, but his right arm was quite enough. He took a professional view of his duties, and would only blow for an accredited organist, in which class he included my mother but not myself. (He also 'pumped up' – the water – every Friday evening at the rectory.) Then there was Charlie Gant, the parish clerk, who also was missing a limb – in his case a leg, for which had been substituted a peg like Silas Wegg's in *Our Mutual Friend*. This, as in the case of Ellis, in no way impeded him in his duties – barking out the responses, digging the graves, and playing clever variations on the three church bells. He was often about the church, but he would never blow. I tried to bribe my brother, but I was rarely successful. But on Saturday afternoons when my mother went to 'do the flowers', she would, out of the great goodness of her heart, run to and fro between the flowers and the wheel, giving it a few turns.

One Sunday morning in the middle of winter, the lawn, trees and bushes covered with snow, my mother woke me to say she had lumbago, and I should have to play for the morning service. I must have been about ten. Unready as I was, nervous, and sorry about my mother's lumbago, I had achieved an ambition. She, much disliking having to play, seized her opportunity, and never played the organ again. After that the church services, even the Sunday school, when I played the harmonium, were a joy to me. And Ellis would now blow for me.

On weekdays we two boys 'helped' in the garden. That was my father's word: we thought of it more as forced labour. The garden was between two and three acres in extent. A drive led from the road up to the side of the house, where was a broad sweep of gravel and the neo-gothic front door and porch. Up this drive had in the old days come the carriages, with plenty of room to turn round. The gravel had grown thin, and now its chief function was to supply us with weeds. The bicycle traffic did little to keep these down; and the driveway and the broad sweep had to be constantly hoed and raked. It was not a task for which one volunteered; but that was only – and I suppose was considered by my father to be – child's play. It was said of him that he could make everything grow; and make anything, and everything, grow, he did. The front and side walls of the house were covered with creepers, which had to be clipped. At ground level, following the bays and angles of the rectory, were sloping grass banks, like flounces, most awkward to mow. Looking from the windows one first saw the pansy beds (which I had weeded), and then, flanked by very large beds (all to be kept dug, planted and weeded), was the rectory lawn, large enough to accommodate in turn, during the summer months, a cricket pitch, a tennis court, croquet, and the church fête (the grass cut fine by a handmower). Below the lawn was a strip of woodland, with wild flowers (Nature's boon). Behind this lay the extensive fruit and vegetable garden; and at the bottom was a belt of trees concealing us from the road. But my father had felt this not to be sufficient. Gardeners, as is well known, like to extend their territory; and he had extended his by taking in, along the length of the domain, at the side opposite to the drive, a part of his glebe land. Here were many more flowers, vegetables and fruit bushes, a grass path (called the 'long walk') stretching from top to bottom, and lastly the orchard, of apple, pear and plum trees, with a quince, and a Siberian crab-apple.

All the grass had to be hand mown, the edges cut, the grass gathered up; the beds dug, sown or planted, weeded and, in a dry summer, watered; the vegetables and fruit picked, and some distributed in the village; the fruit trees sprayed and pruned. The work was prodigious. I never remember a gardener, though

Charlie Gant occasionally came in the summer to cut the 'hedges', meaning in this case the grass 'edges'. With his unoccupied trouser leg rolled into a cone behind, he extended the long handles of the shears in front of him, and appeared to have three wooden legs.

Naturally my father needed help in the garden; and we all enjoyed the results, as he reminded us. My mother was exempt; and my sister was not drafted, though she was welcome to take a part if she chose. My brother and I became semi-skilled labour. We were not allowed to prune, that being delicate, skilful work – enjoyable, we thought. I do not know that my father ever expected to make gardeners of us: it was simply that he could not cope with the garden in any other way. But my sister did become an enthusiastic and expert gardener.

My father had enemies in his garden – the blackbirds. They did not eat the fruit: they picked large single holes in the apples, pears and plums, and opened them up for the wasps, so that we could not eat them. My father shot the blackbirds; and kept for the purpose in his study, which overlooked the lawn, two guns, loaded. My godmother said he should not have done that, with small boys in the house; but that was after the event I am about to mention. One afternoon, when he was out, I went to his study, took one of the guns, the double-barrelled one, laid it on the table, and played with it. I particularly wanted to see whether it was possible to pull the trigger back, and return it to the cartridge so slowly that it would not explode. I did this twice, with each trigger, successfully. Not quite satisfied, I did it a third time, and the gun went off. Frightened as I had never been before, I restored the weapon to its place against the wall, and jumped out of the study window, getting caught up in the large berberis below, then in full bloom. After that, with what aplomb I could command, I walked round the corner of the house, and came upon one of our two maidservants – Doris, the cook, a heavy girl – sitting outside on a chair in a fainting condition. Through the kitchen window came hysterical cries from Ethel, the successor to the red-head. Then my mother came running out. Her relief at seeing me overcame other reactions. Doris too was recovering. My mother and I went to the study: I had shot a deep hole in the stone surround of the fireplace. My mother sent me to my bedroom, while she took my sister to hers, and we awaited the dreaded return of my father. When he came back, and had digested the unbelievable, he gave me a sharp beating with the heel of a slipper. He did not hesitate over corporal punishment when he thought it was deserved. (When I visited the rectory a few years ago the hole was still there. But the place was subsequently bought by a plumber, and he has doubtless plugged the hole by now.) It was most foolhardy behaviour: the sort of experiment that must end in disaster in order to be complete. It was the first of a number of rash things I did in my life.

With the coming of the Great War the two maids went. From then on the only help in the house came from Mrs Garthwaite, a stout, affable woman in a broad-striped apron and a cloth cap, who came on Mondays to do the washing. She had to light a fire under a large, brick copper, and kneeled before it, asking 'Now, are ye goin' to bon or not?' My mother did the cooking on the kitchen range, where there was also a 'boiler' to supply hot water. We took our baths in a hip bath. There was in the nursery a bath as grand as those designed by Lutyens, encased in mahogany with a lid, but too much hot water was needed for that. It was difficult to get any help. No one could be found to clean the church. We kept hens and pigs as a contribution to the war effort.

There were often soldiers in the house, either in khaki, or in blue hospital dress. They came to have papers signed, or for personal advice, or simply on a social call. Some, who came with their young ladies, were – it seemed – in a great hurry to marry them. My father offered the men cigarettes out of a packet of ten Woodbines he kept in a drawer. My mother made tea. The only drink kept in the house was a quarter bottle of brandy for medicinal purposes. Social drinking was not practised by the cloth. A 'martini' was a species of rifle: the Martini-Henry.

Occasionally, at night, a Zeppelin came. The Hull docks, and oil storage tanks in the parish, were the targets. During air raids we all came down, and my father would go out into the garden in his brown dressing-gown, as if to protect us. He disregarded the possibility of falling shells from our anti-aircraft fire. We saw a Zeppelin one night, caught in the search lights, the shells bursting round it: a sight of beauty and awe.

My brother and sister and I were taught our three Rs by a succession of governesses. They also taught us manners, table manners, posture, and the polka. It all stuck, except the last. We went on to a dame's school in Hedon, a mile away. Reading aloud was my father's province, and rightly, since he was a better reader than anyone I have ever heard, outside the cathedrals and colleges. We would stand before him, and read out passages from the Bible.

'Keep your voice up at the commas', and 'Let your eye run well ahead' were his admonitions, which it is a pleasure to pass on.

When I was nine, and my brother seven, we went away to school. Hymers College, Hull, is a large public school, a day school; but there was then a small boarding-house, and we went as weekly boarders. At first we travelled by train, walking to Hedon station; later the bicycles were brought into service, and we cycled the eight miles to the school. We had to ride right across Hull, and there were tramlines all the way. The instant either bicycle wheel coincided with the groove of a tramline, one was hurled from the machine into the traffic. That often happened to me especially, and I would scrape my bare knees when I fell. The bicycle had to be left somewhere to be straightened out; and, as scrape came upon scrape, my knees got into so septic a condition that I could escape football. On some Monday mornings we would stop on the way to have breakfast at my Aunt Emily's, who still lived with my Uncle Herbert at The Grange, Marfleet, which was no longer a farm. She made hot cakes, like muffins, delicious with Lyle's golden syrup, in green tins. I always liked to go and see Aunt Emmy, preferably by train. Marfleet had a station, and the station-master's name was Train. Their gardener's name was Bush. At Christmas Aunt Emmy would take us all to the pantomime, and from this entertainment we would come away with romantic ideas. I would play her some of her favourite songs, always nostalgic, like 'Little Grey Home in the West', and 'The End of a Perfect Day'. My Uncle sat playing patience on the dining-room table. They both married during the war, and my Aunt's nostalgia then dated back no further than the wedding: she requested 'The voice that breathes o'er Eden', and 'Lead us, Heavenly Father, lead us'.

At school I was not at first happy. I was bullied by the older boarders, and took against all forms of games and sport. I went about with a sorry face, and was known as 'Sorry Dale', in contrast with my brother, who was good at games and sports of all kinds, and was called 'Merry Dale'. In course of time, however, and by an all-out effort, I won the quarter-mile, and lost the offensive epithet. In the end, when I was prefect, Editor of the school magazine, and the Under-Officer of the Officers Training Corps, I was enjoying school. The Headmaster, C. H. Gore, was a keen amateur musician, and acknowledged me as leader, under him, of the school music. The Second Master, J.V. Saunders, was the house master. He had a beak like a dodo's, and was known as Neb. He was the senior Classics master, a philosopher, and he taught me to appreciate Greek and Latin literature, and to admire tolerance and wisdom. He had a splendid disregard for examination results. For the Higher Certificate Examination we had to prepare, thoroughly, the first eighteen chapters of the Acts of the Apostles, in the Greek. By the time of the examination we had reached a point half-way through the second chapter, the rest of the time having been given to countless digressions into philosophy, religion and politics. I did not pass the examination. The failure was not entirely due to him: for instance, in English, the two plays of Shakespeare I had barely read. I was too busy doing things I liked better. Also I was ill in bed with mumps shortly before the examination. My failure did not matter much, as my father could not afford to send me to the university. But I learned a valuable lesson: that to pass an examination it was necessary to work for it.

My brother was destined for Cranwell and the Royal Air Force, and did not take the examination seriously either. He excelled in athletics, both at school and later: the mile, and long distance running. He was a good shot as well. He possessed a powerful catapult. One afternoon he took aim at the school clock, which looked down on us from its lofty turret. Unexpectedly, he hit it, and smashed its face – it had only one working face. He was not beaten, as I had been for my experiment in ballistics; but his pocket money was stopped for a very long time. Neb Saunders was amused by this incident.

Soon after the war my father exchanged livings with the vicar of a parish on the Yorkshire Wolds, Wharram-le-street with Wharram Percy. He wanted a smaller parish. I disliked the move, for a number of reasons. The principal one was that I could no longer play the organ for the church services. We had to remain at school for the term; and at Wharram there was no organ anyhow. There was a harmonium, played by the schoolmistress, Miss Wallace, who was both organist and choir. Under a very wide hat, rolling like a ship at sea, she expelled gusts of wind in hymns and psalms; and with all feet to the pumps, as it were, directed equal quantities into the harmonium. The instrument was at the back of the church; and she always had enough control over her whole output to bow if we came in late.

Then my father was now only a vicar, not a rector; and the house was a vicarage, instead of a rectory. I thought this to be a come-down. The vicarage was smaller and, though of much later date, more primitive than the rectory we had left. There was no pretence at running water: it all had to be pumped. The house had been designed by the wife of the patron of the living, Lord Middleton; and she had failed to provide the vicar with a study.

There was a further, most cogent, objection to the move: the garden was a wilderness of couch grass and all known weeds. The outgoing incumbent was a committed non-gardener, and he had been there for many years. Months and months of toil were in prospect.

After an auction sale of our surplus furniture at the beloved rectory, the move was made. My brother and I cycled to and from school at the beginning and end of term, and at half-term. The distance was 37 miles or so, and there were steep hills. My sister, at Bridlington High School, travelled by train. In the holidays we all helped in the garden, where the labour required was penal. Most of it was done by my father. In the course of time he turned the garden into a show place. Admirers would be guided round it after evening service in the summer months. The full tour, with comments and discussions on the origin, history and promise of the plants, took upwards of an hour; but I was not expected to remain for more than five minutes.

The church proved to be an object of particular interest to architects and antiquarians. It was small, solid, Norman, with some Saxon work remaining, including a rare horse-shoe chancel arch. Neb Saunders came, with friends, and an unwieldy camera on a stand, and he got jammed at the top of the ladder in the trap-door leading into the belfry. There were other things of interest in the parish. 'Street' in Wharram-le-street indicated the old Roman Road running north, Ermine Street; and 'Percy' in Wharram Percy referred to the Percy family, Shakespeare's Hotspur. There was a second church at Wharram Percy, long disused, and in decay. The church lay in a valley, isolated, the only access to it being across the fields. My father collected some funds and had it restored; and in the summer he held the evening service there on two Sundays in the month. It was a romantic spot. There was said to have been a medieval village there, the inhabitants of which had been removed by the Black Death. We all thought this a fairy story. But subsequently the archaeologists appeared and excavated the foundations of the medieval village. It is now Britain's prize exhibit of the *genre*. It is a consequence of this, I suppose, that the church is in ruins again.

Summer was one thing, winter another. It was very cold on the top of our wold in the winter. The water froze overnight in the jugs in our bedrooms, and we had to break the ice to wash. There were great drifts of snow, four or five feet deep. The garden disappeared from sight. Thixendale, the next village, the blind vicar of which was a close friend, seemed to hold the record for deep snow; and until recently it regularly figured in *The Times* as being in the Davos class. Moreover Lady Middleton had contrived to place on our vicarage a roof which was not proof against the snow. When this came, as it always did, during the Christmas holidays, it blew under the tiles and onto the floor of the roof loft. My father would go up into the loft, and shovel the snow through the trap door into the room below, the box-room, where my brother and I were waiting to receive it. We reshovelled it all out of the window into the garden below – all of it, that is to say, that had not gone down our necks.

For my parents the move to the Wolds was a good one. My mother had a smaller house to manage, and my father a smaller parish. I do not suppose there was a population of much more than one hundred in the village and the outlying farms, which were very large. The villagers were welcoming, church-going, and friendly, and the farmers were gentlemen farmers. My father was happy to be living once more amongst the hills, and to have distant views. The Archbishop of York, Cosmo Gordon Lang, came to hold a confirmation; and my father, on taking him into the garden to show him the view, was delighted when the Archbishop said that he 'almost' envied him. Some of the neighbouring clergy were odd as ever. One had the sourest face I have ever seen. Another always wore a large white hat, inside and outside the house, kept bees, and was constantly stung on the face. They seemed to go for the white hat. The best was the bachelor vicar of Garton-on-the-Wolds. He left his parish first thing every Monday morning, took the train to London, and remained there until the Saturday. During the week death alone could recall him to his duties. He supplied the gravedigger with prepaid, self-addressed telegraph forms on which he had written the simple message: 'Funeral on . . . at . . . '. The post-mistress filled in the day and hour, and despatched the telegram.

In the holidays, and as the garden took shape, I began to recognise some advantages possessed by Wharram over Preston. It was in genuine countryside, whereas Preston was not. Though

I cycled two or three miles to practise the organ at another church – that of the sour-faced vicar, who strongly disapproved of such liberties – it was not cycling country. There were steep hills, green pastures, golden cornfields, woods and streams, and I happily walked amongst them. We could not afford family holidays, though some years my father exchanged parsonages with someone for a week or two, families exchanging too. And my brother and I would go and stay with our farming uncles up near the moors, bicycling there, seventy or eighty miles in the day. We cut down the thistles, took part in the haymaking and harvesting, and walked sick cows, who wanted nothing so much as to lie down. My Uncle Tom was the thriftiest of all possible farming uncles. Seeing me put the soap in the water when washing my hands, he told me that that wasted the soap: I should wet my hands first, then take up the soap.

A strict upbringing, no doubt, and during and after the war, austere. The food at school was thin. There we could say 'jam tomorrow' only on a Monday or Thursday. At home a cold house, paraffin lamps, paraffin stoves. But jam every day there, thanks to my mother's care and my father's fruit garden: Victoria plum, black plum, damson, red currant, black currant, apple and blackberry, apple jelly, quince jelly, crab-apple jelly. Even the blackberries came from the garden. My father did not approve of our gathering them from the hedgerows: they should be left for people unfortunate enough not to have gardens, he said. Or for the blackbirds.

II

Almost a Solicitor

IT WAS necessary to choose a profession, and of professions there were four: the Church, the armed services, the law, and medicine. Archbishop Lang had wanted me to go into the Church; but my father made no attempt to persuade me that I should do so, nor my brother either. I do not remember that he ever suggested it. One of my brother's godfathers was Captain Reginald Stock, R.N. (retd), a courteous gentleman with a quiet, slightly piping, voice and a finely cut white beard. He wanted my brother to go into the Royal Navy, which meant Osborne and Dartmouth. But Captain Stock found out that the rules had been altered; to pass through those two establishments was no longer a certain path into the Royal Navy. A cadet might be allocated to the Merchant Navy, which was looked upon as an inferior service (it was not 'armed'). My brother chose the Royal Air Force, then in its infancy. As for me, I had no wish to go into the services, armed or not, or to become a doctor. That left the law. But I had something else in my mind, at the back of it.

I spent much of my spare time on music. I had an organ lesson every fortnight, and I was allowed out of school to practise on two evenings a week, and on Saturday afternoons when I could escape football or cricket. There were three good orchestras in Hull, and my teacher was J.W. Hudson, the conductor of the Philharmonic, a Mus. Bac. of Oxford or Cambridge, and a thoughtful musician. But he was fragile, and died in his fifties. His orchestra was taken over by Sir Henry Wood, and I by W.F. Mahony, who played the horn in the Harmonic Orchestra. I played the clarinet in the school orchestra, such as it was. I accompanied much of the school singing.

I began to think of music as a career; of living entirely in the world of music, my white tower the organ loft of a cathedral such as Ely. My mother rather favoured the idea. But it did not survive my father's practical wisdom. He did not attach much importance to this world's goods, and once, to teach me the value of money, gave me a certificate of Deferred Ordinary Shares in the Hull and Barnsley Light Railway Company, which had become worthless. His view was that it was sufficient in life to earn 'a competence'. But he doubted whether a musical career would provide me with even that.

There had never been a lawyer in the family. But it happened that my closest school friend, Harold Payne, belonged to a legal family. His two older brothers, both of whom I admired, had joined, or were joining, the family firm, Payne and Payne; and he would do the same. The work seemed to be interesting, involving a good deal of time in the courts. The Payne partners evidently derived from the practice rather more than a competence, judging by the houses in which they lived. That was all I knew about the law as a possible career. Harold showed me a book on Roman law. It did nothing to put me off.

The law was decided on; music would make an ideal hobby. It worried my father that I seemed to have no interest in anything which would generate outdoor exercise. He was quite right; I had, and still have, no such interest.

A solicitor had to be found to whom I could be articled. Payne and Payne already had their full quota of articled clerks. My father's solicitor in Malton, eight miles from Wharram, was ready to take me without the usual premium. I should have been able to live at home, going there by train (we had a railway station at Wharram, half a mile from the vicarage). But I wanted to be in Hull, for the sake of the wider experience available there.

The decision on my future caused no excitement amongst my school-masters. They reacted as though the law was a profession unknown to them, and they wished it to remain so. It was not a distinguished way to leave their school, to become an articled clerk to a solicitor in the town. On the walls of the school hall was a series of boards (like those in old churches setting out the Ten Commandments) listing in gold lettering the names and achievements of departing scholars. I did not appear up there.

The solicitor to whom I became articled was Priestley Cooper, of the firm of Scott and Cooper, he being the son of the original Cooper. The founders of the firm, Frederick Arthur Scott and John Spyvee Cooper, were still about. The latter had retired to the Lake District, from where he frequently descended, in knickerbockers and walking-boots, to 'examine the books'. A lot of noise, caused by his boots on the wooden stairs, and his hearty voice, accompanied him; and the earning partners, Priestley Cooper and Charles Irwin Cockin, and Mr Day who kept the books, failed to appreciate the zealousness of his attentions. Mr Scott was Victorian in appearance and manners. He had a great Gladstonian head and broad red face framed by white side-whiskers down to the corners of his mouth; and he wore a high collar and stock, and a reefer jacket and stove-pipe trousers in a broad check. He came to the office two or three times a week for an hour or two, and sat at an enormous desk in the room occupied by Mr Geo. H. Smith, the managing clerk, and myself. Mr Scott seemed to attend entirely to his private affairs. He took a grandfatherly interest in me; and when I put into order the house telephone system, which had not functioned for years, he gave me warm approval. But he never used it, nor did anyone else.

I was instructed in my work by Mr Smith. We sat opposite to one another at desks with sloping tops, under a skylight which gave us plenty of light. Mr Scott, sideways on, with his back to us, had the benefit of a window giving onto a totally dark yard. Behind my chair was a walk-in safe. In the winter the first thing Mr Smith did was to put a match to the coal-fire. 'Subject to that' – as I was learning to say – he began the day by unlocking the safe, disappearing inside, and coming out with a bundle of deeds – any deeds would do – which he placed before me. From this material it would be my task to make out an Abstract of Title, the first step in the conveying of a piece of property. Under Mr Smith's tuition I took two or three sheets of stiff, pale blue paper, brief size, and doubled them over from the left, in narrow folds, so that, when the sheets were straightened out again, there were four margins of about an inch each. It would have been simpler to rule the margins with a pencil, but this was not allowed. Mr Smith had a ruler, a long black rod, which he referred to as 'little Benjamin' – 'their ruler', he would explain, his eyes gleaming at me over his spectacles, quoting Psalm 68. But the ruler remained with him: it seemed to possess a faint disciplinary air. The paper prepared, I went through the deeds in chronological order, entering the date and description of each, beginning in the appropriate margin: left for a Conveyance, the second for a Will, the third for a Vesting Assent, and so on. It was clearly a good way to learn about the practical side of conveyancing. Later came the real thing: a client was selling No 8 Gertrude Villas. The Contract of Sale, which had been drawn up by Mr Smith, or by Mr Cooper himself, and the deeds, were handed to me, and I began on the Abstract of Title. The delivery of this to the purchaser's solicitors was followed by the receipt from them of Requisitions on Title, a series of questions about the property, some of them inane enough, with blank spaces opposite for the replies. There might be Further Requisitions on Title. Eventually would come the drafting of the Conveyance. Or I would try to draft a Contract for Sale, or a Will, under Mr Smith's guidance. I do not remember ever consulting books of precedents – there were plenty of precedents in the safe. Mr Smith was a mild little man, with thin sandy hair and a pale moustache, but of considerable sharpness of mind. He would give me kindly advice, always looking at me over the top of his steel-rimmed spectacles, across the piles of paper which formed a ridge between us. When I went up the stairs to talk to Mr Cooper he also looked at me over his spectacles, but his were gold-rimmed. I was grateful to Mr Cockin for not wearing any. The partners, so far as I could make out, were engaged on business of much the same kind as occupied us downstairs, but did not actually do the work. They saw clients, and wrote, or dictated, letters, copied into a letter book, which I saw the next day.

I had bought a bowler hat, and wore it when I first went home for the weekend. My father was in the garden, and saw this figure coming up the road; but did not recognise me, and called out 'Good morning' over the hedge. He said the hat was like an 'extinguisher'. It was rather an extinguishing weekend, as I had to read out, as one of the lessons next day, Luke xi 46: 'Woe unto you also, ye lawyers'.

There was a Hull Law Society, on whose premises was a library. When I could find a reason, or an excuse, I went there, to roam amongst the law books, to make a closer acquaintance with some of them, and to investigate a point of law if I could detect one in my work. *Stephen's Commentaries on the Laws of England*, in four volumes, was the prescribed textbook for the solicitors Intermediate Examination. The title puzzled me: for if these were merely commentaries on the law, where did I look for the law itself? In the case of Real Property law, one of the principal subjects, I soon found out. It was the time of the introduction by Lord Birkenhead and his successor as Lord Chancellor, Lord Cave, of the great reforming Property Acts 1925; and it was made clear by the Law Society that candidates taking the examination in 1926 (my year) would be required to know both the old law and the new. Articled clerks had to attend lectures once or twice a week, and to us in Hull there came over some young man from Leeds University. He was obviously a learned lawyer but he was not always coherent. Occasionally he would falter, stop, and find himself in a slough of confusion; and we used to make sure of getting him muddled over the equitable doctrine of conversion. One of these young men was Ivor Jennings. From time to time I slipped into the County Court, where as likely as not one of the elder Payne brothers was appearing. Occasionally I saw a barrister in wig and gown: either Waldo Raven Briggs, an aggressive little man from London, or our local William Henry Owen, who was a lay preacher, and inclined to whine when he spoke. If the two were on opposite sides, they went for one another like fighting cocks.

On leaving school I had joined the Territorial Army, the 50th (Northumbrian) Division Signals. As Under-Officer in the Officers Training Corps at school I enjoyed the parades and camps, the authority, and I suppose the officer's uniform. My father had encouraged me, thinking that as a Second Lieutenant in His Majesty's Territorial Army I should be bound to have fresh air and outdoor exercise. He made a mistake, and so did I. We did nothing but sit about in the Officers' Mess; and I was no drinker. There seemed to me something hardly genuine about the whole business. Again my innocent mind asked questions. If we constituted the 50th Division, what had become of the other 49? And why 'Northumbrian'? If the place existed, it was certainly miles away from us in the south of Yorkshire. I pass quickly over the regrettable sequel: a notice appeared in the *London Gazette*, '2nd Lieut. W. L. Dale resigns his commission'. Resigning a commission cost money: we had to pay His Majesty one or two hundred pounds, found, I am sure, by my mother.

Then came Goxhill: I was appointed organist of the parish church there. So far, so good. But it may not be known that the Goxhill to which I refer is a village in Lincolnshire, some three miles from the Humber. To get there I had first to walk through the streets of old Hull with the quaint names – Whitefriargate, Bowlalley Lane, Land of Green Ginger, in which the solicitors had their offices – to where the paddle steamer from Hull to New Holland berthed. The crossing took twenty minutes, after which I caught the train to Goxhill. I made the return journey on Friday evenings for the choir practice, and on Sundays remaining there for the day. I had the use of the sitting-room of a good lady in the village – an ardent non-church goer – who gave me lunch and tea; and I had supper at the vicarage before catching the train back. The vicar was a low-church, simple, and obstinate man, but kind and friendly. He went about in a frock coat and shovel hat. The choir was poor, and sometimes went on strike, against the vicar, who knew nothing about music. The organ was execrable: it had only half a pedal board. Still, it was a job; and brought me in £12 or £15 a year. And on Sunday afternoons I got some reading done.

In the summer of 1926 I went up to London to sit for the Solicitors Intermediate Examination. There were four or more papers, the last on the subject of Trust Accounts and Bookkeeping, honesty and efficiency in which are very necessary in the conduct of a solicitor's business. This much I learned from the visitations of John Spyvee. The textbooks insisted on a system of bookkeeping known as 'double entry'. I did not see the sense in making two entries where one would do, still less did I understand why one would put any entry in one place rather than another. In the examination we were confronted, as I had feared, with the task of drawing up a balance sheet. The problem was to know whether a given item should go down as a debit or a credit. The lengths to which the authorities in these matters went in perverting common sense seemed to me extraordinary. I could only do what I had done when studying: give to the matter the best consideration I could, carefully weighing the pros and cons – we were given plenty of time – and if my mind said 'debit', enter a 'credit', and *vice versa.* In this way I arrived at a credit total in excess of the debit – or possibly the other way round, it did not seem to matter. What mattered was that both sides should add up to the same figure, and this I easily achieved by cooking the figure to be inserted in the side which was short.

I passed the Solicitors Intermediate Examination, with Honours, I seem to remember, in some papers, probably Real Property and

Conveyancing. I evidently satisfied the examiners as to my knowledge of Trust Accounts and Bookkeeping.

The final examination was three years away. I began to read for the degree of LL.B. at London University, which can be taken externally. I was not overworked by Scott and Cooper, or by Holden Scott & Co, as the firm shortly became, the result of an amalgamation. For me the change was not for the better. I lost my friend and mentor, Geo. H. Smith, who was offended by the changes and retired. The new (to me) managing clerk was not sympathetic; my desk was in a room so badly lighted that I had to work under an electric light bulb; and I found it hard to accept the new, and senior, partner, who was not of course called 'Holden', at all seriously. He usually came to the office in shooting clothes, and did not seem to me to be a lawyer at all. I spent more time in the library and the county court, and joined the Young Conservatives Association. I won a Public Speaking Competition. I became fascinated by what was called 'The Wireless'. At home I made a receiving set, and whenever anything became audible on it members of the family, including outlying members such as my Uncle Arthur, who had married my Aunt Emily, came and listened to the Morse signals with respect. I was elected to the Committee of the Hull and District Wireless Society, and eventually could hear on my home-made set the voices of the BBC at Savoy Hill.

I advanced a step in my hobby-career as organist. I had enjoyed my trips by water to Goxhill, breathing what was almost sea air, at any rate when the weather was good. But it was a long way to go, for a poor return. There was a vacancy at St Columba's, Hull, within easy bicycling distance. It was a young church, with a young and enthusiastic choir. The vicar, who had two other churches under his charge, was Rural Dean of Hull, and of exuberant vitality. My predecessor had begun to reform the music, by introducing a novel way of singing – pointing, as it was called – the psalms. That beautiful poetry came alive again. I went ahead with this, and there was a little trouble with some of the congregation, who found themselves tripped up in their singing. But the choir took to it all so naturally that soon everyone became convinced of the rightness of the 'new music'. One of the choir boys had a voice in the same class as that of Ernest Lough, of Temple fame. We won prizes at the Musical Festival; and I myself won the organ competition. My salary was £25 a year.

An organist has been described as a combination of a musician and an acrobat; and to enable him to see behind his back he has a looking-glass above the music desk. One Sunday morning a girl came through the looking-glass. I will call her Alice. Hearing some young voices singing 'Onward Christian Soldiers' with martial ardour, I glanced into my mirror and saw the sound came from a company of girl guides spread along the front row of the congregation. Nearest to me stood their captain, and she had red hair. Before the congregation dropped down for the blessing, and out of my mirror, I looked again. The captain's hat was bent up at the side, and I was not mistaken: the hair was a subdued but glowing red, above a pretty face.

Unluckily I had chosen a Bach fugue for concluding voluntary; and by the time I had finished playing, the girl guides, with their captain, had melted away. I could hardly give chase in the streets. As it turned out there had been no need. The guides were entering a singing competition, and I was soon giving them, on Wednesday evenings, a little coaching, in the presence of their captain, hatless. On the first evening, at once, I was struck by the pain of disillusionment: her hair did not seem to be quite that beautiful red I had taken it to be: it was less glowing, a shade subfusc. Had I glimpsed someone in the looking-glass who was an *ideal* Alice?

No matter. I do not remember how I crossed the divide between public worship and private places. It was probably the bicycle that brought us alongside one another. Alice, like me, lived some distance from the church, and bicycled there unless it was raining. Church parade occurred only once a month, but Alice took to coming nearly every Sunday. My machine called for her machine. A few months older than I, she had a job as a secretary, and lived with her parents in a house the ground floor of which was occupied by Newmarch, Ritchley and Mainprize, selling medical supplies. This shop was a part of the scenery, and had long puzzled me: I could not comprehend how it was that all these three gentlemen, with their resounding names, making the second half of a hexameter, were required for the carrying on of a business which was certainly not extensive, notwithstanding its proximity to the Hull Royal Infirmary. In the light evenings, when I said goodbye to Alice, I tried not to see the window display of thermometers, bedpans, enemas, and other medical hardware – and software as well.

There was nowhere much to take her out, but we occasionally went to a concert. Neither of us liked the cinema; we preferred the fresh air. We went for bicycle rides into the country; and sometimes on Saturday afternoons – we worked on Saturday mornings – we took the train to a secluded dale further afield. One Sunday afternoon I was invited to tea. Alice's mother was jolly, friendly, and pretty, with blonde hair. Her younger sister was plump, and friendly too. The father was dark, morose; he did not seem to enjoy my presence. I was only invited once. But not long afterwards, my father, gardening in Wharram, broke his truss, and asked me to call in at Newmarch, Ritchley and Mainprize for a replacement. Already embarrassed by the nature of my errand, I was overcome with confusion when there faced me over the counter, in a white coat, Alice's father. Looking up the name in his card-index of customers, he turned to me more disapprovingly than ever, seeming to regard my conduct as deceitful. Whereas, since Alice's surname was Glazebrook, and I had never connected her with the business transacted below, I thought it was his conduct that was deceitful. The revelation had no effect on my partiality for Alice. But when I later introduced her to my mother at the Musical Festival, and by way of credential explained that her father was 'Newmarch, Ritchley *and* Mainprize', the effect on her was less than impressive.

With my reading for the LL.B. degree, and my other activities, I had plenty to occupy my spare time. But I was beginning to think that life as a solicitor would turn out to be dull. Conveyances, wills and trusts did not hold my interest. I enjoyed points of law, which rarely arose in the practice of Holden Scott & Co; and I liked court work, avoided by the firm. But a claim for damages for misrepresentation on the sale of a business arose against an old client of Mr Cooper's, a lady who had acted quite innocently. She besought us to take the case. Its preparation, and the briefing of counsel, were entrusted to me. It went to the assizes at Leeds, and was tried by Mr Justice Wright, afterwards Lord Wright. I sat behind counsel, and we won the case.

This was heady stuff. My imagination soared to the Bar as a profession. But I hardly dared contemplate it. I – or, rather, my father – would throw away the £380 paid for my articles, and the rest of the money, and time, spent on preparation for the solicitor's profession. I should have to begin all over again: pay Bar fees, live at a more expensive rate in London, give up St Columba's, probably Alice; embark, with no resources and no connections, on a notoriously hazardous career. Moreover, my father would soon be retiring. But after much discussion my mother thought she could manage to find the money, especially in the light of the encouragement I had had from the new lecturer from Leeds, J. L. Montrose, a brilliant if unorthodox lawyer, who was later professor at Queen's University, Belfast. I was to complete my five years of articles, but at the beginning of the fifth I was to enter Gray's Inn, and begin to keep terms.

Accordingly, I went up to London for periods of three days, stayed at one of the hotels in Southampton Row, ate my dinners and drank the wine, and sat for the Holt Scholarship at Gray's Inn, which I was awarded. I was given an oral examination by Professor F. H. Lawson, one of Oxford's, and the Inn's, most distinguished constitutional and comparative lawyers, and this contact developed into a firm and, for me, inspiring friendship, which continued until his death.

Towards the end of this fifth year of articles I began to search the *Church Times* for advertisements for organists in London. In one a vicar was seeking an organist who would revolutionise his Victorian church music, at a salary of £100 a year. He went into some detail, specifying, amongst other items he wanted to be rid of, 'Jangler in G'. We corresponded, and I obtained the post. With the Holt Scholarship, I should have an income of £180 a year.

I wound up my life in Hull, saying goodbye to Holden Scott & Co with thanks, but not much regret. My father asked Mr Cooper for the money back paid him for my articles, but he did not get it. My last appearance at St Columba's was at the dedication of a new church building by the Archbishop of York, known to his Oxford friends as 'fat Billy Temple'. I had breakfast with him. He was friendly, witty, and needed many lightly boiled eggs to feed that enormous frame.

Alice was at all the services that day. I parted from my first love outside that shop window. She had come out of the glass, and behind the glass she vanished. We did not write.

III

The Bar

GRAY'S Inn, smallest of the four Inns of Court, lies in the angle between Holborn and Gray's Inn Road. From Holborn there is a gateway and roofed passage just wide enough to admit a carriage and pair, or a motor car, and a single pedestrian on the pavement. High over the gateway – it is actually over the pub next door, in my time Heneky's – a large clock, its two shining faces looking up and down Holborn, acted, and still acts, as a guiding star for anyone seeking the Inn, and a warning if he is late.

On that evening in November 1928 when, straight from King's Cross and the Bonnington Hotel, I went to dine in Hall for the first time, I was late. The hands of the clock stood at five minutes to seven. I ran down Holborn, through the gateway, past Francis Bacon, and into the robing-room, which was combined with a lavatory. It appeared to be deserted. But out of the cluster of black gowns hanging against one of the white glazed walls, there emerged a figure as if in camouflage, black-haired, black-suited, white-faced, one Smith. He hurriedly fitted me with a gown, and said that, if I did not 'look sharp', I should find the door locked. At this I lost my wits, and put into his hand a £1 note: that, and my rush into Hall, constituted a single action. As I went to the nearest vacant place, the Treasurer entered at the far end of the Hall, with his company of Benchers, and I heard the door being locked.

Grace was said in Latin, and we climbed into our seats on the long benches, the tables covered by white tablecloths. The dinner was substantial: soup, fish, meat, sweet and cheese, with a decanter of wine, or a pint of beer in a silver tankard if preferred, port and coffee. The cost was 3/6d, from which may be judged the extravagant amount of my tip to Smith. There were thirty or forty barristers dining, at the tables on the left as one entered, and a greater number of students, including a lady or two. The meal – the eating part of it – went forward at a rapid pace. We sat in 'messes' of four, and in the course of it were required to give several toasts: each one of us toasted the other three in turn, by name; then my mess, through the mouth of the senior (judged simply by position), toasted by name each member of the mess above it, and was similarly toasted in return; and then – unless at the bottom of the table, as on this occasion we were – we toasted the mess below us, which was reciprocated. Strips of paper were passed up and down with the names. About twenty minutes to eight a concluding grace was said, the Treasurer and his brood of Benchers withdrew, the door was opened, and one was free – but not encouraged – to leave. A few did so – it would be generously assumed that the barristers had work to do – but nearly everyone remained, drinking the wine. Before long, however, from the whole Hall there arose a shout: 'Up, Junior . . . Up, Junior.' It grew in impatience: 'Up, Junior . . . Up, Junior.' I saw that everyone was looking at me; and I realised, to my dismay, that as the last arrival I *was* the Junior. I stood up. Immediately the shout arose: 'Down, Junior . . . Down, Junior'. I sat down, only to provoke the renewed shout: 'Up, Junior . . . Up, Junior.' Bewildered, I rose again. The man next to me told me to ask for permission to smoke. Turning towards the top of the Bar table, and again prompted by my neighbour, I called out: 'Mr Senior, have we your permission to smoke?' It was granted.

After that the conversation grew louder. We students were largely strangers to one another, and came from many different backgrounds. Most were of my age, and many were at the university or had just left it: Oxford, Cambridge or London. There were also older men, already settled in life, having no intention to practise, but wishing to be members of a distinguished institution. There came a point during the drinking of the port when someone sitting at the Bar table rose in his place. Calling out 'Mr Senior' once or twice, thus quietening the hubbub, he addressed to him a complaint: that a member of the adjoining mess was improperly dressed. 'The customs of the Inn prescribe that members dining should wear a dark suit – whereas the gentleman in question has thought fit to attend in a white suit with black stripes.' He asked for the maximum penalty to be imposed for this serious breach of the rules. I could not help but look down apprehensively at the blue serge of my jacket clearly visible under my gown. The accused was called upon to defend himself, and he did so by asserting that his learned friend must to some degree be astigmatic, as he was in fact wearing a black suit with a white pinstripe. After further exchanges Mr Senior gave judgment. The suit of clothes in question undoubtedly fell below the standards laid down by the ancients of their Honourable Society, but the offence was not a flagrant one. He would not impose the usual penalty on that occasion, but merely issue a warning, which he did. On my asking my neighbour what the usual penalty was, he told me it was a bottle of port. Conversation was resumed, and I left about half-past nine.

My first evening at the Inn was more or less repeated thirty-five times, except that I arrived in Hall rather earlier, and the clock ceased to reproach me. I had to dine three times a term in the four terms in the year, for three years. I was not limited to that. The dining term lasted three weeks, and one was free to dine every night if one wished. But during my first year I could not do so, as I was travelling up from Hull. After that I was living in London, in what was called 'digs' in Muswell Hill, but I rarely dined at the Inn more often than I had to. I did not much enjoy these famous repasts, on which the Inns of Court place such great importance. Originating in the thirteenth century the Inns were places of residence and education for barristers and students, who took their meals in Hall, received instruction from Readers, and from the holding of moots, and attended service in the Chapel. It was a collegiate life, like that at an Oxford or Cambridge college, which physically the Inns of Court still resemble. Today's requirement from the student, that he shall dine in his Inn a minimum number of times, is the vestigial remainder of the college life. Dining in that ancient Hall, the gallery of oak from the ships of the Armada, the portraits of Queen Elizabeth and other monarchs looking down on us, was a privilege. There would be there in person, to stimulate our ambitions, Lord Birkenhead, formerly Lord Chancellor, or Tim Healy, the one-time associate of Parnell, who was Treasurer my second year, or Lord Atkin, the most distinguished judge of the time. But I found the after-dinner charades childish; and the one or two friends I made at the table I did not see at other times.

There was also the spendthrift tip to Smith. The amount, nearly 600% of the cost of the meal, was fantastic. And I felt bound to produce it every time – just as the Pope, as I later learned, having kissed the tarmac on his first journey to a foreign land, feels bound to do the same on every subsequent visit abroad. Besides that, I discovered that no one else gave Smith a tip at all, except possibly on call to the Bar.

I attended some of the courses of lectures at the Inns of Court in preparation for the Bar examinations. The lecturers were distinguished scholars. Sir William Holdsworth, author of the stupendous *History of English Law*, in 18 volumes, descended from Oxford to lecture on Equity. His words were difficult to take in. A tall figure with white hair and a large straggly moustache, he read his lectures in a thin, high, inexpressive voice. A similar performer was R. W. Lee, author of the prescribed text-book on Roman Law, but Lee seemed more human. Ralph Sutton, author of another classic, on the Sale of Goods, was almost jolly. We were a little awed by the great men, and did not venture to ask them questions – certainly not Holdsworth. He was said to be composing his history in the Codrington Library after dining at All Souls, taking a bottle of port with him, and writing all night.

I largely acquired my knowledge of the law from the books in Gray's Inn library, and those borrowed from the admirable Law Lending Library run by Gibson and Weldon, the law tutors in Chancery Lane, and read at home in my digs. These digs had been found for me – 'wheedled' would be a more accurate word – by the vicar of St George's, Hornsey, when I went there as organist. I had a small sitting-room, a small bedroom, all meals, and quiet, for the weekly sum, so far as I can recollect, of 35/-. I was more comfortable there than I have ever been in my life until I married. The church was a quarter of an hour's walk away, down Muswell Hill, and I was able to go and practise every day if I wished. The organ was new, adequate, and well placed, with a detached console, so that I could view the choir and congregation without the aid of a mirror. It was of course electrically blown. The choir too was adequate. The voices were not quite of the quality of the Yorkshire voices; but the members of the choir, boys and men, were musical and intelligent, and ready to respond to new ideas. My predecessor had rampaged, rather than played, on the organ, with the usual result that the choir had left it to him to make the noise. I accompanied them quietly, and their response was quick and noticeable. It was easy enough to be rid of 'Jangler in G': replacement by Gibbons in F took some time, but it was done. In due course I introduced a few young ladies into the choir; they formed a stable element amongst the more volatile boys, as at St Columba's.

The vicar, Dr C. E. Simpson, was an eloquent preacher, and a scholar, holding degrees in arts and in law as well as in theology. He and his wife were very good to me, and had me to supper every Sunday evening. They made me feel as much at home in their vicarage as I was in my father's; and Dr Simpson was wholly behind me in every step I took to reform the church music. He had a sister who owned a nursing-home in Welbeck Street, and a limousine. She put her car and chauffeur at the disposal of the Simpsons for a summer holiday; and they most kindly took me with them, exploring the West country and its cathedrals, finally reaching Capel Curig at the foot of Snowdon. There they left me for a week, happily, as they saw they were leaving me in the company of two young women architecturally as beautiful as the cathedrals. The girls were tall, built to last, and always wore white sweaters. But they were susceptible to the weather, and I had to climb Snowdon by myself. I found the mountain slushy. In the evenings we sat round a log fire, and the owner of the hotel interested us in the works of D. H. Lawrence. But at the end of the week the girls went back home to Birmingham, and I to my digs in London.

I began to pay attention to one of the young ladies of the choir. Cecilia was pretty, with neat blonde hair, and eyes the colour of honey. She had a scarcely noticeable lisp, being fractionally short-tongued, and the effect was very attractive. I sometimes went to her house for tea on Sundays, and we played tennis at her club occasionally. In her white shirt and shorts she looked most charming.

I worked hard for my final examinations – for the Bar and the London LL.B. I obtained a second class in both. Call day arrived, 17 June 1931, my twenty-fifth birthday. We who were being called wore evening dress and a barrister's gown, and I gave Smith two pound notes. The ceremony took place before dinner. The Under-Treasurer read out the names, and in turn we went up to the dais. The Treasurer shook hands, and said 'I hereby call you to the Bar and do publish you barrister'.

The dinner was especially good, and there was a glass of champagne in addition to the usual wines. After dinner the Treasurer made a speech, and when he and the Benchers had gone Mr Senior made a speech, and proposed the health of the new barristers. We rose in turn to respond, but most of us were shouted down. There was commotion and festivity, and it was a happy evening, except that I had no champagne. Crowded as we were on the benches, my neighbour sitting on the sleeve of my gown, I had crashed a sauce-boat onto my glass. It was not perhaps the best of omens.

I bought a wig and gown, with blue bag, at Ede and Ravenscroft's, price 14 guineas, and I was ready to enter chambers as a pupil. But the long vacation had to be got through. Cecilia's parents generously took me with them on a family holiday to Cornwall.

On my return I looked at the notice board at Gray's Inn, and saw an announcement about the H. C. Richards Essay Prize, awarded annually for an essay on a subject of ecclesiastical law set by the Masters of the Bench. The subject that year related to the rights and duties in the parishes of clergymen, church officers, and people; and as I knew something about this from the practical angle I decided to compete. I spent the months of August and September digging into old tomes in the libraries of the British Museum and the Inn, and reading the cases. I won the prize. I have always suspected that I had no competitors. However that may be, my essay won the praise of Lord Atkin, and he recommended it to Butterworths for publication. He wrote a Foreword, and the book appeared in 1932 as *The Law of the Parish Church*.

Gray's Inn had yet another benefit to confer on me. The Inn not only made me a grant of 100 guineas, the pupillage fee, but found me chambers in Essex Court, as the pupil of P. B. Morle. Morle was one of the busiest juniors – a barrister who has not become a King's (or Queen's) Counsel – in practice; and he was reputed to know the *White Book*, the enormous volume containing the rules governing litigation, better than anyone at the Bar. He rushed from court to court, appearing in two or three cases simultaneously, and at 4 p.m. hurried back to chambers for a sandwich and conferences. He never ate lunch, spending the time in the 'Bear Garden' as it was called, where barristers, solicitors, and their clerks, jostled one another to obtain the ear of one of the Masters, to get directions as to the next move in an action. Armed with the usual counsel's notebook I would accompany Morle to King's Bench Court III (say), where he had a libel action before Mr Justice McCardie; he would perhaps cross-examine the defendant, then he would leave me there, and disappear to Court VI, where he was defending in an action for fraud before Mr Justice Swift. In course of time the uncouth face of his clerk would bob up at the side of the court, and I would be summoned to the other court.

When Morle had a leader (a King's Counsel) this would not be too bad, but he seldom did have one. I had little opportunity to read Morle's papers, and I often knew nothing about a case before going into court. I was terrified that the moment would come when, in Morle's absence, I should be called upon to rise and address the court. That moment did come, in an arbitration before a tribunal of the National Poultry Farmers Union. We were claiming a large sum in damages for having been sold hens which we said had fowl paralysis, and had contaminated our whole flock. Morle gave the opening address and then vanished. I was left, without even having glanced at the papers, to carry on by extracting the principal evidence from our agricultural client. Floundering along, I hit upon some important technical point, which was taken up by the tribunal; and after that I left the running to the poultry farmers, who eventually decided in our favour. Coccidiosis, or fowl paralysis, must have been rife, because we had another similar case soon after, but we were for the respondent this time. The same thing happened: without my having read the brief, Morle left it to me to cross-examine the claimant. I had learned something about the disease by this time, the tribunal did not intervene to help me, and we lost.

It was all good experience for me, but not necessarily for the client. Morle never paid me a penny for the work I did for him. I was earning nothing. After six months of my pupillage I was offered a tenancy in his chambers by Clive Salter, who was practising in Hull, on the North-Eastern Circuit. The offer was tempting as I knew the solicitors up there; but on the other hand I must give up my pupillage and with it the second half of my grant from Gray's Inn. But the Inn was sympathetic to my needs, and I went. I joined the North-Eastern Circuit, which included the assize towns of York, Leeds, Durham, and Newcastle, and Quarter Sessions at Hull, Beverley, Northallerton and elsewhere. My first brief was for the defence of a man charged at Beverley with committing an indecent assault in the village where I was born. I knew the exact spot. I was handed the brief in court, where there presided Lord Irwin, later Viscount Halifax, Winston Churchill's Foreign Secretary. A Grand Jury of 23 men and women had first to return a 'true bill', that is, to examine the evidence for the prosecution, and decide whether it would justify putting the accused on trial. While they were doing this I had a chance to read the papers, and I could see no defence to the charge. The Grand

Jury sat in a gallery, and bills of indictment were passed up to them, and passed back, in a kind of shrimping net. The indictment in my case was returned with 'no bill' endorsed on it, and my client was discharged. I collected my three guineas all the same, and later joined the magistrates for lunch, when they expressed their views of Grand Juries, and assured me they would have a better – they meant a worse – case for me next time.

I never appeared at Beverley again. I prosecuted or defended at Hull and Northallerton (where the Circuit maintained a particularly well-stocked cellar), and at York Assizes (where I made great rents in the cloth of the billiard tables at the Royal Station Hotel). But I did not take to criminal work, any more than I did to snooker. I preferred civil cases in the Hull County Court. I occasionally went to London to see Cecilia, accompanied by the reproaches of my clerk, who thought I should remain on the spot.

But I was not paying my way. I had the expenses of lodgings in Hull, rent of chambers, fees to the clerk, and travelling on circuit. I had no income except what I earned. The solicitors were certainly not falling over themselves to brief me, though Payne and Payne were kind and helpful. The truth was that there was not a lot of court work there, and Clive Salter naturally had the larger share. My parents helped so far as they could, but my father had retired, and they were living in Buckinghamshire.

I decided it had been a mistake to localise in Hull, and went back to London. With the help of friends I found chambers in the Temple, at 3 Dr Johnson's Buildings. It was a small set, consisting of C.T. Le Quesne KC, Frank Gahan, and H.C. Leon. It was the pleasantest thing in the world to be back again in the Temple, and in such agreeable chambers. H.C. Leon, who was later a County Court Judge, and became widely known as a best-selling novelist under the name of Henry Cecil, became a close friend for life. Frank Gahan, a Canadian, a first-class lawyer with a Privy Council practice, and a tutor at the Law Society, was always ready with his advice. They were both bachelors. C.T. Le Quesne – 'Q' as we always called him – was friendly, an earnest man, a Baptist preacher on Sundays. He was leading a most miserable professional life. Having had a first-class commercial practice as a junior, he had taken silk – and then day after day he sat in his large room, where I had a desk, doing nothing. I only remember one substantial brief, on which he overworked, by insisting on an unreasonable number of conferences, which alienated the solicitors. Q was an outstanding example of the hazards of the profession: an able and busy junior, with a family to support, who ruined his career by prematurely taking silk.

Harry Leon had a busy common law practice, and was briefed by good firms of solicitors. He was a clever lawyer and a good advocate. He was able to put some work in my way, particularly in the Chancery courts, where he was not at home. Neither of course was I. On one occasion I had to make an application to Mr Justice Farwell, who always sat with his eyes closed and his mouth open. (There was a story that a young counsel had once flipped an ink pellet into the judge's open mouth.) I applied for the grant of a patent for the 'Eddy Beer Nozzle', which put the froth into beer. The judge at length stopped me, saying that those who 'knew the practise of the court' were aware that such an application could not succeed. This amused them back in chambers, where I drew half the brief fee.

Some of the judges were more cutting: Lord Hewart, for instance, the Lord Chief Justice, who usually made up his mind at the beginning of a case who was going to win it; Mr Justice Swift, who had a famous Lancashire accent, and would tap hard on his desk with his ring if he saw counsel whispering; and the wizened Mr Justice Avory, who was severe but fair. I once heard Avory interrupt a member of Morle's chambers, known for his somewhat incoherent speech, after he had been speaking for ten minutes opening an appeal, by saying 'Mr G, would you tell me, I haven't gathered yet, who you appear for?'

I was acquiring good experience, and making a little money. I was living in a boarding-house at 90 and 91 Guilford Street, run by a friendly couple named Walter. I made other good friends there. I was once again supplementing my income by earning – only £80 a year this time – by means of my hobby. I had been appointed organist and choirmaster of Christ Church, Albany Street, near Regent's Park – an Oxford Movement Church. The choir, men and boys only, was not quite up to the quality of the previous two. The organ, though limited in range, had three keyboards, and was blown by means of two pumps, the blowers, two brothers, standing by my side behind the curtain. Their pumping was distracting, and I found it almost impossible to stop them talking and eating boiled sweets during the sermon. I found it difficult to keep discipline over the Cockney choir boys; and one evening, when I was letting them into the church for choir practice, they pelted me with snowballs. Fireworks time was also hazardous.

The vicar, who had been an Army chaplain, was a martinet. One day, going to play for a wedding, I went for a walk in the Park, and got lost in that vast expanse, keeping the bride waiting in solemn silence for some time. This was incompetent of me, but I should have preferred the vicar to leave it to me to decide whether to waive my fee. He lacked brotherly love, and did not once invite me into his house. I made a friend of his curate, and on Sundays we often had lunch together at Lyons Corner House.

On weekdays I lunched at the Law Courts or occasionally at the Plane Tree restaurant, a pleasant little place in Great Russell Street. There was a girl who often went there: she had a pale skin, straight black hair, a long neck, and wore a small fur hat like a Cossack's. Russian, perhaps, I thought. I had ceased to see Cecilia, and had given up my old friends in North London. I became completely absorbed in the Plane Tree girl, but I did not know how to make an approach to her. She remained a painting to me.

For some reason I had the idea that in order to know girls one must be able to dance. I don't know where it came from, as neither Harry Leon nor Frank Gahan, who seemed to know plenty, ever went dancing. But I decided I must make the effort. Every day there appeared in the Personal Column of the *Times*, then on the front page, an advertisement: 'Gem Mouflet, teaches dancing, quickstep, tango. Accompanies out.' I telephoned the number given, and a few evenings later I attended Miss Mouflet at her upstairs flat in Piccadilly. She was not glamorous; but she was pleasant, well built, and had particularly strong, finely shaped, confident legs. She was I suppose about thirty, and wore glasses. She tried me out, in her one room, with a double-bed in it, covered by a brown rug. For a few evenings we gyrated round and about the bed, to the music of her gramophone. Some little progress having been made with the quickstep, she suggested I should take her out for the evening, to the Savoy. Naturally I had never been to the Savoy, and I was nervous about the cost, but Gem seemed to be a good sort, and to the Savoy we went. The evening passed well: warmed up by the dinner and the band I even tried the tango. 'We must come here next time,' said Gem enthusiastically, as we left. But the next time never came. 'Accompanying out' to those standards was much more than I could afford; and the brown rug was never disturbed by me.

In any case I had again to consider my financial situation. I could not live on my scant brief fees and organist's salary. I was already doing some lecturing – at Frank Gahan's instance – at the Working Men's College in Crowndale Road, but this was considered an honour, and was unpaid. Now he introduced me to the Law Society, and I did some adequately paid lecturing there. But it was in the mornings, and this took me out of Chambers, where I should have been sitting, waiting for work. To add further to my income, I took on some work for the Metropolitan College of Law, which conducted correspondence courses. I was assigned the law of bankruptcy – appropriately enough – but I knew nothing about the subject. I had to read it up in the evenings, and would sometimes sit up in my bed-sitting room (now a smaller room) far into the night, and without dinner, to correct and comment on the students' papers.

There were other considerations which were compelling me to face the fact that a career at the Bar was likely to be beyond my reach. It was a time of severe recession, and this had a noticeable effect on the amount of work about. Frank Gahan himself – to say nothing of Q – was having a thin time. Even at the best of times it was reckoned that it would be at least five years, and more likely nearer ten, before a young barrister could earn enough to support himself decently. And most of my young competitors, even if they had no private income, lived at home, free of expense. Then there was young Quintin Hogg, called to the Bar the year after I was, brilliant in himself, and the son of a Lord Chancellor. A friend of Harry Leon's, he was often in our Chambers, and I began to realise that some devilling was going to him rather than coming to me. I felt this to be unfair. But the Bar is highly competitive; and I have no reason to complain of lack of generosity on the part of Quintin Hogg in later days.

It was the hottest summer in London that I remember, and in court wigs were discarded. After term had ended paper work kept us sweltering in chambers well into August, and I still had some correcting to do at night. At last, towards the end of the month, I took the bicycle I was allowed to keep in the hall at 91 Guilford Street, which I used for going to and from the church, and set off for ten days holiday. At Waterloo I took a return ticket to Guildford for myself and the bicycle, and somewhere in the direction of Dorking I found a room in a bungalow with an overgrown garden. I remember little of this holiday except some facts appertaining to my landlady. I took a dislike to her. She was untidy, rather dirty, wore a large conical straw hat which she never removed, and spent her time in the garden instead of the kitchen. Meals were late and their content open to complaint. As the days passed she showed an inclination to be possessive, and tried to get me to stay and weed the garden rather than frolic off to Hindhead – where my father and mother had had their honeymoon – or to the Devil's Punch Bowl. She had the qualities of a witch, and I began to fear she would try to prevent my leaving at the end of my stay, by puncturing my tyres, or something of that sort. But I pedalled off.

I took a mid-morning train back to London. The compartment I entered at Guildford was empty. On the seat there lay a copy of the day's *Times*. I had not seen a newspaper at the witch's. Looking down the Personal Column (Gem Mouflet was still there) I saw an announcement by an English solicitor that he was looking for a young barrister to assist him. He was practising in Jaffa, Palestine, and there was a box number. I wrote. The solicitor, Mr S.O. Richardson, was on holiday in England, and I went to see him. We came to an agreement that I should commit myself for a year. It seemed a providential solution to my immediate problem. I should earn my living without giving up my career as a barrister.

My parents were dismayed at my decision. My brother was already out in the Near East, with the RAF at Abu Sueir, and my mother could hardly face the prospect of losing me as well. My sister was working at the University of Lyon. But I had to say goodbye to my parents, to Christ Church Albany Street, and to 3 Dr Johnson's Buildings. Frank Gahan and Harry Leon gave me a parting gift, and took me out for the evening. They asked whether I should prefer a really good dinner, or a quick meal and a show. I said the latter. They sighed, and took me to the Ivy. They thought me naive, as indeed I was.

IV

The Double Bar – Palestine

I ARRIVED off Jaffa on the Lloyd Triestino ship *Vienna* at 5.30 in the morning, when the sun was rising behind the hills of Judea. Said to be one of the oldest towns in the world, Jaffa is built on a slope facing the sea; and its roofs and turrets, a pearly pink in the haze, gave it the appearance of a fairy city. It was a moment of beauty, and of excitement. The P & O liner *Strathaird*, bound for India, full of E. M. Forster characters, with some of whom I had made friends, had dropped me at Port Said. I was alone. From the *Vienna* I was put into a lighter, containing a customs officer. As we chugged softly into port, in the bright sun, he asked me what was in the large flat box, which I suppose did look like a crate of ammunition. I explained that it was a parting gift from friends. 'It is a keyboard', I said. 'Ah! A musical instrument. There is a duty of 100% *ad valorem.*' 'No', I said, 'it makes no sound.' 'A silent typewriter?' he asked; 'Duty of 33 1/3% *ad valorem.*' 'No again,' I said. 'It is like the sawn-off keyboard of a small piano.' 'But what is it for?' 'To keep one's fingers supple.' The officer looked into his loose-leaf book. 'A sports appliance then, duty nil.'

A taxi took me to the Jerusalem hotel, the better of Jaffa's two hotels. It was owned by a German family named Hardegg, strong Protestants, who had been there since Turkish times. They had named the bedrooms after the books of the Bible. Looking down the corridor, I read 'ISAIAH . . . JEREMIAH . . . EZEKIEL . . . GENTLEMEN . . . DANIEL . . . ' A bustling little Arab installed me *chez* RUTH. Above the door, inside, hung a text in fret-work:

'ABIDE HERE FAST Ruth ii 8.' I placed the sports appliance on the table, and unpacked.

After breakfast I went to the office. It was not far from the hotel, but Richardson had sent his car for me. As we drove down one of the main streets I was forced to conclude that Jaffa within was very different from the enchanted city I thought I had seen from without. The streets were poor, the buildings shabby, near to decay; the people, all Arabs, were miserably clothed, dirty, some in rags. Through the open windows of the car there entered, not the perfumes of Arabia, but a mixture of nasty smells.

We slowed down at a blank wall, across which was painted, in large, unsteady capitals, 'PROHIBITED TO PISS HERE.' 'Glad to know,' I thought to myself, as the car drew up round the corner. Cassim, the driver, took me up an outside staircase to the first floor, where was a brass plate: 'Richardson, Turtledove & Co, Solicitors'. Richardson, sitting at his desk, and not wasting time by enquiring about my journey, talked about the work, the clients, and the general state of Palestine under the British. A solicitor from Birmingham, he had been in the army during the 1914-18 war, had ended his service in Palestine, and had remained there. In his fifties, he had a sharp but good-tempered face, thin whiteish hair, grey eyes, a parchment skin, and a very wrinkled forehead. As he talked, he tended to look away from me, in the direction of the window, which was over the street. The sound of Arabic gutterals came up, and of great expectorations.

Richardson took me along to his two partners, whose names I had seen on the notepaper: 'S. Turtledove, Member of the South African Bar, Advocate at Palestine Bar,' and 'J. Papo, Advocate at Palestine Bar.' Turtledove, about forty, was indeed like a bird, almost the skeleton of one, with a white, feminine face, and a very long beak. Papo, in the next room, was younger, thick-set, bouncing, of warm friendliness, and with a lively sense of fun. He was a Palestinian, a Jew of Spanish origin, a bachelor. Turtledove, born in South Africa, married, concerned himself solely with the Jewish clients. Papo, less discriminatory, brought in anyone he could lay hands on. He was competitive. He had once thrown an icecream at a near-naked rival advocate on the beach at Tel Aviv. On the way to my room Richardson introduced me to the clerks present. As it was a Friday, the Arab staff was not there. The room I was to occupy was bare except for a desk in light wood, locally made, the top covered by a sheet of glass, and a chair or two. The double window stood wide open: I smelled urine and looked out. Richardson explained: the merchant who was his neighbour had put up the prohibition notice, with the result that those in need used the yard beneath my window. He was bringing an action against the merchant – exactly what the cause of action would be I did not gather.

My employer had been a bachelor himself until not long before, his home the Jerusalem hotel, where he had picked up several clients. He had married a girl from Sutton in Surrey, and I had dinner with them that first evening. He had a house with a small garden on the outskirts of the town, on the opposite side to Tel Aviv. Doreen Richardson was not much over thirty, graceful, fair-haired and welcoming; and two or three months pregnant. I enjoyed the evening. They had an Egyptian cook, Subhi, a tall, dignified figure, sloping upward and backward from the bottom of his stomach. He wore a long white *abayeh*, and a red *tarboush* on the back of his head. He looked pregnant as well. Subhi had made the stew, and my hostess the lemon custard. Doreen called her husband 'Richie', as did everyone else. I never heard his Christian name, only saw it, in affidavits.

On Sunday I went with Richardson to Jerusalem, where he had a consultation. Jerusalem is 39 miles from Jaffa, and stands at an altitude of 2500 feet. As we climbed, we left the sandy soil behind, and the countryside became greener: there were olive trees and fruit trees, and vineyards in the valleys. The road became steep and dangerous, with acute hairpin bends, and Richardson, in his semi-Arabic, gave warnings to Cassim. The borders of the road were strewn with the rusting remains of wrecked vehicles, as on a battlefield. The new Jerusalem had been built under British rule, and it was a city of striking beauty. Ronald Storrs when Governor had decreed that buildings should be of the local stone, which was the colour of light gold. The effect was as harmonious as that of a Cotswold landscape – 'Jerusalem the golden'. The air was dry and clear, the sky a sparkling blue. I took to Jerusalem as quickly as I had taken against Jaffa. Old Jerusalem was best looked upon as a museum with live exhibits. It was dirtier and smellier than Jaffa; the cobbled streets, some eight feet in width, were largely built over; and the inhabitants were sitting about amongst the donkeys and hens, and the baskets of fruit and bread, all covered with flies. Throughout Jerusalem was to be seen an astonishing variety of nationalities and costumes.

Our conference was with a leading Arab lawyer named Abuhadra. He was an impressive and affable old rogue, who had been a judge. Adapting himself to the new regime, he wore a brown European suit with a *tarboush.*

Richie and I spent the night at the King David Hotel, luxurious in its oriental magnificence. He said it was the most expensive hotel in the world – but not for him, as he had special rates. I cannot remember what our case the next day was about. The court was composed of a British president and two Palestinian judges. I remember the president telling the advocate on the other side that he had not put down half his claim, and the lawyer's reply that there was no more room on the form. But the real point argued was whether there should be a majority of British judges on the court, for which Richie strongly pressed. His request not being granted, he obtained an adjournment, and went to see the British judge in his room. He came out with a smiling face.

Back in Jaffa, at sea level, I felt depressed. I went through the motions of playing a Bach prelude on my appliance, but the dumb thing only deepened my frustration. I had asked my friends in chambers for a stupid present. I had better have done as Albert Schweitzer did in the Belgian Congo, and practised with my fingers on the table and my feet on the floor.

I went down to dinner. I intended to keep a diary, and I took my black exercise book with me. A menu went the round of twenty tables, and I jotted it down:

Dinner the 20th November 1933

the landladies soup

—

beef tongue
green peas

—

mutton cutlets
boiled potatoes
beetroots

—

stuffed tarte

—

Fruits
Turkish Coffee

My diary continues –

> We are waited on by a lanky African in trousers and a white jacket, and a little Arab in a white dress. The African gives an 'a'right' to everything you say, whether he understands or not: the latter clatters about making a dreadful slushing noise with his lips, and barks at you. The chief efficiency of both is to take your plate away before you have finished what is on it, but no one is very sorry to say goodbye. The proprietor's son makes a speciality of hovering in the background, with the rubber-bodied suavity of a Savoy waiter, with a dish of beetroot. On my left front sits the lean judge of the district court, who, in a voice the sound of thin shrapnel, complains about the butter. In front sits a fat Norwegian, who looks like a great toad, sitting with his knees open and his hand on his stomach. On the arrival of the soup there is immediately heard a gentle soughing . . .

Next morning I went to the Ottoman Bank to open an account with the three months salary sadly paid to me in advance by Richardson. The full blast of garlic across the counter from four-and-twenty bank clerks drove me back to the wall. I sent the office boy in future.

The office of Richardson, Turtledove & Co never closed: the Moslems had Friday off, the Jews Saturday and the Christians Sunday. So a Palestinian weekend lasted three days, when it was never Sunday, yet always Sunday. I did not go to the office on any afternoon, but remained in the hotel to work for the Advocates Examination, the following February or March. I began a series of letters to Harry Leon, which he kept, and later returned to me. I shall frequently quote from the letters and the diary as giving the truest picture of my thoughts and impressions at the time, jejune though they may be.

In one early letter I told Harry that I found the English in Jaffa generally uncongenial, uncultured, and some untrustworthy. One of our clients, Kelley, a partner in a fruit firm, was indeed a pathological liar. The hotel was a place of desolation, the food uneatable. I even lamented the lack of exercise.

> There is nowhere to walk except on the beach, and it takes a long time to get there. I thought of skipping and tried to buy a length of rope, but nobody would sell me a piece. I suppose they thought I wanted to hang myself.
>
> On the credit side, the work in the office is varied, interesting and substantial. One day we have the local manager of the Imperial

Tobacco Co wanting help with his business; the next a police officer comes in with the pathetic request to know whether he is married or not. We have letters from all over the world, and there are innumerable problems in Conflict of Laws . . .

The weather is very pleasant now. Almost continual sunshine, with a slight nip; and the oranges are ripening. I shall send you a case.

Ramadan came. Nothing passed the lips of the Moslems between sunrise and sunset. The office boy would not lick the stamps. But I was overcome by joy when Harold Hardegg came to my room to tell me that I could play the organ in the German church when I liked – at 5 piastres an hour. I went straightaway. It was a poor contraption.

My diary proceeds –

20 December I go to Richie's at 6.30. Cassim has refused to eat in the house and gone home against R's express orders. We go in the car to fetch the judge (whose name is Copland) from the hotel, but he has ordered his own car. When we get back we find Cassim has arrived whimpering, and he is forgiven.

R. spoke of the 'good old custom' of sending servants to the police for a beating, with a note. He had a good servant in Egypt just after the war, but sometimes he was a nuisance. On one occasion R. sent him to the police; but the man gave a friend 2 piastres to deliver the note, and was never heard of again.

Judge Copland tells us that during the afternoon he was asked to settle a dispute between the wives of his two process servers, but he turned them out. This led him to relate how the wives of two of the judges in Jerusalem (Baker and someone else) had a violent quarrel over the garden wall, and Mrs Baker threw the other's cat over the wall. The quarrel went to the other judges, the Chief Justice, and finally to the High Commissioner. But it had not abated.

The judge is being very party-mannered; and I feel pleased with myself as, when we are saying our goodbyes, I manoeuvre him into a corner, where he steps backwards, knocks over a table, and smashes two expensive glasses.

22 December The judge is still complaining – he is expected to grant an injunction against the further appearance of red cheese.

Papo and Turtledove very nearly fight this morning (Richardson being away for 10 days).

23 December At a party I meet one or two new people – one nice couple named Bundy. I hear of the man who went to a hotel in Gaza for the night, and was taken to a large empty room where they speedily put up a bed. He was tired and went to sleep. When he woke up in the morning he found twelve other people there. Someone tells me of his preliminary interview at the Cliff hotel here – the manager stood talking, and a cockroach slowly climbed up his trouser leg and over his stomach and finally into his waistcoat pocket.

After the party I go to a piano recital at the Ohel-Shem hall in Tel Aviv. Large uncomfortable hall, full and people standing. Concert begins 20 minutes late. Every one of the audience is a Jew: I am nearly in the front row. The audience will not sit down until the pianist comes in. During the concluding fugue of the Bach-Busoni Fantasia a spider descends on my head. I manage to beat it off without serious disturbance, but it could only have gone up its web ready to pounce again. At the interval I try to change my seat, but without success.

The Jews are bad-mannered. They make some approach towards a civilisation and culture in Palestine, which is more than the British do. But they shove, shove, stand blocking the gangways, move in the wrong directions, and not a word of apology.

Christmas Eve I go with Papo to tea with two Jewish (Palestinian) girl friends of his, in their house in Tel Aviv. People constantly come in. Various girls keep arriving though they do not come into the room we are in, until I begin to think the place must be a brothel. All the others speak Hebrew, and seem surprised that I do not. There is a piano and I play to them, and one of the girls sings and plays a Schubert song well. They are all very nice indeed, and the singer-pianist rather charming.

I don't know that I can continue to think the Jews have no manners. They all listened like mice while I played, and while the girl sang. Whereas Kelley reads, and his friends talk!

We drink tea, and eat a piece of cake with a spoon. After that I go with Papo to the Palatine hotel, where there is a tea dance. Rather bored and do not stay long. I mention to Papo about the manners, but he says this is merely the rude among them. Still, Papo hops off as soon as I have ordered a drink for him, and dances – 'duty dances' he says.

Have the Jews much of a sense of humour? I made a good story out of the spider for them, and they all remained perfectly solemn.

At the hotel Harold Hardegg was giving a party for his family and the servants, and they were singing German chorales in four parts. Next morning, Christmas Day, Aziz, the Arab waiter, came to my room with a Christmas card, and a bottle of champagne and some pastries, from the Hardeggs. I invited the judge to share the refreshments, but he had received a like gift, and knew the champagne would be flat and the pastries stale. We drank some gin in his room, and had lunch together.

In the New Year I went to Jerusalem to appear in an arbitration arising out of the Jerusalem main drainage scheme, which had imaginatively provided for our clients to build a large sewer under a Moslem cemetery. There was snow in Jerusalem. Back in Jaffa the thunderstorms and rains began, and continued for some days.

Ramadan was due to end on 16 January with the new moon, and the Arabs had organised anti-Jewish demonstrations for the day. It was then not so much the rate of immigration that was troubling them, as the fact that areas of land were being sold, by their own people, to the Jews. The Arabs were coming into the towns for the day, and battalions of Royal Scots arrived. The day came; but the moon was not sighted. The feast day was postponed, and the demonstrations fizzled out accordingly. It was the moon's fault.

My brother Reggie managed to fly over from Egypt, via Transjordan and Ramleh, but he was with me for only an hour or two. My social life intensified. I went to a fancy dress party, conceived as in the style of Louis Quatorze. This was beyond my resources, and I borrowed the day-dress of the outside porter of the hotel, who touted for customers at the port; he parted with his clothes for a small sum, for the evening. They consisted of a blue woollen jersey with 'Hardeggs Jerusalem Hotel' emblazoned across the chest, the usual Arab baggy, white pantaloons, and a white *kufieh* for my head. There was no time to give the clothes a wash, which they badly needed. Before I went I showed myself to the judge, who had gone to earth for the day to escape the party. I found him sitting bolt upright in bed, with every appearance of being in court, except that on the wall above his head there hung, in place of the Royal Arms, a pink hotwater bottle. My costume was the laugh of the evening, particularly when the charming wife of the Assistant District Commissioner, covered in sequins, found at the end of our waltz that she was unable to detach herself from my woolly chest.

The examination approached, and I went to Jerusalem ten days ahead. It was tourist time, and accommodation was difficult to find, but they took me in at the YMCA. This was like no other YMCA in the world. It had been the gift of an American millionaire, and outside it looked like a mixture of the Taj Mahal and a public lavatory, inside like a blend of Solomon's Temple and Maples. There were two grand pianos, and in the concert hall what would have been a fine four-manual organ had it been complete. Many of the stop knobs were dummies. The millionaire's money had evidently run out before they could put in all the pipes. No trumpets.

To Harry I wrote –

The examination lasted ten days (with a Palestinian weekend in the middle). The object of the examiners was to trip people up, not to find out what we knew. About 40 Jews, 10 Arabs, and myself. You never heard such a hubbub and confusion of tongues. What with this, an attendant coming round with ashtrays, interpreters and general disorganisation, we usually started about 20 minutes after time. One day it was an hour and 10 minutes as the stencil had not been working keenly enough. There were a number of casualties. The second day a gentleman sitting near the door slipped out as soon as he had received his paper, and was discovered sneaking back later, full of illicit knowledge. Groups were from time to time discovered talking, constituting mutual assistance societies. And towards the end someone was found to have hit upon the ingenious device of taking away a blank answer book, filling it with copious notes in Hebrew, and then pretending he was merely copying out his answers. This brought the Roll of Honour up to four.

I like Jerusalem and I shall try to get myself established here. I have been taken up by the Archdeacon (and his intelligent and attractive young wife) who needs an ecclesiastical lawyer to help in the various messes in which the Anglican Church here finds itself. I expect an invitation to dine with the Bishop. I have already had a client who had been to see the Greek Orthodox Patriarch, and then the Chaplain of the Anglican Cathedral, who had sent him to me. He is an ex-Major with a wife in Australia, and came with his 'fiancée' to enquire how safe it was to commit bigamy in Palestine: would embracing the Moslem faith help? The Greek Patriarch was quite ready to marry them. The advice I gave them I shall not commit to paper. I think this is a good beginning. Almost as good as Richardson's best case, when he was asked to advise certain litigants who understood that it was no use offering money to a certain judge, but would a present of women be favourably received?

The weather is just now perfect. The tourists are flocking in and this morning the Princess Royal *and* Harewood arrived at the King David opposite. There are lots of Americans, who 'guess they can see what there is in this little country in half-an-hour.' They are entirely in the hands of the Arabs, who nag and bully and drive them; and I am constantly reminded of the lady who declared that if she had known there was so much about Palestine in the Bible she would have brought one with her.

With the examination behind me, I was able to give my whole time to the office. Richardson was the only non-Jewish Englishman practising in Palestine, and all the English companies, and some of the wealthier Arabs, were his clients. His fees were high. His way with a new client was to listen – his head cocked to one side and looking at the window – to half the story, then say: 'Well, you'd better let us have £15, and we can go into it.' One day, doubtful whether we ought to take a case on moral grounds, he sent the visitor in to Papo while we discussed the ethics. But in two minutes Papo entered beaming, holding up a £50 note.

Richardson was shrewd, intelligent, and careful; but secretive, and mean over money. He knew everyone in the country of any importance, and was Palestine correspondent for the *Daily Mail*. He admitted to knowing no law: he had begun to practise before Palestinian law had taken shape. He had some business interests, and was a director of Spinneys, who had retail stores over the Near East. At a board meeting, when Mr Spinney, the managing director, had said rather dismissively 'Of course, Mr Richardson is not a business man,' Richie had retorted 'I'm not a bloody lawyer anyhow!'

I wrote to Harry on 9 April –

> We are just now undergoing an alteration from winter to summer. It is not spring, but we are banged violently about from very hot to cool, until I suppose in a week or two the real hot weather will set in. Often we have the hamsin blowing from over the desert, which fills everything with sand and dust. I have bathed twice, but the sea is rough. There is a plague of fleas or something – I have been very uncomfortable for the last day or two . . .
>
> So our friend Moira tells you I am altering a little. For the better, so far; but I shall soon have gone far enough. I promise to cable when I do anything dishonest . . . English people here grow into dreadful liars . . . I have no hesitation in telling a client I will have nothing to do with him, if I think he ought to be told: but just now I have no direct interest in the profits! I am discovering that the Palestinians, particularly the Arabs, think that if you do not give them advice which will enable them to cheat someone, you have given them bad advice.
>
> I am not happy over prospects generally. Richardson has had pending against him for some time an action for negligence. The plaintiff is a Jew living in England, and he is claiming damages against R. for not complying with instructions given him as far back as 1928, in foreclosure proceedings. The plaintiff is an unpleasant man, and is also threatening disciplinary proceedings. Everyone knows about the case, and it is not a good time for me to think about joining the firm. R. worries about the case so much that he has

neglected other matters, and is often impossible to speak to. Other people in the office have been neglecting their work as well. Since my exam I have been clearing up a number of messes which never ought to have occurred – and writing more or less untruthful explanatory letters to complaining clients . . .

Two ships are stranded on the rocks, one exactly opposite the swimming club, and making a stink. We have visits from a series of more or less dishonest clients wanting to know how to get more out of the insurance companies than they are entitled to.

This afternoon we have had lengthy visits from two brothel keepers. One a lady with an old established practice in Cairo, who moves in the highest circles. She is very wealthy, clever, and still very good-looking in profile – quite a Mrs Warren. The other is a man lately turned out of Germany who is trying to re-establish his business near the office; and the police are bullying him.

I had originally agreed to go to Richardson for twelve months, and it was difficult to get anything out of him about his plans. But he had taken a house on Mount Carmel for the summer, and agreed to increase my salary to £400 while I meanwhile ran the office. I began to go to Jerusalem every week to lecture at the Law School attached to the Hebrew University. I deputised for Norman Bentwich, who had been Palestine's first Attorney General, on Public International Law, and on Evidence for the Attorney General then in office, Harry Trusted, who was occupied on a long political murder trial. I travelled in the Arab buses, and often stayed the night at the YMCA. I enjoyed the lecturing, and even more the change to the dry and cooler altitude. I told Harry Leon –

It is quite like the Law Society – except that at the Law Society the difficulty is to start people talking, while here the difficulty is to stop them. I have a mixed lot. A number of Jews (mostly German), Arabs, and a policeman with his head covered with bandages and sticking plaster, a fluctuating number of women, a few Government officials and, whom I like best, a tall, thin, long-bearded Jew in a skull cap, who sits in front of me and nods his assent to everything I say. Then afterwards he attacks me with a torrent of questions. Last time he was missing. At the beginning of today's class he asked me if I would tell him 'in a word, what the last lecture was'.

Richardson is mostly away now and I am busy. I am living in his house which improves life considerably. I have hired a piano – a most abominable thing, which smells. Everything is busy here now because of the Levant Fair – the other side of Tel Aviv. Eight weeks ago there was nothing but sand dunes: now there is a well laid out Exhibition, with permanent buildings, stadium, green grass.

The Fair has had another result. I have fallen violently in love with an extremely attractive girl who is out here from London for a week or two. She is the daughter of an orthodox rabbi: but she is anything but orthodox – most engagingly intelligent, and we argue by the hour. Most stimulating. But difficulties! There are the Jewish anti-British feelings, which she shares, and the British anti-Jewish feelings, which cling to me, though I do not share them. I want time – years of it; and there is only a day or two. The affair will slip out of my fingers.

There is an unexplored family of daughters belonging to the British magistrate. They live in a sort of medieval castle surrounded by a high wall and a moat in the form of an irrigation reservoir. I am told one has red hair.

But no one could come up to my beautiful rabbi's daughter, so clever is she. Did I say argue? Not always.

Again, dated 16 June –

My rabbi's daughter returned to England some weeks ago – she does child psychology work at Guy's. Her father was born in Hungary. Both his parents were murdered in a pogrom there. Her father ceased to be a rabbi when he got to England, and has been a successful businessman.

You ask about the Jewish anti-British feeling. I do not think the Jews have much real cause for complaint against the policy of the British Government – except perhaps the latter restricts immigration rather too severely: though this is a difficult question. But they have in my view a good deal of cause of complaint against the general incompetence and laziness of the administration here – as has everyone who has the misfortune to be compelled to submit to it. To take an example near at hand. The Chief Justice was given comprehensive powers ten years ago to make Rules of Court in all matters of procedure, remedies, and so on. Up to now next to nothing has been done. A good deal of the procedure here is most antiquated and reform is badly needed: it moreover lends itself to abuse. It is well known that the present C.J. (a charming Irishman, with eyebrows like little pigs' tails) is merely sitting still until he retires on a substantial pension (which will be in about two years time). Meanwhile the only Rules of Court of a general nature he has ever made deal with the clothes which advocates must wear in court. Yesterday the Court of Appeal gave an important decision to the effect that the funeral of an advocate's grandmother was not sufficient reason for the adjournment of a hearing.

But I have digressed. This is one reason for anti-British feeling. But I think there are deeper reasons – which are racial. The Jews here are not only a race but a nation – or at any rate their object is to be a nation. They are apt to ignore completely the Arab side of the business. They see within their ranks persons well competent to govern and lead them; and they are impatient of British control – and show it. This irritates the British – who are incapable of distinguishing one Jew from another, and imagine them all to be equally overweening, equally rude, equally pushing. The old anti-Jewish prejudices come back and grow, and in turn give rise to similar feelings amongst the Jews. The Mandate is of course a very difficult task – because of the unique position: we conquered a country, and then neither left it to the inhabitants, nor took it ourselves, but have given it to a third party. But John Bull does undoubtedly make the mistake of treating the Jews (most of whom are far more intelligent and cultured than he is, but not so polite) as if they were ignorant savages. One difficulty is that a large portion of the population – the Arabs – are indeed ignorant and backward. But really, if G.B. held a mandate over (say) Germany, would she send an elderly general to govern and legislate for it? As far as the Jewish half of Palestine is concerned, the analogy is not far from a true one. And the fact that only half are Jews, and the other half Arabs, does not make the administration less difficult, but doubly difficult.

But to turn to personal matters, I have been so busy that I have not had much time for 'exploring'. Last week I had a succession of skippers in to see me, all handing me charter-parties. Some of them made such lovely pictures, that the next thing I buy, after a car and a piano, must be a cinematograph. I particularly liked a Norwegian with a huge wet hand, an enormous size altogether; he had a very broad face, and beneath it a minute stiff collar and very tight bow-tie. Small piggy eyes, and rimless pince-nez. In one case I seized the ship. This threw all the court officials into a state of bewilderment, as they had never had such a task before. They asked the judge what to do. He said 'Nail the writ to the mainmast.' They came back, and said 'Which is the mainmast?' This move brought the Turkish Consul down from Jerusalem; but I held fast and I got our money.

It has been very hot here recently. It is very damp too – like living in a mountain mist. One is never really dry. I have struck out my own line in dress. I decided that cooler and cheaper than the conventional tropical white would be a pair of thin light trousers and a short-sleeved open-necked shirt. I am much cooler than anyone else.

For the time I stay here. But for how long I don't know. I am much dissatisfied, and often miserable. I had no conception of how depressingly boring life could be. I feel very lonely . . .

On 18 August –

After I had pushed the authorities a little I managed to be called to the Bar here on 30 July. Before the Chief Justice I declared in a loud voice in open court that I was neither an undischarged bankrupt nor had I been convicted by a criminal court of any offence involving moral turpitude. The C.J. then shook hands over the counter, as it were, and I was handed my licence. There were some fifteen of us. The C.J. made a short speech of discouragement, saying he hoped none of us intended to practise, as there were enough advocates already.

The words were no sooner out of his mouth than I was instructed in two cases, a criminal case and an election petition . . .

I have not yet found anyone to replace the rabbi's daughter. The whole female outlook is very depressing. I don't really like Palestine any more. It is more tolerable now that I am qualified and can do all the work; it is amusing (provided one has not been too flattened down by the moist heat); and even exciting at times. On the other hand, out of working hours, there is nothing to do that interests me except work, read, write (a little) and play the piano. I get so bored by my fellow Jaffarians that I hardly ever go and see them. I am very busy now, when all reasonable creatures (including even, I am pleased to note, yourself) are merryminded and on holiday. The man Turtledove, and the man Papo, are both in Europe; Richardson is half his time at Haifa; the managing clerk has left; and the result is that I have to do nearly all the work of the office, with a very inefficient staff. There is a lot of new stuff coming in too – secret purchases of Holy Sites (for fabulous sums); a girl of twenty married to a New York gangster, in terror of her life, and anxious only to obtain the baby from the husband; a rich old woman wanting to avoid the operation of the laws restricting devise by Will by turning her decrepit self into a limited company; a man yesterday bashed on the head with a chair by his nephew, his brother looking on, because he had bought his brother's land in bankruptcy; semi-fraudulent company directors trying to get a stay of winding-up proceedings out of a suspicious judge, who is supposed to be on holiday; a charming Polish Jewess whose sister has had vitriol thrown at her by her (the sister's) husband and is in terror of her life, but who unfortunately discloses the fact that she (my visitor) is married and living happily with her – very lucky – husband. All very interesting, but it is impossible to tell what half the people are saying to you . . .

Your question about how long it seems since I left England is difficult to answer. When I think of England I have an uncanny feeling. It seems as if I am dead and in another world; but if only I could just step back across the threshold I should be alive again; a minute and a few feet and I should be there. It is not so much time that lies between us as space and consciousness.

I was still living in Richardson's house. He would be there when he was down, and there was often a paying guest, someone on his own for the time being. I was housekeeping with the help of Subhi, who greatly amused us. His English was devoid of plurals, and everything was 'he', including the washerwoman, a cricket, and the cheese. Other pleasing eccentricities of speech were that prunes were 'beetroot', and paraffin 'paraffill'. But it was too hot and humid for me to want to eat; and the house was noisy, at the corner of a main road, and in a district where men shouted, carts rattled, donkeys brayed, dogs barked, and jackals howled, all the night long. Trouble from the Jews was expected. I was able to read a little, particularly Aldous Huxley. He used a word I did not know the meaning of – 'imberb'. I sent to London for the Shorter Oxford English Dictionary.

Papo had returned from his holiday in Spain. The Polish girl continued to come to the office. I could not understand why, as we had dealt with her sister's husband; and I mentioned it to Papo. 'She comes to see *you*,' he said, surprised that I had not realised that. I pondered. The girl was a beauty, a peach, blooming, voluptuous. But she was a client – it would be wrong. Besides, even if she could forget her husband, I could not: no doubt the family had a stock of vitriol. 'No,' I said to Papo. He shrugged his wide shoulders.

At the end of August I went to Cyprus for a short holiday. I stayed for ten days at the small hotel at Troodos, 5,600 feet up, where were log fires and feminine society. By the third night my energy had returned to a remarkable degree, and I did not go to bed at all. I went with one party to a dance at Platres, and on return joined another, risen from bed to ascend Mt. Olympus and see the sunrise. On later days I went for long walks amid magnificent scenery.

Back in Jaffa I found the dictionary had arrived – two huge volumes – 'imberb' was not in it. I took up my diary again, which I had neglected since I had begun to write to Harry. I find the following –

> *September 20* The nights are cooler. There is a freshness in early morning.
>
> *September 21* I have tussles with Eliash, the leading Jewish lawyer, and an able advocate. In the Court of Appeal, while waiting to come on, I heard one of his arguments with the Chief Justice. Judge

Plunkett (known as Judge Necessity, knowing no law) had given a decision which even he could see was completely wrong. He thereupon 'cancelled' it. The Court of Appeal held that he was unable to do that. Eliash was appealing from the original decision, and the Chief Justice said, 'But there was no decision when you appealed.' Eliash: 'But the Court of Appeal has held that the cancellation is nugatory.' Chief Justice: 'Yes, but the Court of Appeal's decision is not retrospective'!

H.E. (the High Commissioner) is not popular with the officials. He can be like a little country squire going round his estate. Pollock (the Assistant District Commissioner) and a Native (Palestinian) Official were going round with him near Ramleh.

H.E. (seeing some women in a field stooping) What are those women doing?
Pollock: (simultaneously) { Weeding, sir
N.O.: Sowing corn seed, sir.
H.E. (snorts)
A little further on they see another group of women stooping.
H.E. What are those women doing?
Pollock: (believing that the N.O. knows best): (simultaneously) { Sowing corn seed, sir
N.O.: (on the principle that the British are always right) Weeding, sir
H.E. How can you be such fools? Go and see.

Pollock and the N.O. set off towards the women. These, seeing the two men approaching, and the motor cars, grow frightened and begin to walk quickly away. Pollock and the N.O. break into a trot. The women begin to run, and P. and the N.O. increase their pace. The faster the women go, the faster go P. and N.O. until they are haring after them. When they are about a kilometre away H.E. becomes angry, tells his driver to blow his horn, and P. and N.O. trail slowly back over the field.

September 22 Subhi tells me this morning that 'pussy-cat he fall down lavatory'. I inspect and find that the pussy-cat who is Subhi has smashed the porcelain cistern lid to smithereens.

Cocktails with the Bundys (my favourite people) at 7.45. Then to Swimming Club for picnic supper. All very jolly and Eve B. most vivacious. A few dances, then a bathe. Full moon. After the bathe feeling energetic, efficient and sober, and I went for a walk into the moon. Its radiance was caught in the upward fold of the waves just before they turned over, and the light ran forward and stretched out in flashing silver ribbons.

September 25 I hang about in District Court all day waiting for my sodomy case to come on. At 4 p.m. told tomorrow at 9.

September 26 All the morning defending Mohamed el Mansi – attempt on a boy under 16 and against his will in the Apollo cinema (no offence if of age and consenting. Rather it is a national pastime, quite in accordance with Arab public opinion.) The complainant cannot be found. Judgment reserved until tomorrow.

In the evening two British policemen come to dinner. They join for 2 years, no previous training – police school in Jerusalem for 3 months, then job. They stay until after 11 p.m. drinking whisky and smoking from public school tobacco pouches. For an hour conversation entirely amongst these two and Richie, and is a sheer disparaging commentary on the Jews. R. was in his element. All his terrific weight of feeling against them carried him along, and he threw out remark after remark to their detriment, which was agreed and capped by one policeman (who would agree to anything) and less by the other – but he is naturally quieter. Complaining about lack of town-planning in Tel Aviv. How absurd! How can you expect an immigrant population coming in by the thousands (announced in *Palestine Post* today that Jews in Tel Aviv now 102,000) to town-plan? They must get something up to live in as soon as possible. The noise – the noisy men on Mt. Carmel! (Here I spoke for almost the only time – 'We have a certain amount of noise in Jaffa'). The lack of humour (true, but what else can you expect?), the arrogance (natural)! After an hour I think R. thought he was overdoing it, and the conversation turned.

September 27 Convicted – 2 years. Copland obviously prejudiced and ridiculously vituperative. Verdict probably according to the truth, but hardly according to the evidence.

Two very nice and long letters, one from Harry. Extremely sympathetic. What a very good friend he is! A Jew, and worth all the English out here in intelligence, culture, character and breadth of sympathy.

Two Arabs came in the afternoon about their bus. One a marvellous man: a yellow robe, large puffy face, a deep rosy pink all over to the bottom of his tarboush, with here and there a brown spot the size of a long pea. Round his tarboush a yellow band. I began in a bad temper with having to read through a lot of incomprehensible English; and because Richardson had seen them before, and the Traffic Commissioners, and then passed it all over to me. Then R. said I had better see the District Superintendent of Police, and I told him he should, as he had seen him before. R. told the Arabs (through our interpreter, Saba) that I would see him and they asked if I was a Jew. This made me absolutely furious. I don't mind being mistaken for a Jew. It was the gross stupidity and silly national partisanship which infuriated me. What does it matter? I was going to do something for them.

September 28 Rude again to Richie.

Turtledove returns, excited, talkative, and pursuing anxious enquiries into what is all over and done with.

September 29 At 10 p.m. I set forth for the dance given by Gerald (one of the clerks) at the City Cafe. I was, as usual, the only Englishman there – and I think the only non-Jew. I dance with Miss Jaffe (typist) and two South African girls. The South Africans don't like Palestine and hate being lumped together with what they call the Polish riff-raff etc. Many English and American Jews the same.

The dancing an amazing sight. There is a great shaking of the buttocks. One man holds his partner as he would hold a watering-can, and another trundles her along as if she were a wheel-barrow. The floor was extremely crowded but this did not prevent people tearing down like steam engines.

October 6 Subhi tells me that Spinneys' delivery boy has 'converted to be Jew and to marry Jewess tomorrow. If not good wife he turn back into Arab'.

And about the man who 'make the coffee mince'.

October 11 Kelley comes into the office, trying to get out of a contract. I note down his latest pearl: 'I can only admit having promised to make a gratuitous nudam pactum, which, I maintain, is easily revocable or lapsable'.

Pollock and Copland to dinner. They both seem reasonable about the Jews. The Judge really is judicial, impartial, about the Jews and Arabs.

Cassim skids driving Richie's new car when on a frolic of his own, and damages the front and mudguards.

October 14 I have to move out of the Richardsons' house as they are back, and I cannot face the Jerusalem hotel again. I move to the Ritz hotel, Tel Aviv, the best there. No Englishman has ever lived in Tel Aviv; and nearly everyone in Jaffa is aghast, and Richardson thoroughly alarmed. The hotel is on the edge of the cliff (if you can call it a cliff), and I have a corner room with a large balcony over the sea. Rather expensive – over £20 a month.

October 17 I have an enormous task to get what I want, bed moved, second bed moved out, boxes moved, chair in, marmalade. Two attractive chamber-maids, but one speaking no English, the other very little. I have to pay extra for hot baths but as there is never hot water I don't spend much this way. So far as I know no one else ever uses the bathroom.

October 18 By now I have all in order, flowers in my bedroom.

Physical culture much in evidence – rushing up and down the seashore, or hopping, bending, kicking, twitching. Am feeling much better. Sitting on the terrace to eat lunch my appetite immediately returns. Allenby Street like Oxford Street – long line of cars, a joy to see all the lighted shops at night, and everyone walking happily in the streets.

Very curious way of making the beds, with one blanket tucked into an enormous pillow case. Am I expected to get inside it? I do not know enough Hebrew to ask. Nor to ask someone to remove the cast-off chamber-pot, white enamel with a blue rim, which lies jauntily on one edge outside my window.

Big fine girls working with the men, in shirt and trousers. One laying bricks. A bricklayer is paid £2 a day, a plumber £3.

Papo and girl friend (South African) come to dinner.

October 23 I see notices on doors of doctors –

'Specialist in Woman and other Diseases'
'Diplomatic Midwife'

November 4 Going in to breakfast every morning I say 'Shalom' ('Peace') to the proprietor, who booms out his Shaloms with the solemnity of an archbishop on Armistice Day. Opposite me sits a man whose nose bends through an angle of at least 40° from the perpendicular, eating as if his one idea is to mix up inside him things from as many dishes as he can possibly get hold of. He ends breakfast by eating spoonfuls of jam straight out of the pot.

November 17 HERE A YEAR

Advert in Palestine Post – 'Experienced Housemaid wanted for Friday afternoon to Saturday night every week.'

I get onto the bus and find Cassim driving (at last sacked by Richardson). He loses the way. He earns £9 a month – R. paid him £5.5.

I had resumed my lectures, going up to Jerusalem twice a week. Richardson strongly disapproved of this, and of my living in Tel Aviv. He thought this last a blatant display of pro-Jewishness, whereas I was only wanting somewhere civilised to live. I found the Jews in general intelligent but ungracious, the Arabs gracious but unintelligent. This was perhaps, in a nutshell, why the British preferred the Arabs. But both were stubborn. Sometimes it was the Arabs, sometimes the Jews, who were creating the disturbance. Richardson would still not make any firm commitments, though he wanted me to stay. I ordered a car, an open 4-seater, a Morris 8.

Unexpectedly a letter arrived from Frank Gahan, in the smallest handwriting it is possible to imagine – 90 letters, 25 words, of his script would cover a postage stamp. After saying he gathered 'that at times you get fed to the teeth with Jaffa and find that the filthy lucre which flows in a persistent stream into your pocket is but poor compensation for being an exile from the pure air of Guilford Street', he told me that the Colonial Office was thinking of appointing a fourth legal adviser: if I were interested, I was to write at once. He said a good deal more, mainly calculated to put me off.

Of course I wrote straightaway. I heard nothing for weeks, until I was suddenly summoned to an interview with J. Hathorn Hall, Chief Secretary to the Government of Palestine, who chatted a little, told me the Colonial Office would ask for references, and advised me completely to cover my previous career – the Colonial Office would assume that any time not accounted for had been passed in prison.

There was another wait; and there came another letter, but from my mother. My father, who had been ill for some time, was growing worse. I booked a passage on a French boat sailing to Marseilles; and, not knowing whether I should return, I left Palestine on 9 December. I did go back, thirty-five years later – but it was no longer Palestine.

V

The Colonial Office

FROM Marseilles I took the train to Paris, went to the Folies Bergères in the evening, and was in London the following afternoon. My parents were living in Yorkshire again, and it was not until the next evening that I reached them at the Old Vicarage, Wold Newton, Driffield. My father was very weak, eating nothing, and he died on Boxing Day, at the age of 82. He suffered no illness, no pain, and seemed simply to be tired out. I have not much doubt that he had exhausted himself by gardening: once more he had taken on the neglected garden of a parsonage. He was buried at Garton-on-the-Wolds, the parish of the bachelor vicar I have mentioned earlier, where we had close friends. The church is a beautiful Norman and early Gothic building, its interior entirely covered by Victorian murals. From the churchyard is a long, quiet view of the Wolds, stretching north.

There came a request from the Colonial Office that I should go to Hull for a medical examination. My Air Force brother, who had arrived from Egypt in time for my father's funeral, advised me to drink three glasses of water before setting off. I did this; and I set down the result, to discourage others from doing the same thing. After a walk of a mile or two to our local 'halt', and a journey in a train which stopped at every station, I felt in no condition to undergo a medical examination; and I still had half-an-hour to kill before the time of my appointment. At the doctor's, the man was not ready for me; and I had to keep moving round his waiting-room table, bent double. At last I went in. 'Make yourself comfortable,' he said, indicating an armchair. 'I shall ask you a few questions before I begin to knock you about.' 'If you please, doctor,' I said, and explained my predicament. He sent me into a corner with a capacious vessel. Time went by. I could hear him fidgeting with his papers, then stepping to the window and snipping at his nails. When I at last handed over my receptacle, he said he had never known anyone before to fill the beaker. 'You must be more nervous than you look,' he added. He disappeared, reappeared, looking cross. 'Not a drop of urine there,' he said; 'pure water.'

The Colonial Office was evidently satisfied, however, for a letter came offering me the post of Legal Assistant at a commencing salary of £365 a year. A few days after that I found myself entering the small doorway in Downing Street opposite No 10, and I was shown in to Sir Grattan Bushe, the Legal Adviser. He occupied an imposing room on the first floor, two or three doors away from that of the Secretary of State himself. Bushe was a small spare man with flat grey hair, glinting brown eyes, and an impish look. He gave me a sound piece of advice: not to commit myself to paper for several days. He took me next door to the Assistant Legal Adviser, Harold Duncan; and he was not long in handing me over to the Second Assistant Legal Adviser, Kenneth Roberts-Wray. I was to share a room with him, but the room was not yet ready; and I was installed at a long table in the legal section of the library. While I waited for something to happen, I looked about me. The library was the size of a reasonable church, well lighted, with a number of studious figures sitting at tables in shirt sleeves, and – a curious feature – a gigantic reticulated python sailing through the air at clerestorey level. A massive terrestrial globe stood on a table near to mine.

A blue-uniformed, red-faced messenger, puffing hard, arrived with a pile of files, in various colours: green (Mediterranean and Pacific Department), brown (Economic Department), blue (General Department). Suddenly I realised that I had arrived at the moment of truth; and that truth was, that I knew nothing about the British Empire. Here were all these countries, with I supposed millions of inhabitants, whose fate, it appeared, lay in my hands; and I did not even know where they were (excepting Palestine). My duties had been explained to me by Roberts-Wray: to examine the laws, as they came in, of about fifty legislatures from the 'legal point of view'. If a law transgressed the requirements of a colony's Constitution, or was unfair – for instance if its effect were discriminatory, or it imposed excessive penalties – it could be 'disallowed'. I knew nothing about colonial law, and learned there was no book on the subject later than 1913. It was a dull and monotonous task. I varied it by getting out of my chair, going to the terrestrial globe, and establishing where these places were. It was not always easy to find them; and one day, trying to discover St Helena, I pushed the whole world off the table, and it fell to the floor. The shirt sleeves rushed to the rescue; and it was seen that a new rift, unknown to geographers, had appeared right across Africa. The globe was taken into the care of the Office of Works for many, many weeks.

I moved in with Roberts-Wray, and he taught me my job. He was most conscientious, and he had a legal mind of the highest quality. He had more hobbies than anyone I have ever come across: he was a devout philatelist, a persistent photographer, an amateur pianist, and a serious ball-room dancer; a keen golfer; and a horticulturalist within the limits permitted by his suburban house and garden, where he and his first wife Joan often entertained me. Though he did not always approve of me, we became firm and faithful friends.

Harold Duncan was in most respects the opposite. He was conscientious, but over-conscientious; and without a legal mind to correct this. He was prone to enter into points of administration rather than of law. Someone had once addressed a minute to him which ran: 'Mr Duncan, If you will advise on the policy here, I will take care of the legal aspects.' Duncan was tall and erect, an old Etonian, seldom seen without the tie, unmarried, lived in Warwick Square with a frenetic looking sister, had no hobbies, and went to Cromer for a month for his annual holiday. Bushe had told him that he was unenterprising over his holidays, and Duncan said to me: 'How can he say I am unenterprising? When I go to Cromer I swim every day, for a mile out to sea, a mile along, and then a mile to shore again.' He had travelled in earlier days, receiving some part of his education in Germany; and he had, I always thought, retained something of the Junker about him. He never invited me to his flat. But he expected me to do some of his work for him; and I was ready to do it, partly because it was through his acquaintanceship with Frank Gahan that I had heard of the Colonial Office job, and partly because that way I obtained a little variety.

There was, for instance, the great matter of the consecration of the Bishop of The Gambia and Rio Pongas. For the consecration of a bishop, even a colonial bishop, there must be a mandate from the Sovereign, read out at the ceremony. There was no precedent for the case, because foreign territory was included. Duncan asked me to draft the document, and I telephoned the legal adviser to the Archbishop of Canterbury for some assistance. He was inclined to make light of the matter. 'Why,' said he (I had once seen him: he wore a loud, black and white check suit) 'Why, at the consecration of the Bishop of . . . ' (naming a popular prelate) 'I took an old lease along, and read from a draft.' I drafted something, took it to Duncan, and passed on what the Archbishop's lawyer had said. Instead of reassuring him, the story shocked him, and made him more worried than ever. He said we should consult the Foreign Office; and along we went, traversing a labyrinth of corridors, to see Sir Stephen Gaselee, Foreign Office Librarian, and an acquaintance of Duncan's. I soon saw why. On entering Gaselee's vast room I saw the Old Etonian colours, and more; I had before me the figure which had caused me great joy a few days before, walking in St James's Park in the hot sunshine, in an old top-hat and morning coat, and carrying an untidy umbrella. We sat down and he perused the document, the top-hat and gamp hanging on a peg above his head. He wore a high wing collar, his colours tied loosely round it in a bow tie, as if in a constant effort to keep his large, flabby head attached to his shoulders. 'It looks all right to me,' he said; and we were about to rise, when he had an afterthought. 'By the way,' he asked, 'where *is* Rio Pongas?' Duncan looked at me: 'Where *is* Rio Pongas, Dale?' I had to say I did not know. Gaselee went to the far end of his room, hauled down Gazeteer after Gazeteer, and could find no trace of the place. 'It surprises me . . . It surprises me . . . ' he kept repeating; 'where did you get it from?' 'The Archbishop,' Duncan and I replied as one. Gaselee continued his search – thud, thud, – and at last turned back to us. 'It is a river,' he said.

The story went down well at tea time. Tea with biscuits was served by the messengers. Persons of the rank of Under-Secretary and above had little trays brought to their rooms; and one or two others did the same, of whom Duncan was one; he kept a cake in a drawer of his desk, using half a sheet of the blue minute paper as a plate. But most of us coalesced into tea-parties; and there were ten or a dozen – Assistant Secretaries, Principals, Assistant Principals, Roberts-Wray and myself – in ours. The Colonial Office attracted some of the best entrants into the civil service, and every one of the group had been to a well-known public school, and to Oxford or Cambridge, except myself, and the economist amongst us who had been to the London School of Economics and Political Science. Clever men, probably all with firsts, they had acquired an expert knowledge of the particular colonial territories, or special subjects, with which they dealt. They were seriously concerned to promote the interests of the colonial peoples, but this did not rule out wit, anecdotes, a Greek or Latin quotation, realism, or a sardonic comment or two. I felt at first too ignorant, too raw, too recently 'up from the country', to do much but listen. But gradually I obtained a foothold, and in course of time made some good friends: Frank Lee, who eventually became Permanent Secretary to the Treasury, and on retirement Master of Corpus Christi, Cambridge; Philip Rogers, another future Permanent Secretary; Andrew Cohen, later Governor of Uganda; and Christopher Eastwood, who came to grief over Crichel Down. Other members of the tea-party were Sydney Caine, the distinguished economist, and Anthony Bevir, who became Winston Churchill's Appointments Secretary. Anthony Bevir told me that he had once shown his own library, of which he was rather proud, to Stephen Gaselee, who had thereupon remarked that it would make 'nice reading when convalescing after influenza'. The atmosphere of the Colonial Office was almost cosy: we had coal fires, and the Permanent Under Secretary of State had a chamber pot in a cupboard in his room.

Brooding over the legal scene sat Bushe, in his large room overlooking Downing Street. He was of Irish extraction, a penetrating lawyer, outspoken; he hit hard at humbug, and could be sarcastic, not to say cynical. Bushe fought to secure for the law, and for the Colonial Legal Service, its rightful place in the government of the Colonial Empire. It was largely due to him that in East and West Africa a professional magistracy had taken over the magistrates' courts from the district officers. I did some devilling for him. Difficult questions were arising out of the administration of the Mandate for Palestine. In 1917 the Balfour Declaration of 'sympathy with Jewish Zionist aspirations' had stated that the British Government 'view with favour the establishment in Palestine of a national home for the Jewish people, and will use their best endeavours to facilitate the achievement of this object, it being clearly understood that nothing shall be done which may prejudice the civil and religious rights of existing non-Jewish communities in Palestine . . . ' Its terms were incorporated in the League of Nations Mandate, and the British Government, appropriately enough, had been given the duty of carrying them into effect. I had witnessed the problem from within, and had noted the figures of Jewish immigration in my Diary. With the passage of the Nuremberg Laws, depriving Jews of citizens' rights in Germany, the influx increased; and I now had a small part in the efforts of the Government to hold the balance between Arab and Jew, and to keep order. Questions of international law arose; and Bushe's patience at times became exhausted. I once heard him almost turn the good, sometimes impassioned, Eric Beckett, a Foreign Office legal adviser, out of his room. Nor had Bushe any sympathy for those in the Colonial Office who spoke of the 'spirit of the Mandate'. That, he once told them, seemed to be 'the soul of surrender'.

But my proximity to the seat of power by no means compensated me for the lost independence and freedom in the carrying on of my profession. My staple work continued to be the examination of the Colonial Ordinances, and that was dull enough. But worse was the silent and sedentary nature of my present occupation, in contrast to the constant moving and talking of life at the Bar. And I never met any new people. Apart from a short occasional conversation with Roberts-Wray, whose concentration I felt – or rather he felt – should not be interrupted, I sat in silence, hour after hour, day after day, looking at the files, reading the Ordinances, and – in nine cases out of ten – writing 'No legal obsons' as my conclusion.

I cast about in my mind for an alternative occupation, and I had some wild thoughts. Why had I not chosen the stimulating life of a doctor? I went so far as to read a medical book or two, and look at the regulations for qualifying. But it was out of the question to expect my mother, from her small income, to support me for years, and I soon gave up the idea. But so desperate was I that I applied to the Home Office for a job as a probation officer: that would provide human contact. But I was not accepted.

There was no such thing, by way of relief, as mid-morning coffee or tea. At lunch time there was a general exodus. My colleagues disappeared through Treasury Passage and across the Horse Guards Parade to their clubs: Roberts-Wray to the Oxford and Cambridge with two companions, and Bushe to the Union Club, where he joined Sir Thomas Barnes, the Treasury Solicitor, and the cynicisms filled the air (according to report). I did not know where to go – Whitehall does not abound in eating places. I usually went to the Thistle Tea Rooms in Victoria Street (that 'Street of Lost Causes' as Frank Lee used to call it), where I ate

Toad-in-the Hole. Twice a week or so I had a sandwich and a glass of beer in a pub, and went to St Stephen's Rochester Row, where I had permission to play the organ. This usually made me late back; and I can still hear the reproachful sound of the two tenor bells of the Abbey ringing to evensong – *Re Do, Re Do* – 'You're late, You're late.'

I was appointed to an inter-departmental committee to work out a model Workmen's Compensation law for the Colonies. Sir John Shuckburgh, the senior Under-Secretary, was the Chairman; and I sat next to Sir Alison Russell, who had been Chief Justice of Tanganyika, and was an expert draftsman, author of *Legislative Forms and Precedents*. I suffered some chagrin when, about the fifth meeting of the committee, Sir John Shuckburgh passed a note down reading 'Who is sitting next to Russell? Home Office?' Alison Russell and I became great friends. He had a flat in King's Bench Walk in the Temple, was a member of the Savage Club, was – it was understood – separated from Lady Russell, and altogether lived a life of some style. He used to invite me to the Savage Club for dinner. He wanted me to join; but I found the talk, revolving as it did round the minor poets, above my head. I did though have an agreeable talk on the hearthrug with Sir Flinders Petrie, who had been excavating in Gaza. Alison Russell later died in Venice, not – again one understood – unaccompanied. A stylish end!

Another little incident interrupted the even tenor of my life. I had not, after Jaffa, returned to 'the pure air of Guilford Street', but had taken a room in Nottingham Place, near Baker Street. From Piccadilly Circus my way to the office lay down the Duke of York's Steps, and across the Horse Guards Parade. One summer morning I found my progress blocked by a rehearsal of Trooping the Colour. A little vexed, I sought a way round. It seemed to me there was room for me to walk behind the horses – some fifty of them – standing with their backs to the long wall ending at Treasury Passage, which was my target. I was not interfering with the solemnity of the occasion in any way, and I went forward. I had reached about the twenty-fifth pair of hooves – I was keeping a rough count – when I received a malicious kick on my left knee, almost crippling me. I decided I might as well go on as turn back, and without further kicks I limped to safety, and to Roberts-Wray. In the war he had served in a mounted regiment, and he showed no sympathy.

I took three or four days 'leave', as I learned to call it, and went to Salisbury, where I had a friend. I did not see much of him. I sat all day in that lovely Close, reading, breaking off occasionally to go to a charming little restaurant outside the town called the 'Old Mill'. I was reading Axel Munthe's *The Story of San Michele*. As I sat under the spreading chestnut trees, the grey walls of the cathedral before me, the spire soaring into the clear blue sky, I realised my good fortune in having left Jaffa behind me. I have always thought of those few days as idyllic: for a perfect English holiday, give me warm sunny days, the shade of green trees, a Cathedral Close – a garden would I suppose do if there were a wide lawn and distant flower beds – and an absorbing book.

I left Nottingham Place and took a small flat in Marylebone High Street, above a milliner's and nearly opposite Sagne, the patisserie. I had little furniture, but it included an upright Bechstein on hire purchase. My mother came to stay with me for a few days. Together we heard on the radio the solemn voice of the announcer telling us that 'the life of His Majesty is drawing to its close'. King George V died in January 1936, to be succeeded by King Edward VIII. This was followed within the year by the unhappy crisis of the Abdication, so admirably handled by Stanley Baldwin. The legal advisers to the Colonial Office were legal advisers to the Dominions Office also, the Department responsible for our relations with the self-governing Dominions. Our King was their King, and our Queen would be their Queen; and they were entitled to have a say in finding a solution to the problems raised by the King's determination to marry Mrs Simpson. Constitutional questions were involved, on which Bushe's views were sought, besides broader questions of propriety (in the hands of the Archbishop of Canterbury, who was Cosmo Gordon Lang of Wharram days), of personal freedom (handled by the Hampstead intellectuals), and of popular opinion (probably indifferent, as voiced by the conductor of the 11 bus, who called out 'Simpsons in the Strand – the King's Arms'). I was sufficiently in the picture to know that, at least from the Dominions' point of view, the King's decision to go was a wise one.

Now that I had my Marylebone flat, I did not quite know what to do with it. I saw Harry Leon from time to time, but I had few friends, and I never met any young women. In spite of the Sex Disqualification Removal Act of 1919, which had thrown open all professions to women, I never met one in the Administrative Class of the Civil Service, or in the ranks of the legal profession. Again, the old problem: where to meet them? The only answer I had found was – in a restaurant. Part of the charm of the 'Old Mill' near Salisbury had lain with the two girls who ran it. After five or six lunches or suppers, and a tea-time visit or two on my part, we had become well acquainted. One of the girls had later come to London, but the charm had faded. I always dined out, and in Marylebone there were one or two acceptable and inexpensive restaurants. In one in particular there was a beautiful blonde cashier, but she turned out to be impregnable behind her statuesque cash register. Even my brother, who came to stay with me, and who was better looking and more adept than I, made no impression on her. He, a year and a half younger, had returned to England, and was shortly to marry Pauline Levanton, who had been a games captain at Cheltenham. This he did, in Chester Cathedral.

My thoughts began to carry me in that same direction. I was nearly thirty, I had a secure means of livelihood, and I needed a girl. I had a second cousin, a Leonard, of whom I had seen something while in Hull. She was good-looking, fair, with the Leonard aristocracy of feature, quiet, not robust, and knew a good deal about pictures. She also had a wish to be married, or at least to get away from home. She lived in York, and her parents were quite well off: it was surprising that no one had taken her off their hands. She came down to London, and I went up to York. Her brother and his wife rented a cottage in the lake District for the Easter holiday, and Emma and I were their guests there. It rained and rained, as if there were not already enough water in those depressing lakes and fells. The brother and his wife went for long walks, but I do not remember that Emma or I ever left the house. We sat by the fire. I came away engaged to be married.

Emma's parents made her an allowance of £100 a year, and we were married in September 1936 at St Helen's Church, York, going to Hitler's Germany for our honeymoon. Gray's Inn, once more kind, let us a flat, at 2 Verulam Buildings. It was not rich in conveniences. There was a small lavatory with a wash basin and no window, the bath being in the kitchen, covered by a table top and two legs. But there was a spacious sitting-room, overlooking the garden and the catalpa tree said to have been planted by Francis Bacon, and an adequate bedroom. Emma's parents had given us some furniture. On the same staircase lived Sir Bernard Spilsbury, the Home Office pathologist; but he did not call on us, or we on him. Across the garden was a grass tennis court on which we could invite friends to play.

It soon became clear that Emma was indeed not strong. She did not play tennis, or walk much, and was accustomed to going about by taxi. She began to develop a weakness in one of her legs, and had to spend a few days in bed. We had the doctor, who looked grave, but did not say much. She got better; then had an attack in the other leg. She went to St Bartholomew's Hospital, for a full examination. We both of us learned the nature of her illness in the most brutal way. The consulting physician was making his rounds with his attendant students, and when he reached Emma he said to them, so that we could both hear: 'Now here we have a typical instance of disseminated sclerosis'. Neither of us really knew anything about the disease; but we soon learned that there was progressive and incurable degeneration of the muscular and nervous organs, leading to complete paralysis and premature death. It was especially prone to attack young women in their twenties.

Emma had had one or two minor attacks before, and her parents must have been aware of the likely cause, or had shut their eyes to it. But they had remained silent. There was nothing to be done about it: her mother was a mild alcoholic, and her father was pleasant, but weak. We had to face a ruined marriage; and I did what I could to comfort Emma, and she to console me. But she had less and less energy, and an active life was beyond her. We hardly did anything together. Bushe took me riding in Richmond Park. I had had a lesson or two on a parade ground in Jaffa, at the hands of a cavalry officer – not very successfully, as the horse bolted with me, down the streets. Riding in the Park was more congenial, allowing for Bushe's sarcasms. 'It is better to ride under the trees than into them,' he advised me, after a crash.

I took Emma away for holidays. We went one year to Cassis in the south of France, and saw much of Provence. Another year we answered an advertisement in the *New Statesman* offering accommodation for a couple in an American lady's flat in Rome, meals included. We arranged to go; but almost at the last moment Emma felt unable to make the journey, and I was to go by myself. Having learned this the American lady – who, it turned out, had a husband living just round the corner from us in Bloomsbury – sent him to us with a pound of tea, to inspect me.

After a journey lasting nearly thirty hours I arrived at the flat in Rome. It was in one of the streets, near the Villa Borghese, named after the opera composers. I was greeted by a small boy, the son of the American lady, and home for the holiday. He took me round the flat. 'This,' he said, showing me the principal bedroom, 'is where my mother sleeps with the *avvocato*'. For a moment I thought he meant me; but it soon turned out that he was referring to a Roman of the same profession, who was the real reason for the visit of inspection under cover of the pound of tea. My hostess, a large, most intelligent woman, full of laughter, had a thorough knowledge of Rome, and I could not have had a more knowledgeable breakfast-table Beatrice. Each day she gave me my instructions. Her enthusiasms lay rather with the Renaissance and Baroque, than the Classical Rome, whereas what principally moved me was to be amongst the Seven Hills of the Kings, in the Forum where Cicero had made his speeches, and amongst the monuments of Imperial Rome. Naturally my Beatrice spoke Italian fluently and grammatically; and wanting me to do the same she arranged for me to have a daily Italian lesson (in which her Bloomsbury husband, who came for a few days, shared). She suggested that I should spend the last of my three weeks in Italy at Taormina, and I took the boat from Naples to Palermo. At the hotel in Taormina I made friends with a young German naval officer, and we went for excursions together. We climbed Mount Etna on foot, and having gazed down the crater, and not wishing to face all those ashes again on our descent, we went to the funicular car. The operator refused to take us as we had walked up. The Rome-Berlin Axis had come into being the year before, and the naval lieutenant was furious. 'And these are our Allies!' he spluttered, in his polished English.

On my way back to England through Rome I realised that I had learned that I could be for ever happy in Italy. I said that to Emma: she loved it too, having once stayed with friends in Santa Margherita. Not long after my return I visited my Aunt Emily, who was married and living in the lovely Warwickshire countryside. It was then she told me about the Italian presence at my christening. She was still full of romantic ideas. It appeared that the two Italians had, by means of some sort of telepathic implant, laid, on baptism, the ghostly foundations of a new spiritual home for me. That is what it came to, though my Aunt did not express herself exactly in that way.

But Italy and Germany, under their dictators, were on parallel courses of aggression: Abyssinia, the Rhineland, Austria, the Sudetenland. In September 1938, from Bushe's window, I witnessed Neville Chamberlain, surrounded by cheering crowds, return to Downing Street with the Munich Pact in his hand. Though, after delaying so long, we had begun to re-arm, we were not ready to go to war. The two essential elements were lacking: adequately armed forces, and popular support. Nor was the idea then acceptable to the self-governing Dominions, whom we had begun to call the independent members of the Commonwealth. Their support was vital. Hitler occupied Czechoslovakia, and Mussolini invaded Albania. We gave a guarantee to Poland.

At the Colonial Office I had a room of my own by then. A visiting judge or lawyer from the Colonial Legal Service – we called them 'beachcombers' – would sometimes share it. This year I had as room-mate for a month or two a judge from East Africa: with his long thin legs, extended jaw-bones, and beetling figure, his appearance was not unlike that of an over-burdened donkey. But he was very amusing, and I took him to Gray's Inn to entertain Emma. It was an unusually hot summer, and working hours were long. The judge and I sat on the benches in St James's Park from time to time and discussed the probability of war. It hardly seemed credible, under the trees, in sight of the ducks on the lake, the sky a cloudless blue. Then Germany invaded Poland; and on Sunday, 3 September 1939 we heard on the radio the voice of the Prime Minister telling the country it was at war with Germany.

VI

War

MR CHAMBERLAIN had scarcely finished, and the judge and I were still sitting on our park bench, when there came the discordant wailing of the sirens in an air raid alarm. We did not move; and it was not long before there followed the steady note of the All Clear.

Thus began the period of the 'phoney war', as it was later called. Schools carried out prearranged plans for evacuation and moved into the country, children with relatives in Canada or America went over there, wives left town, the National Gallery emptied itself of its treasures. In the cities we went about with gas masks, like the old Brownie box cameras in their cases, slung over our shoulders.

Emma had gone to her parents in York. My mother and sister were in Leeds where my sister was teaching. My brother Reggie was stationed in East Anglia, flying a Wellington bomber. Harry Leon, amongst friends and acquaintances at the Bar, joined the army. I was required to remain at the Colonial Office, legislating the colonies onto a 'war footing'.

In a few weeks time, with no air raids, no invasion, nothing to alarm the civilian population, people began to come back. Wives returned, and sought war work. Emma came back, against her parents' wishes, and we moved to a flat in Dolphin Square, Pimlico, on the Embankment. It was the latest in model blocks of flats, built round a large garden, with a restaurant, shops, and underneath a basement as shelter against bombs.

But Emma was unable to cope with war-time housekeeping in London, and went back to York. I was not well myself. No doubt brought on by my personal disaster, I had developed most painful sciatica, and I could not get rid of it. I began to feel that I too should 'join up', though I was in no condition to do it just then. But when Bushe said they could free me from the Colonial Office, I put myself at the disposal of the manpower authorities. I was posted to the Secretariat of the Ministry of Supply, a war-time Ministry, much needing staff with experience of administration. Before I could join them at Adelphi House in the Strand, I had to make a further effort to get better; and I discovered James Cyriax, an unconventional practitioner from St Thomas's, orientated towards osteopathy. His Wimpole Street ambience was unusual: while I lay prone under most painful kneading by his physiotherapist Nan Harvey, my eyes rested either on the pedals of a harmonium, or on a sort of surgical bicycle, a spectre of a bicycle half made of string. These objects were the property of Dr Cyriax senior, James's Swedish father, who played the one, and rode Harley Street on the other. James was inventing a process of injecting novocaine into the sacro-iliac canal, and after the kneading he would give me an injection. He told me he was going to put me into his first book, since I had two kinds of sciatica at the same time. The day at last came when he – or Miss Harvey, I could not see which – slapped my bottom, and I was discharged.

On my turning up at the Ministry of Supply, I found I was to share a room with a Cambridge don, R. E. Megarry. Other immediate colleagues were another Cambridge law don, Douglas Logan, and V. P. Harries, a nimble-minded solicitor. They had been awaiting my arrival without confidence, expecting an elderly man with an established sciatica, a dust-covered lawyer from what they referred to as the 'Home and Colonial', with *The Law of the Parish Church* (renamed by them *The Pew Opener's Digest*) as his intellectual horizon.

Megarry's job was the requisitioning under the Defence Regulations of land and buildings needed for factory and similar purposes; and evidently to sweeten himself for this task, he consumed numerous chocolates and toffees, which he kept in a drawer in his desk. Sitting opposite him I coped with other instances of the Minister's exercise of compulsory powers. I had a foam cushion on my chair to ward off further sciatica; and Megarry would insert the bell-push between the cushion and the seat, so that whenever I sat down, to begin on a file, the messenger would come in and ask what I wanted. To solve a legal problem we could not use our own legal minds, but were required to consult the members of the Treasury Solicitor's Department housed under the roof of the building. We were extremely well served, for these included two future Law Lords, Colin Pearson and Patrick Devlin. George Corderoy, an established member of 'T. Sol.' as we called it, drafted most of the Control Orders, including the famous one about packaging pails:

> 'The Control of Tins, Cans, Kegs, Drums and Packaging Pails (No 5) Order 1942, as varied by the Control of Tins, Cans, Kegs, Drums and Packaging Pails (No 6) Order 1942, the Control of Tins, Cans, Kegs, Drums and Packaging Pails (No 7) Order 1942, the Control of Tins, Cans, Kegs, Drums and Packaging Pails (No 8) Order 1942, and the Control of Tins, Cans, Kegs, Drums and Packaging Pails (No 9) Order 1942 is hereby further varied in the Third Schedule thereto by substituting for the reference 2A therein the reference '2A(1)' and by deleting therefrom the reference 2B.'

It is hardly surprising that the Order ended by giving itself the title 'The Control of Tins, Cans, Kegs, Drums and Packaging Pails (No 10) Order 1942.'

The Minister was at the time Herbert Morrison. The higher staff was a mixture of university dons, men and one or two women from the professions, the manufacturing industries and business, and civil servants seconded from other Ministries, not all of which had given of their best. The Assistant Secretary in charge of our branch was Stickling, from the Ministry of Labour. He was large, fat and flabby, with round spectacles and a pale face. All day he appeared to do nothing. Whenever one went to consult him he was sitting peacefully behind his desk, his hands folded across his stomach, no papers before him. I once went to him with some proposition which would involve a little thinking on his part; but he excused himself with the words 'I have heavily mortgaged my time until after Easter', which was many weeks away. This pronouncement of his became famous.

On 7 September 1940 the bombing of London began. It was a Saturday, and as I had been invited to the country for the weekend, I luckily missed it. I returned on the Monday morning to a devastated city, and we learned later that on that first night 400 people had been killed. The bombing continued night after night. Emma had remained in York. In my personal life I was adrift again. I had finally got rid of sciatica by a cure consisting of sitting up half the night drinking claret with a delightful companion, and alternating with a night of early to bed and a long, refreshing sleep. I explained all this to a surprised and sceptical Oliver Franks, Professor of Moral Philosophy at Glasgow, and now Assistant Secretary in charge of personnel at the Ministry of Supply. But no one wanted to be living alone. I had made friends at the Dominions Office with Cyril Costley-White, and he and his wife Elizabeth asked me to share the comforts of their flat in Tufton Court, Westminster, where was an Austrian cook, and a visiting sewing woman. During air raids Liz and I played duets on the grand piano. Living above us were two Labour MPs, Margaret Bondfield and Florence Horsbrugh, and they complained to us that we prevented their hearing the bombing. I became godfather to the Costley-Whites' first child, Anthony. But Cyril was posted to Canada, the house let, and I moved to 25 Cheyne Row, the house of another friend, Tony Waterfield, and his wife Honor. Tony, a scientist, had been moved out of London; and I ran the house as a little boarding-house, keeping a room for Tony when he needed it. There were usually two young women, working in one or other of the Ministries, and another man, who was for much of the time my friend Christopher Eastwood from the Colonial Office. The women used our combined rations – except for my sweet coupons, which I was devoting to Megarry's drawer – to cook breakfast, and dinner two or three times a week. We did not do too badly on 4 oz a week each of butter and bacon, 12 oz sugar and 1 s worth of meat.

My brother was engaged in the nightly bombing of targets in Germany. There came a night, that of 10 May 1941, the very night that Rudolf Hess flew to Scotland on his attempt to talk peace terms, when Reggie was shot down and reported missing, later killed. I went at once to try to comfort my mother, who was at the time living in the Warwickshire countryside with my Aunt Emily and her husband Uncle Arthur; and then to Pauline, who was living in Hampshire with her baby son Reggie, and pregnant with my brother's posthumous son, Jim.

Tony Waterfield was posted abroad and I had to give up his house. I was admitted, on the Waterfields' recommendation for good behaviour, to what was impolitely known amongst us as the 'Cattery', nos 96 and 97 Cheyne Walk. These fine Queen Anne houses – Whistler had lived and painted at no 96 – had been bought by Richard Stewart-Jones, with a view to their complete restoration. Richard, who embodied in himself all that is the essence of the

National Trust, had gone off to the war; and he had committed his houses to the care of his sister Diana, for the purpose of accommodating young women of breeding engaged in war work, a man or two not excluded. Diana was well named: she had the face, poise, and kindness from above of a goddess, if one can imagine a goddess stooping to collect ration books. There was a magnificent drawing-room with a grand piano in it, on the first floor overlooking the river, and we were allowed to play it on proper occasions.

By this time I was thirty-six. On Emma's last visit to Dolphin Square I had told her that I had not been faithful to her, and she insisted on a divorce. That meant that I must take the steps required, but I had done nothing. I felt a cad. Besides, I did not know what to do. I did not wish to marry again. I had talked it all over with the Costley-Whites, in circumstances of extreme irony. Cyril had the disease Emma had, but with him it did not develop as it did with her. He and Liz were brave and their spirit was unbroken. Cyril, well-informed, told me how to go about acquiring the evidence the law demanded in a pleasant way, and gave me a name and telephone number. Still I did nothing.

Jimmy Cyriax, who had become a good friend, and was concerned for my welfare in every way, introduced me to a Hungarian girl, a leading young dancer with the Ballet Jooss. Lili was glamorous: she had large black eyes, hollow cheeks, and a playful humour. She spoke English well but eccentrically, with a number of original words, and pronouncing '-le' at the end of a word as if it were the French definite article (Jimmy's father rode a 'bicyc-*le*'). She had left Hungary before the war, and now the ballet company had been compelled to dissolve. She occasionally came to Whistler's House and danced while I played. The goddess was rather pleased. Not so the other girls, who would look in: 'She's like a panther,' one of them said breathlessly. If Lili came to my room, the others would come and knock on the door. Lili introduced me to a musician friend, Clifton Parker, a composer who wrote the music for some of the contemporary films. He and I together played in piano score Benjamin Britten's music for 'The Ascent of F6', the poetic drama by Auden and Isherwood, at performances at the Tavistock theatre in Bloomsbury. The score was so difficult to read, and the light was so bad, that I had eye trouble for some time afterwards.

In September Lili went to 'Montgomerryshire' as she pronounced it, to teach ballet dancing at a month's course. She wrote me letters in what she called her 'cook-parlourmaid handwriting', so characteristic of the time that I reproduce one or two extracts:

> 'The mountains are beautiful (this is overstating, they are really hills, but it is a continental thing to overstate) and the river makes a non-stop noise . . . Now it is foggy and a rain comes down which one cannot see it is so fine. I don't want to offend you but I don't like that (or this?) although I know it is the specialité of this Island and one of the national prides – to have such a fine rain. To me, rain is rain.'

She described her pupils:

> 'More like elephants as they get younger. The old ones are like the lemons one could get the last few days before they disappeared from the markets. Skinny and dry, no juice inside.'

She described a visit to the cinema, with her young pupils:

> 'All the Welsh-es stopped doing nothing, stared at us and got excited after we passed. They had early closing day yesterday, which means that most of the shops didn't open at all in the morning and some did between 10 and 12 a.m. Being a lovely day, they withdrew behind closed windows in the afternoon, and sat there. All this I grasped, when on my way to the cinema I passed the window tiptoeing and looking in. Of course I felt justified to do so, only, because I knew they did the same when I passed in my trousers on the streets. They had a more difficult task to do – tiptoeing on the behinds . . . Would you hate to send a pound of Algerian (coffee)?'

I was invited to Wales:

> 'You can't come on a Sunday to this part of the World. But if you can pinch the Saturday off could you come? I could take you round and show you, how and where they do the tiptoeing on the behind best . . . Don't put any travelling cap on. I always used to think as a kid, that I would not be able to look at anybody any more who goes in such a thing to travel. I saw lots of Englishmen in Italy "doing traveling" in such caps (illustration) . . . Thanks for the lovely coffee, I feel even more cheerful since you can have it twice a day after meals. If you can get a few cigarettes and any chocolates . . . I think everybody is nonconformist in this place . . . can you tell me more about the non-conformists?'

I doubt if I ever did. In the winter Lili decided to marry a compatriot, a composer, and I saw no more of her. But she had stimulated me into taking action about the divorce. As Cyril had advised, I telephoned Mrs X, who operated from a pretty little house in a small street off Knightsbridge (now demolished), and asked her assistance in providing the evidence the law required. Mrs X suggested one Jean as suitable. I resolved to make it a romantic week-end, at the inn at Hungerford. For the train journey I provided Jean with a copy of the *Illustrated London News*. She was a quiet girl – not particularly pretty – fair, slim and lonely; her boy friend had been sent to the West Indies, and she had to earn her living. She was affectionate, and a good companion. On the Sunday morning we went to church, and in the evening we had a good walk. On the Monday morning we took the train back to London. At Paddington, instead of saying goodbye, we arranged to meet again. The law had nothing against that; but Mrs X had, and we did not tell her of the three or four rendezvous which followed.

I enclosed the hotel bill in a suitable letter to Emma, which she sent on to her solicitor. I awaited service on me of the petition for divorce – for weeks. Nothing came. In the end there arrived an intimation that the hotel at Hungerford declined to testify that the girl and I had spent the night – two nights – together. The bill itself did not prove that. I had made the mistake of not ordering breakfast in bed, and there was nothing for it but to begin all over again. Chagrined, as I had to admit that I had not shown legal acumen, I went back to Mrs X and besought her further help. She was not pleased, as she regarded that side of her business as vulnerable – vulnerable to publicity as a result of court proceedings; but she agreed to oblige, and arranged for Jean again, at half-price for one night (I seem to remember £5). This time there was no romanticism. One night in a little hotel somewhere behind Selfridges, breakfast in bed, and to make sure the waiter had something to remember us by I upset scrambled eggs and bacon (Jean did not want any) over the bed and floor. Some months later the petition for divorce was served on me at Whistler's House, some months after that came the five-minute hearing in the Divorce Court (at which I was not present), and six months after that came the decree absolute. I never saw Emma again, or corresponded with her. Years later I learned that she had survived; and I was pleased to learn also that she had married her doctor.

I had worked myself thoroughly into my job as a half-lawyer, half-civil servant, at the Ministry of Supply. John Wyndham joined us to help in the task of directing firms what to make and how to make it; and his aristocratic, Edwardian style – with a little of Bertie Wooster about it – was a great joy to all of us. One Saturday afternoon (today's civil servants might note the day and time) he sat down opposite me – Megarry had moved to another room – and telephoned a laggard industrialist in the Midlands.

> 'What has become of those spare parts?' he demanded in loud tones.
> '. . . . .'
> 'You mean they're not ready!?'
> '. . . . .'
> 'Preposterous. The Minister will have to issue a direction.'
> '. . . . .'
> Angrily – 'I know it's Saturday afternoon.'
> '. . . . .'
> 'To whom am I speaking?'
> '. . . . .'
> 'The FOREMAN! God bless my soul!' And he hung up.

John did not stay with us long. He became private secretary to Harold Macmillan, who was then Parliamentary Secretary, and was later Macmillan's Private Secretary when Prime Minister. John became Lord Egremont, and inherited Petworth from his father, Lord Leconfield. He died young. The last time I saw him I was sitting in the official box in the House of Lords, and he came into the Chamber after dinner. He sat as near as he could, and shouted to me blasphemous comments on the speeches.

I was promoted to be Assistant Secretary, and became responsible for the enforcement, by prosecution if appropriate, of the Ministry's Control Orders and directions under the Defence Regulations. I experienced the difficulties often facing those who have to decide whether a prosecution is in the public interest. A highly competent enforcement branch of five or six officers seconded from the Customs and Excise Department investigated and reported to me. We also policed some orders made by the War Office, in respect of their establishments. One day it came out that directions forbidding smoking, and other loose behaviour, had been posted up at some military establishment, without their receiving the formal signature of the authorised official; they were therefore legally invalid. Unfortunately several offenders had been prosecuted and fined. I decided that, as only a formality was involved, it was unnecessary in war time to spend our energies tracing the smokers over a number of years, beg their pardon, and repay the pound or two they had been fined. My decision was overruled. The Permanent Secretary to the War Office was quite shocked at it. There was another occasion when I took the robust view. Stickling had in early days ruled that whenever a direction was issued under a certain regulation, recorded on the appropriate file, a second record was to be made in a special file. It was a perfectly useless exercise, an example of Stickling bureaucracy; no one had observed the instruction for a year or two; but it was there, and a continuing embarrassment. When Stickling left the Ministry I resolved that it would be in the public interest to get rid of the file. I took it to 25 Cheyne Walk, where we heated the bath water by means of a 'Tortoise' combustion stove, and when no one was looking thrust it into the flames.

Harry Lawson, Professor of Comparative Law at Oxford, who had examined me for the Holt Scholarship at Gray's Inn, came at his own request to work at the Ministry as my assistant. He was a delight to have there. We needed intellectual refreshment. He would sometimes disappear for a long time to the Treasury Solicitor's Department, where he would have long discussions with Colin Pearson, who was also interested in the philosophy of the law. Harry with his sister Betsy, who was with I.C.I., had taken a flat in Chelsea with a piano in it, and later, when I was living alone again, they often invited me to a meal with them. It was a few minutes walk away, and that was a great advantage. One of the tiresome things about life in London during the war – I remember the walking more than the bombing – was the prodigious distances one had to walk at night. There was no transport after about ten o'clock. One had to choose one's friends accordingly, at any rate for late visiting. Kensington was possible for the homeward drag, Hampstead out of the question, Marylebone on the border line. Of course if there were an air raid in progress it was wise to stop for shelter. I was an air raid warden, my station in the bowels of the Home Office, but I was only wanted there once a week. I had tried to follow my friend Tony Waterfield into the river police, but they would not take me on account of my eyesight. After Germany had attacked Russia everyone began to read Tolstoy. There were no theatres, except for the Windmill, with revues ('We never closed'). There was a lunch-time concert every day at the National Gallery, sponsored by Myra Hess, and at which she often played. For pictures, there were always three at the National Gallery, brought up from Wales. I formed the view that all exhibitions should be limited to three pictures.

About the time the flying bombs (the 'buzz bombs') started, which was the summer of 1944, I moved into a studio cottage behind 38 Cheyne Walk. The large studio was composed almost entirely of glass, and was warmed only by a stove of the kind that had engulfed the Ministry file, but larger, and fuel for it was almost impossible to get. Everyone thought my move the height of foolishness, considering that the Germans treated us to 100 to 150 bombs a day of about a ton each, but I was tired of the restricted conditions of Whistler's House. I felt a revulsion from all domesticity. I hired a hand-cart, trundled my few belongings along the Embankment from 96, took a divan bed and a chair and table or two out of store, bought an old Bechstein grand from Harrods, and placed a Tang priest or teacher on a book-shelf, as a household god. The previous occupier, Frederick Thurston the clarinettist, had left most of his blackout curtains. To my extreme indignation the Army and Navy Stores, from whom I had bought wine before the war, refused to supply me with any, as I had not been an account customer. But I got hold of some bottles of Algerian – what should we have done during the war without Algeria? – I bought a handsome brown pitcher with a black rim from Peter Jones, into which I poured the wine, and gave a party. The floor was of wooden blocks, my guests brought their own cushions, and we ate one another's fish-pies. (Fish was not rationed, but was difficult to find, and it was three times the price it had been.) The Ministry of Food had imported large quantities of tinned sardines, or what represented them, from Portugal, but had forgotten the openers. I was compelled to use a pair of pliers, and my complaint to the *Times* provoked a spate of letters to the Editor.

The house itself at 38 Cheyne Walk was occupied on and off (depending on the incidence of the bombing) on the first floor by two sisters who were painters, on the second by another painter, and on the third by Ann Hefferman, an actress and friend of a young actor called Alec Guinness and his wife. A Mrs Wright lived without interruption at ground level, and kindly 'did' for me, though she was also something of a policeman. Access to my cottage was down a hallway past her door, and she seemed to know by instinct whether I had an overnight guest. If I had, in the morning she remained outside washing the front-door steps until we went. She cooked me my rations two or three times a week, though I never asked her to cook for two. Restaurants were open, and were forbidden to charge more than five shillings for a meal. The best ones were crowded out at this price. The 'Blue Cockatoo', three doors away, was my outside dining-room. One ate dinner by candle-light, for half-a-crown, and I often saw friends there. I dined early; and it sometimes happened that, on my return home, someone unexpectedly in possession of a fowl or perhaps offal (unrationed), would telephone and tell me to come to dinner. I would say I had already eaten, they would ask where, I would say the Blue Cockatoo, and they would reply that in that case I could easily eat another dinner. I did. Or painter friends, such as Anthony Devas and his wife Nicolette, whose sister was married to Dylan Thomas, would tell me to join them in a pub. After a glass or two of beer, I would eat again. Hospitality was not limited to single meals. Ted Megarry and his wife Iris asked me to Cambridge for week-ends (Ted was already forming his tastes for wine and Real Property, so brilliantly deployed in post-war years); and Tim Luke, a friend from the Colonial Office, and his wife Helen, would ask me to Bracknell. One summer holiday Jock Logan lent me his rooms at Trinity, Cambridge. Colin Pearson and I went to Edinburgh to arrange for the requisitioning of their iron railings (fortunately the war ended before they could be removed).

A pleasant institution in my corner of Chelsea was the Countess Toulouse-Lautrec. She was married to a good-looking English soldier who was away at the war, and she was somewhat awash. She livened us up with her French wit; and she was the scourge of a little man with a large moustache who for many years had kept the chemist's shop at the corner of the Embankment and Oakley Street. It was a modest shop, but Mr Ward always had enough alker-seltzers and aspirins to go round – I cannot remember anyone wanting any other medicine in those days. But Mr Ward had embossed on his window pane, in solid white lettering, an announcement: ICI ON PARLE FRANCAIS. The Countess, who never prepared a meal and had much time on her hands, paid him a daily visit to grill him: descending on him with her long face and beak-like nose, she would pick his French to pieces. Relief only came to Mr Ward when the blast from a flying bomb blew in his window.

I took up my music again. All my organ music, stored in a warehouse which had been burnt by incendiary bombs, had gone. I had a few piano lessons with a young woman known as 'Dorcas', a pupil of Franz Osborn, the distinguished Beethoven player. It was not long before she told me I could go 'straight to Franz'. She was going away, and asked me to take over her small Persian kitten; she brought it to breakfast at the Ritz. But I am afraid 'Ritzie' – as he was inevitably called – found himself more comfortably off with Mrs Wright; and I gave him to my Colonial Office friend Philip Rogers, and his wife Heather.

My relationship with Franz Osborn developed from a shy pupillage into a close friendship. He had come from Berlin, with the wave of outstanding musicians and others arriving in the later twenties. He was reputed to have been Artur Schnabel's best pupil, who was a pupil of Leschetizky, who was a pupil of Czerny, who was a pupil of Beethoven himself. On my telling him that my ambition was to play Opus 111 (Beethoven's last piano sonata) as well as Schnabel, he took me on. Small and slight in build, and looking much like Disraeli, he had the personality and discrimination of an aristocrat. His lessons, at his flat in Hinde Street above the Palestine Exploration Fund, took up an hour and a half. For the first hour we would talk, I sitting at one of his Steinway grands, he walking about and laughing. Then perhaps Natasha Litvin (Mrs Stephen Spender) would arrive for her lesson and Franz would give me mine, sitting at the parallel Steinway, while she listened (not that Natasha gained anything from my lessons – she was an accomplished pianist). Franz came to my studio and played at a supper party – fish-pie again. One Sunday afternoon I went to the Wigmore Hall to turn over for him. He was playing piano trios with Professors Rosé (who was Mahler's brother-in-law) and Buxbaum, and during the first movement of the opening trio the lid of the Steinway grand fell down with a crash. It was at the time of the rocket bombs, the V2s, and the audience almost leapt out of their seats. The old professors went on sawing away regardless. When we got to the same bar in the repeat, Franz – incorrigible – said 'That's where the lid fell down'; and our giggles lasted well into the second movement.

When, on 29 April 1945, Germany unconditionally surrendered, the public holiday to celebrate the victory, VE day, seemed to fall flat. People were tired; and there was not a great deal to celebrate with. Normal life returned slowly, and it was years before all rationing ended. Harry Leon was back, and I lent him and his gentle, charming wife Lettice, my studio cottage for several weeks. My mother and sister were now living in Reading, where Hilda was a lecturer in French at the university, and I stayed with them.

VJ day came – two days' public holiday to celebrate the end of the war with Japan – and the time had come too for me to return to the Colonial Office. Bushe had become Governor of Barbados, Duncan, who had succeeded him, had retired, and Kenneth Roberts-

Wray was now the Legal Adviser to the Colonial Office and Dominions Office (renamed the Commonwealth Relations Office). Roberts-Wray wanted me back as his deputy. But there was trouble with the Treasury. That Department – which always tended to regard the Colonial Office as Cinderella amongst the Departments – refused to recognise the Legal Adviser to it as top class. It had upgraded, with rises in salary grades, all senior legal advisers' posts except that at the Colonial Office. This was manifestly unjust; and Kenneth declined to accept the decision. Having obtained my support, he courageously – he had three sons at school – took nothing but his old salary as Assistant Legal Adviser. This went on for a year or two until the Treasury gave way. Meanwhile there was a difficulty over myself. The Ministry of Supply did not want to let me go. I was not having this. I had enjoyed much of my work there as a wartime civil servant, but it was time I resumed my proper function as a lawyer. I forced the issue by working for both offices, at lunch time passing down the Strand and up Whitehall. I was released from the Ministry of Supply about the end of the year. Mr Attlee's Government had succeeded Mr Churchill's in the summer, and the Colonial Office was beset with problems.

My studio, with its skylights, had borne the war well. The rain had come in now and again, and damaged some books. But the glass had survived the flying bombs – one had descended on Chelsea Old Church near by – and the rocket bombs. There was a crack in the glass of one of the windows, but I attributed that to the window cleaner. We had a particularly cold winter, and I could not get enough fuel to feed my hungry 'Tortoise'. Transport was still difficult, and the long nocturnal walks remained; there was a general feeling that the Government was prolonging austerity longer than was necessary. Walking down the King's Road late one evening, I caught up with A.P. Herbert, returning to the *Water Gypsy* from the House of Commons. I did not know him, but we chatted amiably, about the divorce law and other matters. I told him of my Hungerford experience. As we turned down Oakley Street, we grumbled to each other about the absence of buses.

'Who is responsible?', I enquired of him as a Member of Parliament.

'Some bloody civil servant', he said.

VII

End of a Raj – Sarawak

THE Colonial Office was faced with a special problem – Sarawak. Like Singapore, Malaya, and other Borneo territories, it had been occupied by the Japanese, and devastated. But with Sarawak the problem was deeper than one of reconstruction. About the size of England, it had for a hundred years been ruled, not by the Colonial office, but by the Brooke family.

The founder was James Brooke, the son of a judge in the East India Company's service. James, having been wounded when fighting in Burmah, bought a schooner, and cruised about in the Far East; and he was sent by the Governor of Singapore on a mission to the Rajah Muda Hassin ('muda' meaning 'the young', the heir) of Sarawak. Hassin had helped some ship-wrecked British sailors, and Brooke conveyed the thanks, and gifts, of the British Government. The country, named after the Sarawak river, was unknown, and the coasts were uncharted. Brooke explored, gained the respect of the local administrators and people by helping to put down insurrection within and piracy from the sea, and was invited to stay and become their ruler. In 1841 he was installed as Rajah, worked hard to deal with piracy, slavery and head-hunting (the habit of the Ibans, or Sea-Dyaks); and brought the country peace and modest development, using nothing but his own resources and the help of a few British friends. Sarawak was recognised as an independent State by America in 1850, and by Britain in 1864. James retired in 1863 to Burrator, on the southern edge of Dartmoor, within sight and smell of the sea.

James, disabled by his wound from having children, had never married, and was succeeded by his nephew Charles. He followed the policy his uncle had proclaimed: 'Sarawak belongs to the Malays, the Sea-Dyaks, and Land Dyaks, the Kayans and other tribes; not to us. It is for them that we labour; not ourselves.' Other Borneo tribes sought the Rajah's protection, and the status of Sarawak was formally declared by Treaty in 1888 to be that of an independent State under the protection of Britain. Charles devoted his whole life to his people, and he governed the country with the help of a few British officers and a small force of Sarawak Rangers. He was an austere and formidable character, and of fierce appearance. He had lost an eye when out riding, galloping into a tree (as I had done); and he had replaced his eye with that of an albatross, which he had seen in the window of a London taxidermist.

Charles's eldest son, Charles Vyner Brooke, had succeeded to the Raj in 1917. He had been brought up in Sarawak, except for Winchester and Cambridge, and entered the Sarawak service; and he ruled over a prosperous country, without racial or tribal conflicts, granting it in 1941 'a modest measure of self-government.' Then the Japanese invaded, and the Rajah, in Australia, remained there for the war. By now he was seventy, felt the reconstruction of the country to be beyond his resources, and said that anyhow 'the time for one-man rule and that sort of thing' had passed. He proposed that he should cede his country to the British Government. To him this was a straightforward offer – and a generous one, considering the oil potential.

To Mr Attlee's Government the matter was not so straightforward. It was not the moment in history for Britain, above all for a Labour Government, to be acquiring a new colony. There were other difficulties. The Brooke family was at odds within itself. Like James, the Rajah had no sons; and Anthony Brooke, the son of Vyner's brother Bertram, known as the 'Tuan Muda', had been named as successor by Charles's Will. But the Rajah had lost confidence in Anthony's ability to govern, an attitude not shared by Anthony or his father Bertram; and they would do all they could to oppose the cession. Anthony's sister, moreover, was married to Arthur Bryant the historian, who had influence in Conservative circles, and wrote for the *Illustrated London News*. Then there were the views of the people of Sarawak to be considered. The Rajah, knowing his people, said they would do whatever he decided was best for them; but Labour Ministers could hardly base their policy on that. Beyond all this, there were legal problems, arising out of the unique nature of the Brooke regime, the 1941 Constitution, and the unfortunate visit to the country by the Rajah's personal envoy, G.T.M. MacBryan, to 'prepare' it for cession. A mercurial character, MacBryan had turned Muslim, married a Sarawak Malay girl while in the Rajah's service, and made the pilgrimage to Mecca. He was now discredited. We had Opinions from the Law Officers, Hartley Shawcross and Frank Soskice, and Lord Jowitt, the Lord Chancellor.

George Hall was Secretary of State for the Colonies. He was a likeable, simple man, who would put his forefinger on the paper when reading, and run it along under the words. But he was good in the House of Commons, and stoutly defended the Government's position against the Conservative Opposition, which had suddenly begun to oppose the idea of colonies. Two MPs, Labour and Conservative, were to go out and report to the House whether cession was 'broadly acceptable to the native communities of Sarawak'. I was to accompany the Rajah as legal adviser. He had a number of discussions with Mr Hall; and it was when he was leaving one of these that I first met Vyner Brooke. He had got pushed behind the heavy door of the Secretary of State's room; and on my being introduced he said: 'You're coming with us? Very nice of you to come. We won't hurry – spend a few days in Cairo.' I had expected, I suppose, a sort of nabob, peppery, with a blue and red silk handkerchief half over his face. Instead, here was an English gentleman, tall, broad-shouldered, with very blue eyes, white hair, and a tanned face – handsome. He eventually got through the door. I received the impression that a Government office was not the place he loved best.

His Ranee had probably never entered a Government building, except perhaps a Customs house. I met her at a party the Rajah gave before leaving for Sarawak, at the Savoy hotel. The Ranee had been Sylvia Brett, granddaughter of Lord Esher, Master of the Rolls; and her sister Dorothy had gone to join D.H. Lawrence in Mexico. The Ranee was small and lively, dark, with mischievous brown eyes; and she wore her Sarawak costume, a sarong and long loose blouse. The Rajah was a shy man, disliked parties, and was nowhere to be seen; and the Ranee was managing a difficult gathering. It was composed of politicians, British officials, Sarawak officials, and a number of glamorous women, outstanding amongst them the three Brooke daughters, known to the press as the 'Princesses'. Leonora, married to Lord Inchcape, was of good height, slim and blonde, her father's daughter. Elizabeth was dark, voluptuous, with great black eyes, more her mother's daughter. She had married Harry Roy, the dance band leader. Valerie was small, fair and impish, with a perfect figure; and she had just married Bob Gregory, the all-in wrestler. I did not much enjoy the party. The guests did not mix well. I got stuck with a retired Sarawak officer, who held me in anecdote while I looked over his shoulder at Valerie's legs. I hoped to encounter the opposition; but neither Anthony, nor his father the Tuan Muda – who was to visit Sarawak while we were there – was at the party. The Rajah eventually appeared, in time for a farewell toast.

James Brooke, in a letter to a friend, had said: 'What better can he or you do than to hire or build an aerial machine, and with your ladies, make a six weeks' flight to Borneo and back; it would sound well in print.' Prophetic, encouraging words, and I kept a full diary; but it is too long and detailed to print here, and what follows is an abridgement.

Our 'aerial machine' was a Sunderland flying boat, taking off from Poole harbour on 6 April 1946. The BOAC coach could not resist a stop at Basingstoke for refreshments; and I was struck by the youthful appearance and vigour of the Sarawak officers returning to their posts, in spite of internment by the Japanese. At Poole were the Rajah and Ranee, and four press men. I was embarking on a flight of 9,000 miles, and it was the first time I had flown. I must have been nervous, for I gave my date of birth one day out; but I did better than the Ranee, who could not remember the year, and had to be prompted by Spurway, the Rajah's ADC. We took six days to reach Singapore, descending on water every evening, boarding a launch, and going to a hotel for the night. Our first stop was Biscarosse, and I ate my first French meal, after seven years of London and rationing. But at lunch the next day at Augusta the consequences of the raw Marsala were such that the Ranee said to me: 'When you get to my age you always know when to be sick.' After Sicily there was the Nile, and Cairo for the night, then Bahrein, Karachi, Calcutta, Rangoon (where we visited the Sheve Dagon Pagoda), and at length Singapore.

We stayed for two nights in Government House, white, clean and shining again after enemy occupation, amongst lawns, flowering shrubs and trees. Lord Mountbatten, Supreme

Commander of Allied Forces in the Far East (the Supremo), agreed the arrangements for returning Sarawak to the Rajah; and we continued in the Sunderland, made a flawless descent on the Sarawak river, and went up by launch to Kuching. An intoxicatingly sweet scent came from the tropical vegetation, cheering people stood on the banks, and the river was full of sampans. I changed handkerchiefs with the Ranee, who needed a large one for waving. There were addresses of welcome, then up at the Astana, the Rajah's residence, where the Malay servants were waiting, there were tears on both sides. In the evening there was a long 'state' drive, the streets lined with enthusiastic crowds. Nearly everyone must have been out, throwing rice. The car I was in kept stalling, and the spectators pushed us up a hill. In the town there were some banners against cession displayed by the Malay National Union, but in the countryside there were demonstrations by 3000 or more supporting it. Many of the Malays tended to be against the Rajah's proposals because they looked upon him as their protector against the Chinese.

The Astana, built by the second Rajah and largely of wood, was on a low hill across the river from the town, with enormous, airy rooms – though not very many of them – and extensive grounds. A member of the Malayan Civil Service, Christopher Dawson, had come with us as 'British Representative'; and he and I decided that he should stay in the town, while I should accept the Rajah's invitation to be his guest at the Astana. The first two or three days were occupied by ceremonies, conferences, displays and parties. The Malayan police band, inexhaustible in wind and repertory, was much to be seen and heard. Many people came to see the Rajah, the most striking being the Sea Dyak Chiefs, sturdy, likeable rogues with feathers in their headdresses; they wore a jacket, a cloth hanging from their waists before and behind, and no trousers. They had taken more than 260 Japanese heads – 'very good heads', they added – and some Chinese heads as well. There was a problem: should they be tried in respect of the Chinese heads? Dawson and I acquired an office across the river: two rooms, and a typist of little use, our main need being paper-weights. I had my first swim for six years, in the Astana pool. A glaring moon, and the deep silence, frightened me out of the water.

Dawson and I went by jeep to Sugu, a Land Dyak village 21 miles from Kuching. We travelled through the jungle, past rubber trees – the raw rubber in sheets – durian trees (a large, delicious fruit with an unpleasant smell), pineapples, bananas, and betel nuts on tall palms; sago on smaller palms, and pepper, looking like hops or runner beans. A bridge did not quite meet the road at either end, and we became bogged, leaving the jeep and walking a mile into the village. The Dyaks build their 'long houses', and the 'street' itself, high out of the wet, on poles. At ground level are the hens and pigs; on the first floor are the living quarters of the family, two or three rooms on an open plan, with a front door onto the 'street' – a wide verandah with bamboo flooring; and the upper floor is left for storage. To quote from my diary:

> The street of the long house is largely covered with rice spread on mats, drying in the sun. A baby is hanging in a sort of laundry bag, on a spring. We take off our muddy boots, the people drift out of their doors, and accommodate us on stools placed on a mat. The men wear shorts only, the women a sarong below the waist, the children are naked. Dawson talks in Malay to the Chief, the people squatting on the floor, the children standing and occasionally shooing away a hen.
>
> A serious-faced woman, her hair in a bun, is preparing her rice. She pounds it in a wooden bowl – which is our stool the other way up – and then, gracefully and deftly, with an unbroken four-in-a-bar rhythm, by a neat wrist action, her long breasts shaking in tempo, tosses the product in flat rush mats shaped like shovels. She edges the rice to the outer edge of the mat, and lets it fall into a second mat, keeping the chaff in the first. This is repeated until the rice becomes whiter and whiter; and from time to time she crosses the verandah to the open side, and winnows the chaff in the slight draught. The chaff falls to the floor between the bamboos, and to the ground beneath, where the hens and rodent-like little black pigs eat it up. Occasionally someone spits between the bamboos.
>
> The Chief has said that the Japanese were much disliked on account of their roughness and bad manners, and the people took to the jungle. Because the Japanese seized their guns, they have nothing with which to shoot the birds and animals robbing the paddy fields, and this is a serious cause of food shortage. They give us coconut oil to drink, chopping off the husks and cutting a large triangular hole in the shell, so that we drink as easily as from a bottle. We eat our lunch – the Chief declares he has had his – leave them some eggs and bread-and-butter, and distribute cigarettes. There is a village shop, they use a little money, but often barter with rice. The men are wild-looking – broadish heads, thick, black bushy hair, many young men (or older boys) with fine physiques; but the older people, especially the women, are very thin. They compare badly with the Sea Dyaks. Some

> of the children have lively, intelligent faces, but not one of them is at school. The girls marry at 12, have their children in quick succession, and are middle-aged at 22.
>
> On our way out we had visited a leper camp, and talked to some of the lepers – noses falling off, one with his feet largely gone. On the way back the bridge now tidily rebuilt – we see a Chinese school, just opened, and full. We talk to a class standing outside, and being instructed in English by a Chinese girl, with a light switch in her hand. Inside are a hundred children or so, most of them boys, tightly packed, and roaring *Do, Re, Mi*.

Back in Kuching we went for a drive with the Rajah and Ranee, then to the Club for drinks, and we sat and watched a lovely sunset, the colours rapidly succeeding one another as in a film. Mountain edges were thrown out like etchings, the palm trees standing up, and the outline of a piece of jungle appearing along the ridge. After sunset the Ranee wanted to move, but the Rajah was in a placid mood, and sat still. He talked a little. He wanted to show us his country and his people; he had a pride in them, and in the way they were governed. But he felt sure that he would best secure their interests, and the country's return to prosperity, if he were to give it up. He thought that he was the best judge of this; and that, as he would be considerably worse off financially, he could not be accused of selling his country to the Crown. He could not really understand what all the fuss was about.

But the next day we had something of a showdown over lunch. The Rajah said he intended to promise the Malay Union that the British Government would spend large sums in the country, and that he would continue to live there, in the Astana. I pointed out that the first could be made to look like bribery, and that the second was not what had been expected. He said that *he* did not want cession – the Secretary of State proposed it. The Ranee said 'Better call it off – if we can do it without loss of face.' I thought this was bluff, and said 'What about Anthony?' The storm blew over. It was necessary to keep up the Rajah's spirits. The Ranee was almost always cheerful, though at times cynical. But the Rajah was inclined to lose heart at any setback, and to lose interest in the whole proceeding.

Then came the visit of Lord Mountbatten and his daughter Patricia. The Rajah became so nervous that his ADC had to find the doctor on the telephone, and ask for the required mixture. (Telephoning in Kuching was a pleasure: one asked by name for the person one wanted, and if there was no response from his number the Exchange located him.)

Lord Mountbatten and his daughter arrived on Easter Monday. It began to pour with rain – the characteristic, torrential rain. But it cleared in the evening, in time for the Tattoo, the occasion of spectacular dancing by the Dyaks; there was also the Khattah, an Indian dance, and a display 'Constabulary through the Ages' by the indefatigable police.

Next day the Mountbattens went for a tour, Lord Mountbatten being insistent that he should be last into the sampan. Back at the Astana, I had a short chat with him before lunch. He asked how things were at home. I told him that some things were still difficult – transport, for instance, and the laundry. 'One needs 29 handkerchiefs,' I said. 'Why 29?' he asked. I said that the laundry van came once a fortnight. 'Then you need only 14 handkerchiefs,' he said. 'No,' I said; 'there are 14 in the wash, and 14 in the drawer, and one extra for the day the laundry comes.' 'No,' he said; 'the laundry brings the clean ones back.' 'Let us start at the beginning,' I said. 'The laundry . . . ' But the Rajah came in. (Long afterwards I noticed that Tristram Shandy, according to his laundress's bill, had in 'one single month . . . dirtied one and thirty shirts.')

There was another downpour during lunch. Mountbatten had ordered departure in jeeps, and he grew agitated about the luggage getting wet. He changed the order to cars. Raincoats had been left, by his almost certifiable valet, on the plane. Turmoil followed, everyone disappearing in turn. We lent the party raincoats, and Mountbatten took mine: 'Ah! Austin Reed,' he said. The captain of the plane telephoned to say he could not take off, and the party should remain at the Astana. 'I'm afraid I disagree,' said Mountbatten. 'We should go, and be ready to take off whenever it lifts. For example' – staring out at the streaming rain – 'at this moment we could take off.' There were more phone calls, but finally the party was marshalled. At the museum Mountbatten had been given a Malay sword, and this had been packed. Patricia had been given by the Rajah a coloured, fabulous bird of wood, nearly the size of a turkey; and this she had half-wrapped in a piece of pink paper. At the last moment her father found her large white hat in a paper bag, and Patricia suggested she should carry the hat, and he the bird. She handed it over. Then Mountbatten's ADC appeared with two bags of secret papers. Mountbatten said the ADC had better carry the bird, and he would take the papers. So they set off down the path, each carrying a Japanese umbrella in the left hand.

Quiet back in the Astana. A torrential visit! Mountbatten had nearly every excellence: looks, intelligence (except in the matter of the laundry), drive, strength, a wonderful memory, and he had told many amusing stories. But he was moody and explosive, and one was not at ease: not because he was difficult, but because he was so restless.

My day usually began at 6 a.m. with breakfast of fish, bacon and eggs, and the especially sweet Sarawak pineapple. I took it on my balcony, and looked at the town across the river. By 7 a.m. the Rajah's 'bread line' was beginning to form below me – a stream of people with small requests. It was the time when I did my writing and thinking, before the heat and humidity impaired one's energy. Then I was ferried in a sampan across the river, broader there than the Thames at Westminster, to our office. The Rajah's institutions of government were being formed again. We now had a Chief Justice, an acting Chief Secretary (J.B. Archer), and a Supreme Council, meeting round a table-cloth. Also we had made a start on the assembling of the Council Negri, the council of the People, or Parliament, which would have to pass the Cession Bill. There were many telegrams to and from the Colonial Office, all in cypher. The Rajah learned that MacBryan was intending to come out, and we asked that he should be stopped.

In the evenings there was the Cinema Lilian, and the Café, or Cabaret, Cathay. At the cinema the Chinese manager, with profuse apologies for being without anything else, gave us pre-war champagne, and this helped with the tedious films. The Café Cathay was owned by another Chinese, Vincent, who had been Spurway's sergeant in the Volunteers; and he entertained us with good Australian brandy, his wife Frieda – who had just had a baby, and danced all night – and sundry Chinese girls. One had to dance with these; conversation became too arduous. Sometimes the Ranee came, and she taught me the Rumba. There was a Malay girl, Sairah, who turned out to be MacBryan's wife. She had been with him on his pilgrimage to Mecca. At first she had spoken no English, did not know how to use a knife and fork, and stayed in her cabin on the ship for five days. She could still neither read nor write.

We went by air to Sibu, the headquarters of the Sea Dyak district. I again quote from my diary:

> Demonstrative welcome; and in one spot, lining the road, there are ten Dyak girls, about 17, in gala costume. Their breasts, very long, firm and pointed, are bare, though some have over their shoulders a short tippet of beads; they wear short sarongs, and from metal rings round their waists hang innumerable large silver coins, which rattle as they walk; rings on their fingers, silver bangles up their forearms, and many have on their heads a kind of two-dimensional crown of silver, with bits of coloured wool at the points . . .
>
> In the afternoon Dawson and I walk through the bazaar with the Ranee, and four Dyak girls join in, hand in hand with the Ranee. A large, motley procession collects behind. A Government officer takes us all for a ride round. The girl next to me is affectionate, and we hold hands for the trip. They give us the flowers from their hair, and the one next to me asks if I will visit her long-house . . .
>
> Next day with Rajah to 'court' in the skittle alley. He reads the Malays an address telling them the benefits of cession, but they do not say a word. The Chinese come in, and petition about their war losses. Then a crowd of Dyaks, chattering and bubbling, who ask to be allowed poison for tuba fishing, increase of pay (both requests granted), and for flags (none available). They ask that a score of men sent to prison for 15 years for the murder of Chinese should be let out, since they did not know whether they were Chinese or Japanese, and 'they had given back the heads'. The Rajah will consider this. They also ask for back pay, following an excellent piece of cross-examination by their Chief, Koh. This is granted. While they go out a weeping woman makes her way in and says her husband has been killed by the Dyaks and asks for free education for her children. An old orang-utan, as big as a man, looks in for a few moments.

We visited the hospital, went to a Chinese garden party where a band played, and saw more superb Dyak dancing at the club. My friend was at the garden party, in a long, dark green sarong and thin, top jacket of pale yellow. As I and the others were leaving, the girl's mother rushed up with many smiles, took my hands, and laid them on her daughter's bosom. The Ranee told me later that it wanted but a gift from me of a cooking utensil to marry us. Next morning I woke to find the orang-utan standing at the bottom of my bed, gazing at me; he had been led there by the District Officer.

There was a further expedition, less romantic, to Simanggong. We travelled up river all day by launch, taking two of the Rajah's boys and the cook, and when we arrived the people swarmed on board. The Rajah held a court again. The Dyaks asked for a grant of weapons, and for permission to start a war with a neighbouring tribe in Dutch Borneo; and requested the Rajah to obtain the return to them of two Chinese heads, which they had smoked but given back. A third Dyak came to join in the argument, and was told by his friends to take his arms off the table. The Rajah's final answer was that he would consider giving them something in lieu of the heads.

In Kuching we found that the two Members of Parliament, David Gammans and David Rees-Williams, had arrived, and Dawson and I visited them on the Minesweeper *Pickle*, which was to be their home. Dawson went off with them next day for their tour of the country, and I applied myself to a spate of telegrams from London. The last cession of a country to the British Crown had been that of Fiji in 1870, to Sir Hercules Robinson; and Sir Hercules had been given power to settle the details. That was not my case. The Colonial Office was nervous, and everything had to be referred to it. There were many question of concern to the Rajah which I had to discuss with him: future visits to Sarawak, a right to occupy the Astana, financial arrangements for himself, his family, and dependents. I would usually find him in the Brooke deck-chair, reading, or doing sums. On one occasion he looked up, and said 'Hurray! I can live till I'm eighty-two.'

The 'diplomatic bag' was broken into while still in the custody of the military; an officer had left it in the back of his jeep when at the cinema, then going on to the Cathay. I had to institute an Inquiry; but it appeared that the bag had contained nothing we could not do without.

Bertram Brooke, the Tuan Muda, arrived before he was expected, with two assistants. They could be seen writing busily on the balcony of their house, and the assistants were observed canvassing against cession in the streets. The Rajah felt unable to do anything to counter this. The leader of the Chinese community, Ong Tiang Swee, 83 years old, gave a magnificent lunch. While we had birds' nest soup (swallows' nests), sucking pig, sharks' fin soup, duck, fish, and ambrosial sweets, with cocktails and champagne, brandy and cigars, much of the conversation turned on the horses, rats and dogs which our hosts, if lucky, had eaten during internment. As we ate, crowds of women and children peered through the doorways and windows. Two days afterwards Tiang Swee entertained the Tuan Muda to a precisely similar lunch, and invited a Government officer as well, which prevented any talk about cession.

The lunch almost knocked me out, but I had to go back to the office to deal with more telegrams. Our cipher clerk, from

Singapore, had been taken ill; I had to do it all, the deciphering and the ciphering, by an abstruse method, like translating from and into an unknown language by use of a dictionary, single-handed. The Ranee had arranged an evening party at the cinema, afterwards at the Cathay. Too many people got drunk. We ate later, or tried to, at a stall in the market. On the way back home we fell into the river.

Next morning, Sunday, I awoke feeling degraded, and worried about the difficulties of cession, which would come to a head that week. But I looked out, across to the town, laughed, and the remarkable sedative properties of Sarawak worked on me. I sat on the balcony in the sunshine, ate breakfast, and watched a father passing below, taking a pineapple and coconut home for his family's breakfast. I went to call on the Tuan Muda. He was courteous and charming, and we kept off any talk about cession. He said he was not asking to see people, merely waiting for anyone who wanted to see him. At that point in walked one of the Government officers.

The two MPs returned, with Dawson, but they were unwilling to talk about their conclusions. Next morning the Council Negri met, the Tuan Muda and his party being also present. The Rajah opened the proceedings, then left. Archer presided; standing orders were suspended for the day; and five or six Bills were passed in less than an hour. When the Council had adjourned the Tuan Muda asked Archer to see him, shook his fist in his face, and called him a traitor to the Brookes.

Next day the Cession Bill was debated, fully, most of the speakers being against it. The Tuan Muda delivered a speech – or, rather, an angry shout. The voting, after a recount, was 18 in favour and 16 against. Archer was understood to say that the Bill had been passed, and he adjourned the assembly. But he had forgotten that the standing orders had been suspended for the business of the previous day only; and I had to point out that the Bill must pass through a Committee stage and Third Reading. Archer abused me violently, and resigned.

Lunch at the Astana was very late, and very appalling. When I arrived the Rajah and Ranee were in joyful mood; some of the Government officers had been across and told them how the proceedings had concluded. I had to break it to them that all was not over; the Bill must be debated again on the next day. The Rajah said: 'Begin all over again, do we? . . . I don't mind . . . Only Hall will mind . . . poor George Hall!' The Ranee was livid, and very unfair. But I had to insist; I expected every attempt would be made later to invalidate the proceedings.

I spent the afternoon making the arrangements for reconvening the Council Negri on the next day, borrowing the *Pickle's* stencil to get out the notices. From time to time Dawson and I tackled Archer, who, after lunch, was more abusive than ever, and resigned three or four times over. In the end we talked him round. On the following day the Council passed the Cession Bill, Third Reading, by 19 votes to 16. The MPs left; then the Tuan Muda departed, with a guard of honour. 'Kindly note', the Rajah said, 'that I am not going to be blown out of the country by a blast from the buglers.' He signed the Bills, sitting in his deckchair. 'Signing away my birthright, like King John at Runnymede,' he said. 'I'll sign anything.' The Ranee was playing patience. 'Looking to see if a handsome man is crossing my path,' she said, as Dennis White, a Government officer, came in, all buttons undone.

In London the MPs reported that the cession of Sarawak would be 'broadly acceptable' to its people. The Supreme Council met, and in its presence the Rajah signed the Instrument of Cession, on 21 May. The Rajah gave a great party at the Astana, and I gave a small one at the Café Cathay. Next day the Sunderland carried us away – the Rajah, the Ranee, Spurway and myself – and we left Dawson behind to administer the Government, on behalf of the Crown. Dennis White (who later became High Commissioner for Brunei) had summed it up: 'Well,' he said, 'there's one thing no one can accuse the Rajah of . . . and that's nepotism.'

Sarawak, under the Brookes, had probably come as near to Utopia as any country has done, or will do. The British Government never, by word or deed, acknowledged the high-minded action of the Rajah in giving it up. The Colonial Office appointed as first Governor Sir Charles Arden Clarke, who had been Governor of the Gold Coast, and was an experienced and sympathetic administrator. Rival factions of the Chinese Communist party and the Malay Union stirred up some disorder; and on his retirement his successor, Michael Stewart, was assassinated on arrival, whilst inspecting the guard of honour. In England Anthony Brooke tried to upset the cession on legal grounds, but he was advised by one of the most searching minds in Lincoln's Inn that all possible loopholes had been closed by the Secretary of State's legal advisers. The country settled down, the Colonial Office's plans came to fruition, and in 1963 Sarawak became a State within the Federation of Malaysia, an independent country within the Commonwealth.

Except for Ascot and occasional visits to Devonshire, the Rajah lived quietly in his house in Albion Street, near Hyde Park Corner. The Ranee lived nearby, in Archery Close, and passed much of the day with him. I visited them from time to time, and took the Ranee to the theatre. We saw Sartre's *Huis Clos* at its first performance in England at the Arts Theatre. (The Ranee wanted the middle of the front row of the stalls, there was no interval, and I had to struggle hard against claustrophobia.) The Ranee had been a friend of J.M Barrie and of Bernard Shaw, and had written stories from her early days. At Archery Close she was up by five or six o'clock every morning, and wrote for a few hours. I knew two nieces of hers, Nancy Shuckburgh (married to Evelyn Shuckburgh of the Foreign Office, son of Sir John), and Pinkie Beckett (married to Martyn Beckett, the architect and Yorkshire squire). They looked upon me with some awe, as actually knowing the lady spoken of in the family as their 'wicked aunt'. She was not wicked, though she enjoyed mild wickedness in others, and was amused at the strange marriages of her daughters Elizabeth and Valerie. Elizabeth was by now parted from Harry Roy, and I was hoping to meet her again.

A public holiday was declared – it may have been the anniversary of VJ day – and Lord Mountbatten was to appear in a march past along Millbank, where the Sarawak Government Offices were. The Ranee invited me to a party there at 8 o'clock, and I asked if I could bring Franz Osborn. It was a very beautiful day. I met Franz in the morning, and we did not know how to kill the time. Everything was closed. There were crowds all over, aimless, and there was no transport. We walked, talked, laughed, found somewhere to have a meal, walked again. We did not want to be at the party too early, and at 8.30 rang the bell. The Ranee appeared on the balcony above our heads.

'You're twelve-and-a-half hours late,' she said, half-amused, half-annoyed.

'I'm terribly sorry', I called up, 'I thought . . .'

'You've missed Elizabeth,' she said.

'I'm sorry,' I said again.

We were very thirsty. 'May we come up?' I called.

'No'.

The Rajah died in 1963. I went to the service in Devon, and saw him laid in the churchyard at Sheepstor, near to James and Charles. The Ranee survived him for some years, and in 1971 wrote an autobiography, *Queen of the Head-Hunters* – an amusing, brave, sad tale.

VIII

Standing up for the Empire

THE Colonial Office moved from Downing Street to Church House, Great Smith Street, just beyond the Abbey. The coal-scuttle, and, we were given to understand, the chamber-pot, had vanished, or at least had been left behind, and replaced by, respectively, central heating and wall fittings. The legal staff was growing: there came Jasper Peck and Hamish McPetrie, and, more junior, Tony McNulty and Tony Rushford. It was a well-organised Office, with a stability derived from the past; and an efficiency necessitated by daily requirements. For the administration of an Empire – especially an Empire in decline – a good filing system is needed. The Colonial Office had one, invented by the Registrar, Ashworth. A 'boot-lace', both ends threaded through the spine of the cover from the outside, held the minutes on the left, and the despatches from the Governors and other correspondence on the right, in chronological order from the bottom. The minutes, often beginning with an analysis of the problem by the Assistant Principal, followed by the views of all concerned, up to the Secretary of State where appropriate, were the repository of Office wisdom. A clerihew about one of the Assistant Secretaries ran –

> He's slow is Mr Acheson
> In passing his despatches on;
> But when he writes a minute
> There's everything in it.

A Colonial Office file had dignity: I should never have dared to burn one.

Soon after my return from Sarawak I was caught up in the Gold Coast ritual murders case – the 'juju' murders as they were popularly called. Five men, convicted and sentenced to death for murder of a minor chief at the ceremonial funeral of a big chief, had three times appealed unsuccessfully to the Judicial Committee of the Privy Council. There had been no miscarriage of justice, and in the Gold Coast (Ghana now) tribal feelings were inflamed. The men's London solicitor, A.L. Bryden, lodged a petition to the King for commutation of the death sentences. This was referred to the Governor, Alan Burns, to whom, as always in the colonial territories, the prerogative of mercy was delegated. He held to his view that there was no case for intervention. There were more petitions, and other approaches; and, every time the date was fixed for the sentence to be carried out, Bryden appeared at our doors with a new blocking pretext. Three times the matter was raised and debated in the House of Commons. Many Labour MPs objected to the death penalty, and the Conservative Opposition, including Winston Churchill, only half-informed on the matter, protested at the delay. I had to see the Speaker to advise him on the constitutional position, and he made a firm statement. Arthur Creech Jones had replaced George Hall as Secretary of State, and he procrastinated. At last Burns let it be known that, unless the law were left to take its course without interference by the politicians here – he didn't say exactly that, but that is what he meant – he could not answer for the state of order in the Gold Coast, and he would have to resign. That brought Creech round, three of the men were executed, and two (whose cases had been subjected to further delay) were reprieved.

After that painful business came the problem, on the international stage, of Palestine. The Colonial Office's task of administering the League of Nations' Mandate was growing more and more difficult. The Government came under increasing pressure from the Jews and the Arabs, and both resorted to terrorism. The Office was guarded and barricaded in a manner till then unknown, though today commonplace. One day, despite this, two members of one of the leading terrorist organisations, the Irgun Zveid Leumi, called at the Colonial Office, signed the visitors' book as such, and were shown in to a startled Assistant Secretary.

The King David Hotel in Jerusalem was blown up, with the Chief Secretary to the Government and other senior officers in it. The country became impossible to govern, and the British Government announced it would give up the mandate, naturally to cries of exultation from some and execration from others. The date fixed was 15 May 1948; and amidst all the tumult we lawyers advised that Parliament should be asked to pass a Palestine Act to end British sovereignty, and provide for continuity in legal matters. I was responsible for settling the provisions of the Act with Michael Hogan, Solicitor General in Palestine, who was seconded to the Colonial Office for the purpose. In explaining to Creech Jones this politically unwelcome measure, as simply as I could, I unhappily used the phrase 'leaving our house in order'. Creech, in turn explaining the Bill to the House, used my words, and was met by more derision than even he usually attracted. An earnest and honest devotee to the welfare of 'colonial peoples', and altogether likeable, he was not a success in the House of Commons.

Another problem, not attracting so much heat, but still controversial, was that of Newfoundland. Formerly a self-governing Dominion, it had been unable to survive economically, and had become dependent on the British taxpayer. The simplest solution was that it should become a province of Canada, but this was opposed here, in Newfoundland, and in Canada. A.P. Herbert, still Independent Member for Oxford University, and whom I had come to know well, was a vigorous advocate of independence for Newfoundland. But a Bill to effect the transfer was decided upon, and I was sent by the Commonwealth Relations Office to settle its terms with the Canadian Government.

In Ottawa I stayed in the massive Chateau Laurier Hotel. The first evening, searching up and down those vast gothic aisles for a drink, I found a bar, entered, and was at once asked to leave. I enquired why. 'You're not allowed in here unless accompanied by a lady', was the surprising answer. I could find no other bar. Insulted, injured, and dry, I went to the dining-room and enquired whether I would be given access there. I was welcomed, and ate my solitary dinner, thinking of the companion who would have legitimated me, so to speak, had she been there, and not in New York. This was Hetty Kantlin, whom I had met in London that summer. A painter friend, married to a sculptress, had given a large party in their studio in the Boltons, that spacious garden village off the Fulham road. The place was crowded to the walls, which were hung with pictures, while the young women were hung with the loose clothes still worn to conceal their thin, war-time figures. But right across the room was a contrasting figure, a girl with a beautiful head, dark hair, white skin, and a bust. When the party began to shrink I worked my way across to her, and introduced myself. Over on a short visit from New York where she was a youthful architect, she was going back the next day. 'Unfortunately' – we both used the word – she had a dinner engagement.

That was enough to fire me with the determination to go to New York, about which I had formed romantic ideas, based on the short stories of O. Henry, the novel *The Lost Weekend*, the advertisements in the *New Yorker*, and the notion of a drug-store, which I gathered was a chemist's shop with refreshments and high stools. I had obtained Hetty's address from my hostess at the party, and we corresponded. The British Government was paying my fare across the Atlantic, and I managed things so that I went first to New York, then to Ottawa, then to New York again.

I sailed from Southampton on the S.S. *Washington*, used as a transport ship during the war, and not yet reconverted for civilian use. There was only one class, and three Americans and I shared an enormous room as a cabin. I enjoyed the voyage immensely, and especially the smell of spices from the land as we approached it, still hours away, and finally the glorious sight of the Statue of Liberty, which seemed to rise almost to the clouds above New York Harbour. Everyone travelling to New York for the first time should go by sea.

Hetty, to my joy, had booked me a room in the very hotel in down-town New York in which *The Lost Weekend* was written. The atmosphere was authentic enough. The first thing I did after checking in was to go to a drug-store, sit down on one of those stools, and say to the man behind the counter 'Do you know, I am doing something I have wanted to do for years – sitting in a drug-store?' He thought I was crazy. I asked him what to have and he handed me a Coca Cola. It was the only time I have ever drunk one.

Hetty herself lived in a one-room flat in Greenwich Village. We began to think of getting married. She took me to see her parents who lived on the Hudson, well away from New York. They were most kind and friendly, though alarmed by this sudden descent of an Englishman with intentions towards their unmarried daughter. And what an Englishman! Their politics were left, and those of some of their friends lefter still. It could hardly be credited that Hetty was thinking of marrying a man who worked in the British *Colonial Office*. But I stood up for that institution.

On my return from Ottawa we decided to marry, in New York. I obtained extended leave from the Office, and asked my colleague and friend there, Jasper Peck, to obtain a few documents for me. The task was onerous, and telegrams passed to and fro. He had to employ solicitors, and on the opposite page I exhibit their bill in facsimile, which I have preserved as a classic.

Armed with the material demanded, we persuaded the pastor of the Washington Square Methodist Church to marry us, which he did, amongst the chintzes of the Church parlour. He afterwards handed us a pretty white booklet of little poems, entitled 'Bridal Blossoms', lavishly decorated with floral embellishments. On the middle page, signed by the minister, was the certificate that we had been 'by me united in Holy Matrimony at New York City According to the Ordinance of God and the laws of New York'. This certificate of marriage had to be produced afterwards to a number of disbelieving authorities. 'Pretty', they said. 'But it's not a marriage certificate'.

Hetty's father was a professor of biology; and as a wedding present he gave me half of a monkey's brain, in lead, life size, which I had admired on his desk. Hetty and I had a few days honeymoon in the lovely Connecticut countryside, and sailed from New York in the *Queen Elizabeth*. I was so attracted by America and the Americans that I thought of throwing away my job at the Colonial Office and trying to earn a living on that side of the Atlantic. But Hetty, twenty-six to my forty-two years of age, had more sense – and anyway had not married an Englishman to stay in New York. I had given up my studio cottage, and was again living with the Costley-Whites, in Cheyne Row. They took us in until we found a flat in Montagu Square. My mother and sister, now living in Reading where my sister was teaching French at the University, welcomed Hetty into the family. She soon found work with Erno Goldfinger, an architect well known, but castigated by some, for his modernist style, which was her style also. At the Colonial Office Creech did not suppress his surprise at what he evidently thought was a precipitate marriage.

Unexpectedly there came another opportunity to go to America. We were heavily dependent on the United States for economic aid,

J.A. PECK Esq.

To Herbert Smith & Co
62, London Wall, London, E.C.2.

Re: William Leonard Dale

1948
24th Nov. To our professional charges incurred in connection with the dissolution of the marriage of the above-named including attending on you when you explained that a certified copy of the decree absolute was urgently required by your friend, Mr. W.L. Dale, for use in the U.S.A. in six days time and you desired to know how to get this today – advising you that a copy decree for use abroad should bear the Court Seal as well as certification and we doubted whether you could get the copy in time and in any case it would involve you in considerable trouble and loss of time and you desired us to endeavour to get it for you and in any case to let you know the date of the decree – special and immediate attendance at the Registry searching for and obtaining date of decree – further attendances explaining the urgency of matter and requesting expedition with the preparation of the decree and that it might be sealed and certified this day – further attendance on you reporting what we had done and that we hoped to obtain the Decree later in the afternoon and that it was dated 25 January 1943 and arranging to meet you at 4 p.m. and hand it to you if successful – further attendances expediting matter and obtaining copy decree absolute sealed and certified and attending on you therewith when you were extremely gratified – in view of time, say 3 13 6

Paid search fees and for sealing and certification. 12 6 — 12 6

£ 4 6 –

and moral support. There were two matters in particular about which we hoped for a better understanding of our difficulties: the economic problems, and our Colonial position. British Information Services (BIS), handling our cultural and information relations with America, was arranging lecture tours. A notice came round the Office asking if anyone would like to go and talk about the Colonies. No one responded. A second notice came round, a little reproachful. I volunteered – an offer received by my colleagues with surprise and a touch of disapproval. It was not the province of a legal adviser to have opinions on colonial policy. Could he be trusted to speak for it adequately? Or – a doubt lurked in some of their minds – might he perhaps be too enthusiastic? But BIS was pressing for a response; and the Colonial Office could hardly confess that nobody was willing to speak for colonial policy. My offer was accepted, especially when I said that I would give up leave for the purpose.

With some advice from Hetty I worked out my lectures. I wished to face the issue: what was the case for the colonies? Sir Alan Burns, one of the best of the later Colonial Governors, did not bring out his book *In Defence of Colonies* until 1957. But I may quote his first page, on which he describes the hostility displayed during the 1950s towards colonies. He says:

> 'From Soviet Russia and her satellites comes the accusation that we exploit our colonies and deprive colonial peoples not only of the wealth that should belong to them, but also of that democratic self-government which is so dear to communist authorities. From India, where the untouchables are still untouchable, come complaints of our racial discrimination. From Latin-American countries, where two-thirds of the Amerindian population are illiterate, we are reproached for the insufficient education given to the inhabitants of British colonial territories. From the United States, which calls its own colonies "possessions", there comes the denunciation of "colonialism". Even in this country there is, in some quarters, a belief that our colonial empire is something to be ashamed of and that, in any dispute between an Englishman and a coloured colonial, the white man is always wrong and the coloured man invariably right. All of this is based on a lack of knowledge and on prejudice.'

The benefits brought by British rule to the dependent territories included the ending of slavery, tribal warfare, cannibalism and some appalling tyrannies; the establishment of law and order, with a sound system of courts of justice, native courts being preserved where appropriate; and the development of education, health, natural resources and communications. Moreover it had been our policy for many years to lead the territories towards self-government, and for this purpose to teach the art of government, to train a civil service, and to improve economic conditions. This policy had resulted in complete independence not only for Canada, Australia, New Zealand and South Africa, but since the war for India, Pakistan, Ceylon (Sri Lanka), Burma and the Sudan. The larger African colonies, particularly the Gold Coast and Nigeria, were on their way to independence. Sarawak was an example of this very process of civilization; and the people had been glad to accept, for a hundred years, government by an English gentleman, with the help of a few officers, and no soldiers.

The object of my lecture tour was not so much to justify the conception of colonies as such – hardly possible with an American audience – but to get my hearers to appreciate this policy of promoting self-government, and to see that it would be disastrous for the people whose interests we all had in mind if the Empire were to be hurriedly dismantled. The Colonial Office feared being pressed into undue haste.

I gave the BIS three titles, to try to meet what would be expected of me by varying audiences. My titles were: 'The Case for the British Colonies', 'Is the British Empire a Going Concern?' ('going' could be in the sense either of 'departing' or of 'active'), and 'Recent Constitutional Developments in the British Commonwealth'. I did not keep my notes, or any record of the tour. A lady made a sound-recording on one occasion, which I afterwards listened to with some dismay; she remarked on the absence of 'punch lines'. My recollection of the lectures is hazy, of what I saw and did in between more vivid.

Towards the end of 1950, then, Hetty and I embarked on the *Queen Mary*, and I saw the Statue of Liberty again from the sea. New York was glistening in the snow, and I watched the skating at the open air rink at the Rockefeller Centre, as if in a painting by Dürer. We spent Christmas with Hetty's family, and in early January I was off. I first went to Boston, where I stayed with a charming, hospitable couple, Bostonians of almost Henry James vintage, laughing at themselves. My hostess entertained me first thing every morning with her efforts to produce fresh orange juice, which she thought obligatory, from her new electric machine.

Each time she put an orange in, it jumped out and across the room, and we had to catch it. We played orange cricket. Their house was in the best part of Boston, somewhere near Beacon Hill, and my host took me to his elegant club for lunch, where I met other Bostonians. I lectured to the English Speaking Union, assuring them that the Empire was not going overnight. One evening I went to Harvard, to address a group of professors. All teachers in American Universities are called 'professors'; but here really were grave, grey-haired, lean seekers after truth, clearly a case for 'Recent Constitutional Developments'. After a six o'clock dinner, a milk and water affair, we adjourned, and I talked about the new Commonwealth – the Statute of Westminster, India, Pakistan and Ceylon independent members and now republics, the position of the monarchy, and so on. They were courteous and attentive, but not I think greatly moved. It was only later that I realised it was not much use expecting American constitutional lawyers to take a serious interest in the Commonwealth. Magna Carta is their line.

My next stop was Washington, and I lectured at the 'black' – the word was not used then – Howard University. There they had chosen 'The Case for the British Colonies', and I gave it to them. My reception was polite but painful, and I felt like St Sebastian with the arrows sticking into him. After that I went to the English Speaking Union, and the arrows were removed, painlessly.

Then came St Louis, and a different atmosphere altogether, almost a different country. I felt that I was meeting authentic Americans, people who had been there for generations, 'natives', not expatriate Europeans. My arrival at the New Hotel Jefferson was complicated by the simultaneous arrival and registration of (1) 'The American Retailers Ass.', 'The Mississippi Valley Ass.', 'The Ass. of Asphalt Paving Technologists', 'The Urological Post Graduate Seminar', and 'The Bandwagon of Infants' Childrens' and Girls' Wear' (I counted myself fortunate to avoid a clash with the American College of Allergists), and (2) the British Consul's baby. The latter led to a lot of extra parties, and during my week there I did not pay for a single meal, except breakfast. I gave a lecture to the English Speaking Union, preceded or followed by dinner. Before the dinner the Chairman took me aside, into the Men's lavatory, and handed me 25 dollars in notes. What speculations ran through the minds of the men standing against the fitted wall, who looked round with curiosity, I do not know. During the lecture, finding myself on a platform with a wall-map of the World behind me, and a long pointer in my hand, I foolishly embarked on a tour of Africa. Over in the west I tried to find The Gambia, but had to give up. 'That place will be the death of me', I exclaimed, throwing away the pointer; and I told them the story of the Bishop of The Gambia and Rio Pongas.

I was taken into the general care of the Senior Judge of the Federal District Court. He was the local historian of Missouri, had received his LL.B. degree from Mark Twain, and had practised in the court – which he showed me – where the Negro slave Dred Scott had sued for his freedom in 1846. Amongst rare characters I met was Charlie Doran, who had been an Irish MP from 1906-8, resigned to become a Sinn Feiner, and was not re-elected. He gave me lunch. The Judge insisted that I should sit with him in court on the bench, and from there effected a series of introductions to persons present. I was required to say a few words, which I did. A number of people came forward, stretched up, and shook my hand. The Judge and one of his friends took me to an old 'saloon'. As we stood at the bar drinking beer, the Judge introduced me to the manager, and praised the establishment. 'Why', he said, 'during Prohibition, I was Prohibition Enforcement Officer. I came in here any time I liked and could get a drink – get anything you liked.' He looked at me with pride. Instead of going back to his court, he took me to the museum. I said goodbye to St Louis with much regret. The consul said my informal contacts had been more valuable than any amount of lectures: I hope so, since I gave only one.

An idea had come to me. San Francisco was my next destination, and BIS had planned for me to be immured in the train for two or three days and nights to get there. I found out that I could fly, and have the time in San Francisco. I persuaded the BIS office in St Louis that the journey by air would cost no more than three days in the train, and they bought me an air ticket. On the way the plane came down for a brief stop at Los Angeles in the middle of the night. I visited the bar at the airport. It was almost deserted; but I retain a distinct photographic recollection in profile of a girl in black and white sitting alone at the brightly lighted bar. She looked every bit as a girl sitting at a bar in Los Angeles airport, in the middle of the night, should look. I wished I had Toulouse-Lautrec with me as my companion, to paint 'The Absinthe Drinker' of the New World.

I suppose I must have arrived in San Francisco when it was still dark. I kept away from the BIS office until it was time to announce my presence. I thoroughly enjoyed my days of freedom there. The city entirely came up to my expectations. The weather was warm and sunny, with some fog by the water. But the Golden Gate Bridge rose above it all, more beautiful that I had imagined. I do not suppose I had been put up at the Mark Hopkins, but I was staying somewhere up there, and the cable car down the steep hill, and then up again, made me think of our cable car rides down and up the cliffs at Scarborough. I lunched on Fisherman's Wharf, and took an excursion to the Red Woods. On the third evening I ventured into a night club, and there encountered the 'Cuban bombshell'. In between her appearances in the cabaret she devoted herself to me. She was pretty, exotic, attentive, and somehow seemed to exude heat. We talked and joked; and I bought – invested in, I should say – a series of bottles. During several hours I identified no other sign of attachment. At last the place closed down, and we left the building hand in hand. As soon as we were in the street a man standing there, unknown to me, came up and pushed me aside. I pushed him back again. He became abusive and violent, acting as if he owned the girl. He was of the same build, colour, and heat as the 'Cuban bombshell' – evidently another of them, but more explosive. I withdrew.

Next morning I reported to BIS, saw Kathleen Graham, the Consul, and realised she knew all about my doings. My San Francisco visit proper began. Early one morning I took the train to Stanford, and addressed a large contingent of undergraduates at breakfast time. I remember the occasion well: the campus of the fine university, the bright, sunny morning, an enthusiastic crowd of lively young people, and many intelligent questions. I had an evening meeting at the Faculty Club, after an early dinner at someone's hospitable table. It followed much the same lines as the Harvard meeting, but I was more successful in arousing their interest. Perhaps it was because I unwittingly made a statement to them of botanical import. Along the trail I had emphasized the economic developments we were introducing into colonial territories, especially in agriculture: new crops, new methods of cultivation. The world was short of foodstuffs, edible oil for one. We had started great schemes for the cultivation of ground-nuts, particularly in Tanganyika, and these produced an excellent substitute for olive oil. This was known in America; and they called it the 'peanut plan'. It was also known that our ground-nuts scheme was not working well. It was no use my trying to gloss this over. I announced that we had found an effective alternative crop – chrysanthemums. I saw a look of surprise on all faces, and pressed the point home. I made something of a joke of it. 'Oh yes', I said; 'their seeds make excellent edible oil. We do not grow them as table decorations for idle Empire overlords!'

For my last day in San Francisco BIS had done well for me: I was to be guest of honour at the monthly luncheon meeting of the Commonwealth Club of California (every State has a kind of nickname, and California was known as the 'Commonwealth State'). The Club enjoyed great prestige, and all the important people belonged to it. I was nervous. We were seated at tables for six or so, with white table-cloths, and glistening silver, but not much else. I suppose there were thirty or more tables, and I was placed on the Chairman's right. He talked to me about the history of the Club, and of their pride in being able to attract to it very distinguished guests. 'Why,' he said, 'every President of the United States since Taft has sat in the chair you're sitting in'. I began to wriggle with alarm. 'Would you mind', I asked, 'if we talked about something else? You are making me very nervous.' He was a kindly man, and sought to reassure me. He turned to me, saying 'Oh, you've no need to feel nervous. You British – all you have to do is to get up and spout. Look at Winston Churchill now! He was here . . . '. The time came for him to introduce me, and I rose. Two men suddenly appeared from opposite directions and placed microphones before me, about eighteen inches apart, and well below mouth level. I tried stooping down and speaking first into one and then into the other, but they completely unnerved me. My address was recorded, but – unfortunately – I never listened to the tape.

On my early morning start for Stanford I had worn the winter overcoat I had brought with me from England. But the day was too warm for me to need it afterwards; and on my train journey back in the evening I put it in the luggage rack overhead and forgot all about it. As my itinerary was to take me to the snows of the far north, this was a serious loss. I had no dollars with which to buy a replacement. The young man who had been looking after me on behalf of BIS placed his at my disposal. This very kind offer I at first felt bound to decline: it was in fact a particularly light, Spring overcoat, no doubt adequate for California, but I was bound for Duluth, where I had heard there were bears. But there seemed no alternative to accepting his generosity; and with the light grey overcoat over my arm I boarded my train. As I watched the Golden Gate Bridge disappearing, tears came to my eyes at the beauty of the scene I was leaving. San Francisco was one of the two places I have visited which have in no way disappointed my expectations. The other is Venice.

I was travelling on the great South Pacific Railway, and BIS had obtained for me what was classed as a 'drawing-room'. I had the compartment to myself, ate in the restaurant car, and went from time to time to look at the view behind us through the wide glass at the end of the train. At night my black steward came to my drawing-room and made up the bed for me. I was in the train for three days and nights, travelling in great comfort, and through fantastic country. We went by Lake Tahoe through Salt Lake City, Utah, where the Mormons have their headquarters, and across the salt flats.

I left the train at Minneapolis, and it was so dry and cold that, when the receptionist at the hotel handed me my key at the bedroom door, the static electricity produced a crackle. After a day or two there, I went further north to Duluth, and I was colder there than I have ever been in my life. I bought ear muffs, and someone lent me a woolly to put under my Californian overcoat. Everyone liked to tell me about the black bears raiding the dustbins at night time.

Then down to the comparative warmth of Chicago, beside the great lake. I had two memorable experiences in the city. I went to a Van Gogh exhibition, then touring America, at the City Art Gallery. Filling my eyes with the light and warm colours of Provence, I was brought up short by the well-known – perhaps even hackneyed – picture of the Sunflowers. I went hot with the shame of it. By a slip of the tongue I had said 'Chrysanthemums', and had repeated the slip from Stanford to Chicago. I wished I had listened to that Commonwealth Club tape. On a lecture tour one cannot issue an 'erratum'.

The other experience was at Pickett's Tearooms, an all-black establishment in down-town Chicago, on the Saturday night. I was a little surprised at BIS's choice of time and place, but I was told I should enjoy the evening. I had chosen 'Is the British Empire a Going Concern?' – or perhaps the Tearooms had – and bills had been distributed announcing the talk by 'The Legal Adviser to the British Empire's Colonial Holdings'. The evening was due to begin at six o'clock, but there was hardly anyone there when I arrived. My hosts were hospitable and welcoming, particularly after the whisky had begun to do its work. I never saw any sign of tea. By degrees people came in and joined us. The room filled with shouts of laughter. We were all in a merry mood when at last the time came to eat, and merrier still by the end of the meal. I was never asked to get up and deliver my talk. I have entitled this chapter 'Standing up for the Empire'; but I think that, at Pickett's Tearooms, I did more for it by remaining seated.

My task in defending colonial rule would have been easier if in 1951 I had been able to see ahead for twenty or thirty years, and perceive the ugly dictatorships, corruption and starvation which would overtake many territories after the withdrawal of colonial rule. But colonialism had to pass. An Indian acquaintance gave it a fair epitaph: 'English policy of ruling other people unacceptable; apart from that, well done'.

IX

Rise of a Kingdom – Libya

THE maisonette in Montagu Square was too large for us. That part of Marylebone, at least our Square, was still in the main residential, with gardens and tall trees, but the slide towards professional and institutional occupation was beginning. The maisonette above us was occupied by an immigrant psychoanalyst and his lady, with whom Hetty, from New York, naturally struck up a friendship. I, from old Yorkshire, naturally did not: I believed in being on good terms with one's neighbours, but keeping one's distance from them – especially from a psychoanalyst. A great many ladies seemed to go up there for couching.

Anthony McNulty, later Secretary of the European Human Rights Commission, and then working with me in the Colonial Office, came to dine with us in our basement dining-room. 'Why do you live like Troglodytes?', he asked in his affable and affluent manner. Tony had, or would have, a house in Cap d'Antibles. The answer was that that was the way we could afford to live – I was still paying maintenance to Emma. But it was not the place we wanted: the rent was high, the rooms were large, they were only half-furnished, and there was no heating, no one to clean. Worse than all this, it was beginning to appear that our marriage was not going to prosper. Our backgrounds were too dissimilar. Besides, I was in my forties, Hetty in her twenties. She was being absorbed into the architectural world. She had found a new and agreeable employer, and together they were designing an important building for the coming Festival of Britain on the South Bank.

We took a holiday in France: first in Paris, on the left bank, then in Provence, sitting at cafe tables, swimming, and visiting those lovely places by train – Arles, Nîmes, the Pont-du-Gard. There was nobody about very much, and that region of the country was still wholly French.

We were offered a smaller maisonette at 13 Paultons Square in Chelsea. Before we moved we gave a party for a Mrs Taylor and her American debutantes. Mrs Taylor we had met in New York, always wearing a small red hat, because, she explained, it helped her to gain her ends. These were to cajole the wealthy parents of developing daughters to send them in her care, and to her substantial profit, on a visit to Europe. It happened that there was appearing at that time, in successive numbers of the *New Statesman*, an advertisement which had caught my eye: a strong Cotswold cider in barrels, accompanied by a warning that it was so powerful an aphrodisiac that it should be drunk in moderation. We ordered a barrel, and invited to the party such young men as we knew. These included Laurie Lee, an acquaintance from Chelsea pub days, who played a tin whistle. We thought he might, at the right moment, pipe the young ladies into the garden of Montagu Square. But either they were genuinely delayed, or Mrs Taylor took fright: they never appeared. The properties of the cider were not scientifically tested – though *Cider with Rosie* appeared some time later.

At the Colonial Office my urge for movement was being satisfied. Having achieved Assistant Secretary level I had a carpet – and it was becoming a magic carpet. It had lifted me to Canada, via the snows of Newfoundland, and across America. Best of all, it had carried me, with intermediate descents to earth, on that magical visit to Sarawak. Nor was it allowed to gather dust. I accompanied Lord Listowel, Minister of State, on a mission to Gibraltar. The Colonial Office was much troubled about the future of the Rock. 'Decolonisation' was in the air, but to think of Gibraltar – with some 20,000 inhabitants and no material resources – as an independent State was absurd. The same difficulty would arise over other small colonies. But with Gibraltar there was a difference, shared to some extent with Malta. It was not far away, and in Europe. The Gibraltarians had no wish to become part of Spain. I worked out a new constitutional arrangement – new for us, though the French had something like it for what they called their 'metropolitan' territories in North Africa. Gibraltar could have a status something like that of Northern Ireland, returning MPs to Parliament. Lord Listowel was an intellectual, married to a Hungarian, Judith, of forceful character. We stayed with the Governor at 'The Convent', as Government House was called. We had meetings with influential local politicians and business men, and a pleasant few days altogether. But nothing came of our mission.

One morning, when Roberts-Wray was away and I was sitting at his desk as his deputy, a confidential letter came from the Foreign Office asking help in finding from the Colonial Legal Service a legal adviser to a new country, the United Kingdom of Libya, created by the United Nations. I immediately thought of offering to go there myself. I abandoned my files for the rest of the morning, and tried to find out – surreptitiously – what I could about this new United Kingdom. I remembered mention in the Acts of the Apostles of 'the parts of Libya about Cyrene', but that description seemed vague even for a United Nations Resolution. The former Italian Colonies of Tripolitania and Cyrenaica, with the Fezzan stretching back across the Sahara, were to be federated into a new Kingdom. Libya would, so far as I could make out, consist of some 700,000 square miles, four-fifths of it sand, with a little cultivation along the coastal strip introduced by Italian settlers. Its only export was grass, esparto grass, to make paper. There were perhaps one million inhabitants – Arabs, Berbers, Italians. Cyrene was the birthplace of Eratosthenes, who had seen the sun at the bottom of a well. Of more concern to me, the Constitution was already written, by the United Nations, and it would have to be made to work. The British would help. A difficult job! But I liked a difficulty. Unknown territory! But I liked unknown territory. When I told Roberts-Wray he was aghast. Not only was he to lose me, for two years at least, but the post was a little demeaning for the Assistant Legal Adviser to the Colonial and Commonwealth Relations Offices: it would be all right, of course, promotion even, for a member of the Colonial Legal Service. But, generous-spirited as he was, he acquiesced. Hetty accepted my decision: we had already half-agreed to part.

But before going to Libya I was wafted to Nyasaland (now called Malawi) to deal with a highly embarrassing situation. The Attorney General there had told us he might have to prosecute his predecessor, William Lockhart Smith, on charges of bribery made by an Indian lawyer practising there. Lockhart Smith had been promoted to be a judge of the Court of Appeal of Eastern Africa, and was one of the best lawyers in the service. The scandal would be enormous. The new Attorney General, Basil Hobson, seemed perhaps a shade enthusiastic, and Roberts-Wray wanted me there to ensure prudence. The accusing lawyer had himself been involved, and the case was tricky. But after a stay of some weeks I was forced to the conclusion that, while we could not be sure a prosecution would succeed, we should not be justified in trying to dissuade the Attorney General, out of regard for a wider public interest, from exercising his responsibilities. It was the question of the 'public interest' again. Lockhart Smith was brought from the bench in Kenya to stand trial in his old territory. A county court judge was sent from England to try him, acquitted him, and said the prosecution should not have been brought. Lockhart Smith resigned and took up private practice in Kenya. Was I mistaken? The question worried me for a long time.

After Nyasaland I went to Swaziland on an errand for the Commonwealth Relations Office, the nature of which I now forget. I stayed with the Resident Commissioner in Mbabane, in a thoroughly English setting, with wood fires, chintz curtains, and a Derbyshire countryside around us. On my way back I drove through a part of the Kruger National Park, failing to see much in the way of lions and tigers, but encountering in Johannesberg the early stages of apartheid.

At last the time had come for me to go to Libya. I left by plane for Tripoli on 30 November 1951, arriving in the evening in the pouring rain. I was met by my old friend Harry Trusted, who had been Attorney General of Palestine, and later Chief Justice of Hong Kong until imprisoned by the Japanese; and by Alan Goodison, a diplomat in escrow as it were. The country was still under the British Military Administration, and I was driven to the residence of the Military Administrator, Blackley, where I was to stay for a few days. This was the Villa Volpi, a beautiful house built by a Turkish pasha 180 years before. There was a very large, tiled, reception room with a good grand piano in it, Mrs Blackley was musical, and I played it after dinner.

Next morning the sun shone. I sat in the courtyard of white marble, with a basin in the middle and fountains playing. Beyond was a large garden with orange and grapefruit trees, date palms, and a swimming pool. The air was warm and brisk. It was the first, and last, blissful moment I passed in Libya.

Evidence of Mussolini was still there. The Villa Volpi had been the residence of Marshal Balbo; and it was his chauffeur who was now our driver. Trusted, who was with the Foreign Office, took me to meet the Ministers, so far as there were any, of the Provisional Federal Government. These were Ali Jerbi (Foreign Affairs and Justice, who had been Mussolini's interpreter – bald and, I judged, wily), Mohammed Othman (Health – a pleasant little squint-eyed Fezzanese, who did not know where Tripoli got its water from), Omar Sharib (Defence), and Mahmoud Muntasser, the Prime Minister. Muntasser was friendly, with prominent teeth which added to his air of smiling affability. I knew no Arabic, and had been having a daily lesson in French in order to be able to communicate with him, but I found that he had been having a daily lesson in English. That day we spoke English, but ever afterwards French. Muntasser had been educated in Italy – as had other Tripolitanians – and that caused him to be mistrusted, especially in Cyrenaica. But he was able, honest and had broad views. He and his son Omar eventually became good friends of mine.

They had nowhere for me to live, no office, no staff – hardly surprising, since 'they' consisted of a Government not yet in being. There was an Establishment Officer (late of the Sudan Civil Service), an official of the Tripolitanian Government, who was supposed to help, but he proved more elusive than most Establishment Officers, and a good deal less competent. Tripoli was still full of American and British families; and there were many United Nations officials, who occupied the only building to have any warmth, the Grand Hotel on the sea front.

After ten days with the Blackleys I moved to a run-down hotel on the sea front called the Uaddan, which was to be smartened up and house a Casino. On the top floor was the 'Officers' Club', for 'officers' in transit, and I was taken to be one such. The Establishment Officer, as was to be expected – he was at heart a water-colour artist – had not told the management I was coming. There was a bathroom with no hot water, bed too short, no arm chair, no writing table, no drawers. Above a gaping void revealing intestinal cables was a notice: '*HOT WATER* is usually available from 6 a.m. to 8 a.m. and from 6 p.m. to 8 p.m. daily *except* on *Saturday mornings* and *Sunday evenings*'; but I soon realised that this referred to the coffee pot of water occasionally brought round. On the ground floor was the 'Bath Club', an officers' club where I ate to the sound of the Forces Programme. But it was cheap living. My room and three meals cost £1 a day, and two large whiskies and soda under 1/6d.

Also I obtained a share in an office, and a secretary to myself. Stanley Weinberg, a Pole of Jewish blood, whose family had been wiped out by the Germans, and who was legal adviser to the Tripolitanian Government, offered me half his room. Stanley, with his ironical humour, put me wise on many matters; and I became indebted to him, and to his Swiss wife Bambi, for many kindnesses. My secretary was Dorothy Haley, the wife of Tim Haley, the Treasurer designate of the new Government. I told her to fix up her salary with him. I passed this on to Trusted, saying I had no doubt they would agree something. 'It all depends what terms they're on', replied that man of the world.

There was not much for me to do yet. Ali Jerbi did not concern himself with Justice, but he ordered two typewriters to give the Ministry of Defence a good start. One of the immediate problems facing the Libyans was the large number of Italians there, settled as cultivators, tradesmen and workmen, and the number of Italian institutions. An agreement about the disposal of Italian property had been made under United Nations auspices, and a Tribunal of three international judges set up to settle disputes. The judges had been there some months, at prodigious salaries, and without work. The Swede implored me to give them some. I attended two Government meetings, but the discussions tended to switch suddenly to goats and their tiresome nature. The Minister-to-be of Agriculture mistook me for an agricultural expert.

I flew to Benghasi, the chief town of the Province of Cyrenaica, where they leaned towards Egypt, unlike Tripolitania, which was oriented towards Europe. I had an audience of the King-to-be, Idris al Sanussi, Head of the powerful Sanussi religious order, and Emir of Cyrenaica. He was over 60, in poor health with perpetual dysentery, and had no children, but was said to be an able leader. He was pleasant and gentle, and kept going well in his feeble, high-pitched voice. He had already had several hours with Muntasser. I also had a frank talk with Mohammed Saqisli, the Emir's handsome, white-haired Prime Minister, who endeared himself to me by telling me he always kept secret documents under his blotting pad. I next saw C. N. Hooper, the legal adviser. I already had respect for him: a scholar, with a better knowledge of Arabic than the Arabs around him, he had, when Judicial Adviser in Transjordan, translated the Mejelle, the Turkish Civil Code, which I had tried to assimilate when in Palestine. He had drawn up Codes for Cyrenaica, but was unable to get them further than his desk. They were pro-British there, he said, and would go the way we wanted, if only they could understand which that was. It was known that we were apprehensive about federation, which had been wished on the country by the United Nations. It became clear to me that federal powers under the Constitution, drafted by the UN, would have to be exercised lightly, or the new 'United Kingdom' would break up. The King would not be able to keep it together; he would not go to Tripoli at all, where a small bomb had been thrown at him when he had gone.

Independence came, on 24 December. I flew to Benghasi again with Muntasser for the celebrations. We learned that Idris had declared a general amnesty for all prisoners of half their sentence, and three public holidays. Ali Jerbi sent from Tripoli to say he could not find the documents for informing foreign Governments of Independence. And a desperate effort was on foot to substitute a new Agreement about Italian property. The celebrations took place in the square, with salutes fired on a gun borrowed from the Americans. There was a large crowd of people, who gave vent to regulated applause. There followed a lunch in the Government building. Faced with a hopeless search for my name amongst the hundred place cards in Arabic, I remembered Hooper's story of King Abdullah who, when losing at chess, would get his opponent out of the room and then move the pieces. I removed a card at random, put it in my pocket, and stood behind the chair until everyone had come in and we sat down. Somehow I got through the meal, stuffing chips and other uneatable material into the carcass of the whole chicken. Saquisli made a long speech, and he was followed by a poet, who had to be stopped. Fortunately, on the way back to the hotel, I cut my forehead on the open boot of the car, and escaped the tea party at the Palace.

The Blackleys left, and embassies raced to establish themselves. The Ministry of Foreign Affairs, which was the same thing as the Prime Minister's Office, borrowed the passport of the Greek Consul, to learn what had to be put on a diplomatic passport. Stanley Weinberg, on returning home after Independence celebrations, found a turkey flying round his flat. It was a present from the Qadi, and as there were sixty Qadis in Tripolitania, Stanley was wondering what he could do with sixty turkeys. An Italian judge sent a bottle of wine, and another left a parcel. Stanley complained of the expense of sending anything in return, now that the NAAFI was closed. This had never happened before; it marked the end of British Administration.

The only Libyan lawyer in the country was now appointed Minister of Justice, and the only Libyan doctor Minister of Health. The Minister of Justice was Fethi Kekhia, who had a doctorate in law from Cairo. He was short, bald, intelligent, with a moustache, and, when not wearing his tarboush, resembled Mr Attlee. His English was inadequate, and we got stuck from time to time, but he liked to practise it. He was inclined to be prickly at first, but it was not long before we were on good terms. There was an initial difficulty over appointing me as Agent for the Government before the Italian property tribunal, to which the Italians had applied for appointment of an administrator. I drafted a letter in the usual form, but Fethi Kekhia objected to the concluding words, 'I have the honour to be, Sir, Your obedient servant'; and the matter was referred to the Prime Minister. He assented if Auni Dajani, a Jordanian, who was Head of the Royal Diwan (or Office), was joined. I said this would not do; there must be one Agent. 'But', said Fethi, 'you will be so busy, drafting decrees, you must have an assistant'. 'Very well', I said, 'I would accept Dajani as my assistant'. The matter was referred to the King. Then Fethi had an idea about the Italian property: draft a decree attaching it all. 'No good', I said; 'there is an international agreement'. 'Well, draft *some* decrees', he said. I told him I had been doing exactly that. 'Then', he said, 'draft a decree setting up a Supreme Court for tomorrow's Cabinet'! This was comparable to a request I had a little later from Ali Jerbi, to draft a Defence Law, providing for the Army, not more than six sections (I remembered our Army Act had some 200 sections). But I had two major triumphs: a letter appointing Pitt Hardacre, the Financial Adviser, as Controller-General of Property, and my appointment as Director of Causes and Legislation, with a letter appointing this official as Agent before the Tribunal. I learned the best rule for drafting for Ministers: put in something wrong towards the end, then they will strike it out and pass the rest of the draft.

I was summoned to the Cabinet to advise on the question whether a proposed concession to a certain bus company was a federal matter. The discussion was over when the Minister of Communications, Ibrahim Shabaan, launched into a heated speech, doubting whether it was proper to grant a concession at all, either to a Libyan or to a foreign company, as it would affect the elections. The Prime Minister said he would leave that to his conscience. I sat wondering what the conscience of a Berber could be like: I decided, on the analogy of the monkey's brain, like a small haggis, with one or two slight coruscations. In the end Shabaan satisfied his conscience by selling his shares in the bus company.

The Ministers went to Benghasi for some time, to be around the King, and there was a stagnant period. We were given offices in the Castello, the large, straggling, half-ruined Moorish fortress. My first room was cold, and I moved over with the collaboration of Ali Sunni, Fethi's nephew and First Secretary, into a room on the sunny side, with a balcony and a view of the sea. There were no messengers, no cleaners, and a telephone which the Italian Representative (the Italians did not deserve an Ambassador yet) mistook for a coffee-grinding machine. I asked the Director of Antiquities to lunch and to show me the mosques. He did not appear until hours late, with all his fly-buttons undone, a thick rim of dirt round the neck of his jacket and rain-coat. I never did see the mosques. I hired a bicycle for a day; it had a large nail in the front tyre, but I rode along. Members of the diplomatic corps, whom I met on my way, stared. Another day I was driven to Sabratha, miles along the coast, and under a brilliant sky saw that enchanting ruined city on the edge of the sea. The theatre, of sandstone, wonderfully restored by the Italians, had three tiers of Corinthian pilasters rising behind the stage. Through the openings we saw the different greens, and further out the slate blue, of the sea.

At the beginning of February I went home for a week. I had my divorce to arrange, and had stipulated with the Foreign Office that I should have a week's leave on 'urgent personal affairs'. Muntasser had not known this, and demurred. But when I repeated the phrase 'urgent personal affairs' he was much intrigued, and gave me permission. I stayed with Jasper and Olwen Peck; and when I left at the end of my week the fog was so thick that there was no transport and I had to carry my bags from their house in Clareville Grove, off the Brompton Road, to the Air Terminal in Buckingham Palace Road. I believe it was the last of London's pea-soup fogs, for the Clean Air Act 1956 prohibited the emission of 'Dark Smoke'.

The elections in Libya took place towards the end of February, and passed off with some violence, but on the whole well. Dr Anneisi, the Minister of Finance, was elected by two votes, but three people who had voted for him confessed to impersonation. On this Dr Anneisi produced three further impersonators who had voted against him, and won the day. One candidate gave his opponent £2000 to withdraw, which he did. Another candidate went off his head with worry. But Muntasser was confirmed as Prime Minister. He inspected a Victory parade of army recruits; and on the rear rank suddenly firing off a *feu de joie*, Muntasser fell flat on his face.

There was an acute shortage of housing and personal goods. Two Ministers were caught late one night moving furniture, including a grand piano, from one house to another, and were rebuked by the Prime Minister. In March I was turned out of my room at the Uaddan, and had nowhere to go. In desperation, and through the introduction of a friend who was giving me Italian lessons, I obtained a room with a Greek, George Tsoucos, an 'exporter'. On my returning there the first evening, the key broke off in the lock, and I had to spend the night with the Army friends with whom I had had dinner. George always wore blue shorts and a pyjama jacket, played Wagner as loudly as he could on his radio and gramophone (it could be heard all the way down the Lungomare), and fried the breakfast eggs in castor oil, which he no doubt *imported.* I decided on a bold move. There was a solid little one-floor house at the far end of the Lungomare, built by an Italian not long before the war, which would shortly be available. It was occupied by one Morison, an ex-Sudan Tripolitanian official, who was leaving. Pitt Hardacre and I both applied to be allocated the house, but I did not see why he should have it. It was true he had a wife and daughter, and charming they were (the wife was German, and liked a sea view), whereas I was single. Still, they had a perfectly good house already. I would have referred the matter to Muntasser, but I was not sure he would decide in my favour – finance was more important than law. I persuaded Morison to take me in as a lodger; the furniture, Government property, had to remain anyway; and when he went he left me in possession, with a maid Elena. Possession, as I explained to Pitt, who was amazed at my effrontery, was nine points of the law, and I would take care of the tenth. Neither he nor his wife ever bore me the slightest grudge; the daughter later came to me for piano lessons.

I met with a few difficulties. Morison having made sure of getting his deposit back from the Electricity Company, the company promptly cut off the electricity and removed the meter ('Of course', they said, when I protested). Elena, who helped herself liberally to the Italian vermouth, left before long; but whether this was due to the influence of the Pope as she was inclined to assert (Morison had a wife in England which apparently regularised the situation, but I was disinclined to argue that point), or of her boy friend, or of American pay packets, I never determined. More important was my need of a piano. The occupants of the Villa Volpi were now the British Ambassador and his wife, Sir Alec and Lady Kirkbride. Sir Alec was a well-known Arabist, speaking and writing the language in a way which brought admiration from Muntasser and others. I tried to persuade Lady Kirkbride to let me have the loan of the piano, for which she had no use. She refused, writing that she 'had no right to let it out of the house, as it was the property of the Libyan Government'. I wrote back saying that I 'had not expected her to turn down my request on *legal* grounds'. I was never asked to dinner there; but then, so far as I heard, no one else was either.

I sent for my own piano. I acquired other necessities, such as crockery, two glass decanters with unnaturally long necks (which Tim Haley asserted were for use by funeral directors, 'one each side of the deceased'), and a mousetrap. This article was home made, from cocoa tins, and would have killed a cat.

The elections over, the testing of federal government began. Muntasser, to begin with, did everything himself; saw all applications for visas (this lasted for one day), and approved the design for the messengers' uniforms. He then told a meeting of senior officials that they were to take the advice of their British advisers. He also wished to imprison some of his political opponents in Parliament, but was dissuaded. I had a long discussion with Saqisli, who wanted to know whether it was Muntasser's view – or, failing him, mine – that the Federal Government was 'more important' than the Provincial Governments. In asking me this he plumbed the depth of his constitutional thoughts, except that when the question of an inter-Governmental Committee was raised, he asked who should be Chairman; and I said Muntasser, always. He asked what would happen if Cyrenaica, instead of coming to the Federal or the British Government for money, went elsewhere.

I knew that 'elsewhere' meant Egypt. At the opening of Parliament the Egyptians, uninvited, were present in strength: a Minister, two high Parliamentary officials, and a former member of the Court of Appeal, now President of the 'Libyan Legislation Committee' sitting in Cairo. Parliament decided to meet for six months in Benghasi, and six in Tripoli. The Cyrenaican President of the Senate gave us joy when he addressed one of the Federal officials thus: 'Thou of the lowest possible breeding, hast thou learnt these manners in America? Take thy hands out of thy pockets.'

Fethi Kekhia was annoyed with the Egyptians in presuming to draft the Libyan laws, but he nevertheless wanted the Egyptian Codes. He made me a few pronouncements: 'You don't want to take any notice of the Constitution – I don't believe it is right for this country'. (This reminded me of what I had once heard Herbert Morrison when Foreign Secretary say to the Legal Adviser to the Foreign Office: 'You don't want to take too much notice of International Law, Mr Beckett'.) Fethi also said that he did not believe that everyone should be assumed innocent until proved guilty. Approving my draft law for conferring on the Italian judges – who had suddenly been deprived of their salaries by the Italian Government – a pension of 1/480 of salary for every month of service, he said 'I see you are a mathematician as well as a lawyer'.

The Ghibli – the strong hot wind coming from the desert – blew for several days. The temperature reached 104.9, and I had to go home and lie down. Everything was covered in sand – it came in under the doors. The members of the Sudan Civil Service, I was told, would at meal times put their plates in their top drawers, and pull open the draw for each mouthful. (I find a bad-tempered note in my diary: 'If ever I meet another member of the Sudan Civil Service I shall knock his block off – it would not be missed'.)

I bought a Hillman Minx, a Convertible, which drew praise from my Tunisian wine supplier: 'Le Sport!' he exclaimed. I wanted an open Jaguar, but that was second-hand, and I should have had to borrow the money from Barclays Bank. When the very affable manager heard I could not drive he cleverly talked me out of the Jaguar on motoring grounds. The Hillman was new, on hire purchase. I had a lesson or two from friends, especially Philip Bradburne, and took my driving test at the hands of the Italian examiner. One did this in one's own car. The morning I attended there was also a girl to be tested. Naturally he told her to get in and drove off with her. 'Follow me', he called, waving his arm at me. I did my best, but soon lost him amongst the tortuous streets of Tripoli. I lost my way altogether. When I eventually located him in his office, he said, waving his arm again, 'Licence will be ready Wednesday'. That is the only driving test I have ever undergone, except that on my return to England the AA man took me once round Trafalgar Square, to enable me to receive a driving licence as a 'visitor' to the United Kingdom.

My piano arrived, faultlessly crated by Steinways. I summoned the leading piano tuner, called the 'maestro': he and his men came and the piano was unpacked, set up, and tuned. As soon as the squad of men had departed I sat down at the keyboard, placed my starved fingers on the keys, and the piano crashed in a belly-flop onto the marble floor. The maestro, resummoned with his team, took offence at my blaming him for this disaster. Piano tuners can be vain. (One of Steinway's older tuners once told me that, after tuning the piano for Rubinstein at the Albert Hall, he had been sitting by during the concert, listening to the applause, and had said to himself 'How lucky I am to be able to bring such pleasure to thousands of people!')

In the middle of my white marble floor was a handsome marble basin, with water in it. One could sit on the edge and watch the goldfish. It would light up, but for some reason there were never any bulbs in the half-dozen holders. To celebrate the arrival of the piano, I bought some, switched on, and electrocuted the goldfish.

I now had a boy, Bushir, a likeable fellow of about twenty years old. I arranged with him to teach me Arabic, six words a day, examination every Friday. If I passed I was to give him ten piastres. He kept the house clean, but was nothing of a cook, or a teacher. During the long humid summer I had no appetite. I went for a meal sometimes to one of the Italian restaurants, none of which were good or even very safe. One day the police guard outside the Wali's house discharged his revolver into my restaurant, which was next door, on the first floor, and wounded a waiter. I preferred the open terrace of a café, the Bonbonnière. I was making some friends amongst the Army officers and their wives, who were quartered at Sabratha or Homs: Grenadier and Coldstream Guards; but there was little entertainment or social life. There was a cinema to which I occasionally went. Over coffee at the Bonbonnière I read a letter from Hetty: her architect boss had proposed to her. There was my second marriage tidied away.

In May a young Palestinian, Anis Qasem, who had been employed by the BBC in its Arab service, arrived from London as my assistant. He was a good lawyer and linguist. We worked well and quickly together: when a draft law was needed in a hurry (as it usually was), we sat on opposite sides of the table and drafted it together – as Gladstone and Thring, the first of the Parliamentary Counsel, had worked – Anis turning our concentrated thoughts into Arabic. I realised the importance Arabs attached to words. Controversies arose in which I could take no part. One concerned the 'remuneration of MPs' which the Constitution required to be 'prescribed by law'. It was argued that Ministers could have a salary in addition to the prescribed 'remuneration', though the only Minister concerned appeared to be Ibrahim Shabaan, who was accumulating directorships in bus companies. We drafted a Bill, but it was not passed. Another problem was the 'Federal Post', or 'Posts', a subject on the Federal list. The Arabists were universally at variance over what this included or excluded, the trouble being, I gathered, that a feminine singular could indicate a masculine plural (a sort of verbal polyandry).

Fethi Kekhia reproached me for 'causing for the first time criticism of the Ministry of Justice'. I was said to have altered something which had been agreed by the Cabinet, while he was away. I convinced him that I had not done so. The second charge was that of unduly favouring the Italians in the meaning I gave to the Property Agreement (whereas of course the Italians thought me non-cooperative). The truth was that the terms of the Agreement were very much in the Italians' favour. Later on, when I had earned the Ministers' confidence as an honest and fair-minded adviser, I told them that the wisest course would be not to pursue their case before the Tribunal, but to make a political deal with the Italian Government, when they would be on much stronger ground; and my advice was accepted. The judges never did have any real work.

Ramadan came in June, with summer hours of work, intense humidity and temperatures well over 100. Not a great deal of work was done. After the siesta I sat in my tiny, paved front garden, and progressed with my Italian, or worked at Hugo's Spanish Course. Sometimes I went for a swim. The piano helped me through long hours of ennui and depression. Bushir my servant wanted to sleep all day and be out all night, and I usually had to wake him in the mornings. One evening, from 10 p.m. to 2 a.m., we had a meeting with Fethi Kekhia about the Codes. I resisted the adoption of the Egyptian Codes because it would mean the importation of Egyptian judges. But I had no alternative to offer. The English legal system could only supply the common law, and that, with its hundreds of reports and text books, is virtually unexportable – 'unimportable' from George Tsoucos's point of view. Another day Anis Qasem and I spent the afternoon in Fethi Kekhia's garden going over the speech he was to make in Parliament in the evening. There was a slight breeze, a rivulet of clear water ran through the garden, and some sheep 'safely grazed' (as we thought) near by. Fethi, in his pyjamas, put the speech down, and we all dozed off. Suddenly he awoke with a start, crying 'What's that?' The sheep were eating his speech.

For the three days' holiday that followed Ramadan, the feast of Eid el Fitr, I escaped to Malta to stay with the Governor, Gerald Creasy, a friend from the Colonial Office. He and Lady Creasy gave me a welcome period of civilised life. I had a curious argument at the dinner table. Lady Creasy, describing the attractions of Malta, said that the dome of the cathedral at Medina was the third largest in the world. I hesitated to contradict the Governor's wife at her own table. 'Surely not?' I ventured. 'There is St Sophia, St Paul's, St Peter's, Rome . . .'. 'Oh, but St Peter's has no dome', said Lady Creasy. 'But surely, Michelangelo . . .' I began again. 'No, St Peter's has no dome', my hostess repeated flatly. I had to accept that, for all purposes within the Island of Malta, St Peter's, Rome, was without a dome.

In September the Government set up house in Beda, a hamlet near Cyrene, where the King had a summer villa. A Tripolitanian official tried to prevent my leaving the province on the ground that I had no exit permit. On the way I noted in my diary: 'The only time I feel happy and well is in the BEA plane between Tripoli and Benghasi – nice bit of corned beef and lettuce, and cold runner beans, for lunch'. We had a four-roomed cottage. The Prime Minister had one room, the Ministers a second, the clerks were in a third, and the rest of us in the fourth; on one day there were nine or ten people in ours. Happy was the man who made the coffee, having the kitchen to himself. We lived in a former officers' rest-home a few miles away, and spent spare hours of daylight exploring the ruins of Cyrene, and the under-water ruins of the port of Apollonia. In Greek times Cyrenaica had been the granary of the Peloponnese, now there were only a few Italian cultivators.

Cottage government was productive. We were all close together, and there was nothing else to do. I drafted laws on some important subjects, including Minerals, Income Tax and Exchange Control. I gave an Opinion on Finance. The Federal Government was living on funds provided by the British Government.

When we moved back to Tripoli I found that Bushir had damaged my car – it had been 'smashed in the garage' he sought to explain; and that some of my English friends, feeling like a party round my piano, had broken into my house. Bushir of course had not been there. I packed him off, and took on Signora Ida, more or less Italian, of uncertain age – say forty-nine – and with an unrevealed history. She was very heavy, sailed rather than walked, and when she laid the table for a meal – which she would not begin to do unless I was present – she sauntered back and forth bringing in one article at a time.

Under '10 February 1952' I find the following in my diary: 'Tony and Cicely Hancock stayed for a week or two – much enjoy their visit.' I had not known them before. Tony was a patient of George Crosby, who, with his actress wife Violet, had taken over our flat in Montagu Square: Tony was in need of a rest, and George had told them to look me up. I fetched them at once from their insalubrious little hotel, and installed them in my house. Tony Hancock meant nothing to Ida, but he meant something to my friends, and a party we gave was well attended. Tony, not yet thirty, was ambitious to be a great comedian, but his nature was quiet and melancholy. Cicely was a great support to him. Tony's gift was his sense of timing, and this is not possible to recapture in a written narrative. I treasure one or two remarkable comments. Stopping at the wineshop on our way to a picnic at Sabratha or Leptis, Cicely and I spent ten minutes discussing the merits of the various Chiantis, the man chose the largest flask, and Tony said, as if till that moment unconcerned, 'Yes, and that's about right in quantity too.' On another outing, gazing in silence in the February sun from the low cliffs above Tripoli, over the placid Mediterranean, Tony at last commented 'It seems a funny thing to say, but it reminds me of Bournemouth.' Watching Ida lay the table piece by piece, a spoon, a glass, another spoon, then the removal of everything because she had forgotten the tablecloth, all for a plate of spaghetti, we planned the worst English meal we could think of:

Brown Windsor Soup, Cottage Pie and Sprouts, Prunes and Custard. They enjoyed my story of the mayor of Tripoli, who, in addition to drawing four salaries, was regularly supplied with fur coats by the directors of the Uaddan, for his *Signora*. They also liked to hear about the Wali of Tripolitania. He had two boxes permanently assigned to him at the cinema, and looked in every evening to make sure that nobody was sitting in them. I told them of the time I had sat and listened to an intolerably long speech of his in Arabic, and said how much I had enjoyed it. 'But you don't understand Arabic.' 'No, your Excellency, but you used the three Arabic words I know.' 'Oh, what are they?' '*Destour* (constitution), *istiklal* (independence), and *Unesco*.'

A friend of old standing, Philip English, who had married another friend, Pat Napier, the daughter of the Lord Chancellor's Permanent Secretary, Albert Napier, also came to stay later for a few days, and suffered Ida's cooking. My social life spread into the diplomatic world, where I met time and again the same people, especially representatives of the United Nations organs bringing Food, Agriculture, Health and Education to the Libyans. I began a friendship with the Italian Ambassador, Mario Conti, and his delightful family, which was to mature in later years. My private social life revolved about my music. Mario Felici, the doctor in charge of the Lunatic Asylum, was a gifted violinist. We played together, and occasionally gave a recital to thirty or so guests: we gave them Mozart, Beethoven, César Franck, de Falla. The Arab listeners liked Mozart especially. A friend, Ronald Diacono, with the Tripolitanian Government but an impresario at heart, arranged some public concerts in the theatre at Sabratha – thrilling evenings. Flavia Marsh, an American pianist who was living in Tripoli, gave a brilliant piano recital – on my Steinway – at the now resplendent Uaddan. I gave an illustrated talk on the Radio on 'The Spirit of Music'.

A formal Treaty had to be negotiated with the British Government, and in the early summer of 1953 I accompanied Mahmoud Muntasser to London for this purpose. Mahmoud stayed at Claridge's, hating the light evenings. On his return he had to face much animosity towards the Treaty, shown in particular by the Egyptian press and by the Opposition in Parliament. But the Treaty, providing for peace, friendship, a close alliance, mutual defence, and financial assistance by Britain, for a period of 20 years, was signed and ratified.

Four oil companies were represented in Libya: Shell (by Maurice Lush, formerly of the Sudan service and the British army), British Petroleum, and a French and an American Company. For some reason known to themselves – perhaps they had caught the idea from Eratosthenes of looking down wells – they thought there was oil. The Libyans scoffed; but still, if the oil companies were foolish enough to want to pay fees for permission to dig up some sand, the money would be welcome. This meant a proper Oil Law, and I should have to draft it. I stipulated that I should remain at my house, away from the office, for as long as the work required; and that I should be free to look for precedents where I thought fit. Fethi Kekhia agreed. In due time I produced a draft Oil Law and Concession Agreement, and this remained virtually unaltered for many years.

The time for my departure was approaching. Fethi Kekhia tried to persuade me to stay, and offered me the post of Chief Justice. I was tempted, but it was time I returned to London. The Colonial Office would not keep my job open much longer, and I could not be sure about a future in Libya. The Ministers gave a party for me at the Uaddan, at which I was able to say goodbye to my many Libyan friends; and at which the convention was followed that if one of the Ministers needed a drink, he was to be called to the telephone. The Prime Minister was ill, and he was in bed when I said goodbye to him; he presented me with an inscribed cigarette box of the soft, local silver. Ida, in floods of tears, packed everything up for me.

With about £200 in travellers cheques, extracted with difficulty from the Treasurer's officers, who reminded me of the stringent law I had myself drafted, I left Tripoli early one morning at the beginning of November, in my open Hillman. I stopped for breakfast with Army friends in Sabratha, and continued westward along the coast. The rains had begun and I had been warned of the likely presence of lakes across the desert road in Tunisia, and marauding Tunisians. There were lakes all right. I drove through them, but at last, in a sea of water, the car came to a stop, the water above the floor boards. There was nothing for it but to take off my shoes and socks, roll up my trousers, gather up my valuables and old guide book, wade to dry land, and sit down and wait. In the guide book I read up Tunisia: 'The inhabitants', it said, 'have the worst possible reputation, and exercise robbery and brigandage on a large scale.' But help came sooner than I had any right to expect.

Coming towards me, stuck in the next lake, was another car, the occupants pushing themselves out. They were Americans from Tripoli whom I knew. They pushed me out, and somehow got the engine going for me. I spent the night in Sfax, drove on through many miles of olive trees, with low mountains in the distance, suddenly came upon an enormous Roman ruin, El Djem, and arrived in Tunis. There I dodged the trams, saw the ruins of Carthage, then crossed by boat to Marseilles, spent a few days in Paris, turned round and drove to Rome via the Riviera, lunched in the sun in the Piazza Navona until a few days before Christmas, and late on Christmas Eve arrived at my mother's and sister's house in Reading. An enjoyable journey home, except that I lost my way near East Grinstead.

In a few years the attempt at federalism in Libya broke down, and the country was unified under a single government. Oil began to flow in 1961, and Anis Qasem was made Chairman of the Petroleum Commission. With various changes of government Mahmoud Muntasser became ambassador in London, and I saw much of him, and later of his son Omar, who also became ambassador. I had done something, with the other British advisers, to get a new country, almost entirely devoid of material and human resources at the beginning, onto its feet. The British Government had nursed the country on its way towards a democratic independence, in contrast with what happened in the Belgian Congo, abandoned by the Belgians to its fate. But Colonel Gaddaffi seized power in 1969, ejected King Idris, and the darkness fell.

The letter from E. B. Boothby of the Foreign Office, which Roberts-Wray received on my return, makes sad reading now, but I venture to quote it in conclusion:

> 'In view of the interest you took in Dale's appointment to the post in Libya, I should like to let you know personally how much we appreciate the work he did there.
>
> As Chief Legal Adviser to the Government of a new country in which a number of distinct and uncoordinated legal systems existed side by side, Dale had to shoulder a heavy task of legislative drafting; and the absence of constitutional experience in Libya or of any tradition of public service greatly added to his burden. In begging him to remain in their employment as a judge of the Supreme Court (at a time when the contracts of many other British officials in their service were being terminated) the Libyan Government paid the highest tribute they could to the wisdom and single-mindedness which Dale had shown throughout his tenure of office.

This was in itself an important contribution to Anglo-Libyan relations. But we have not forgotten how, without ever failing in his scrupulous regard for Libyan interests, Dale succeeded in maintaining a helpful attitude throughout our prolonged treaty negotiations. We are grateful for his patience and judgment during that time.'

X

London in the Fifties

MY MOTHER, highly pleased to see me back in England again, was dismayed at my appearance: an evident loss of weight. As Libya was on the list of 'unhealthy places', the Colonial Office required me to undergo a medical examination; and once more I submitted myself to one of its physicians, on this occasion as dry as the desert I had left behind. The doctor handed me a note to give to the Office, and he left it open, I supposed for me to read; and what I read was that he suspected tuberculosis, and that I should see a specialist. This sent me into a state of panic. All my life I had been afraid of tuberculosis. My mother's two young sisters had died of the disease; but more influential on my state of mind was I think the romantic but consumptive hero – with whom I had identified myself – of Marie Corelli's novel *The Silent House in Pimlico,* which I had read when young. I passed an agonising few days with my mother and sister in Reading, taking solitary – and, I was convinced, my last – walks. The specialist declared that the suspicion was unfounded. But, he added, as if in compensation, that I might develop an ulcer; and he recommended me to eat frequently and in small quantities, and to drink milk. I had never been able to drink milk except as an additive; and to supply me with light refreshments at frequent intervals was beyond the capacity of the Colonial Office canteen. I put my dilemma to George Crosby, still at Montagu Square; and imitating his sergeant-major assistant during the war, he told me to avoid 'soops, stoos and froyes'. This advice, or at any rate the last two-thirds of it, I followed; and I am happy to record that I have never had an ulcer. As for tuberculosis, having once had it, in my mind, the thought of it troubled me no more.

While away I had let my maisonette in Paultons Square, and the last of the tenants had been so destructive that it had to be redecorated and newly equipped. Until I could get back there I took up residence in one of the sets of bachelor chambers to be found in Ryder Street, St James. I was on the fringe of what Sydney Smith, exiled to his Yorkshire parsonage, had referred to as the Great Parallelogram, the area between Oxford Street, Piccadilly, Regent Street and Hyde Park, which, he said, enclosed 'more intelligence and human ability, to say nothing of wealth and beauty, than the world has ever collected in such a space before'. The only person I had known living within it was Gem Moufflet, my dancing teacher; and by 1954 the area was no longer the golden rhomboid Sydney Smith described. But his image of it was stimulating; and returning from my own exile I felt a new freedom, as if I were beginning a new life, and a bachelor life at that. London had changed. There had been important happenings while I was away. Queen Elizabeth II had ascended the throne, and Edmund Hillary had ascended Mount Everest, which two events we had celebrated even in Libya. But there were other changes: Queen Mary, identity cards, ration cards, utility goods, and the last tram, had all gone. The welfare state was in being. But London was still recognisably the capital city of the British Isles. 'Tourism' had not yet begun – 'usu. depreciatory' my Shorter Oxford (repatriated) said about that word. Nor had immigration yet had any noticeable effect. In Soho one found French and Italian, with one or two Spanish, Hungarian and Greek restaurants, but that was part of our pre-war civilisation. The English – we always said – did not know how to cook. I had breakfast at Fortnum and Mason's Fountain bar, lunch at the Colonial Office canteen, and dinner in Soho.

On my telephoning Tony and Cicely Hancock, they gave me a standing invitation to the BBC's studio at Shepherds Bush, to watch Tony recording his weekly TV programme. The recording session was followed by a drinking session, which enabled Tony to relax, with his script writers and a friend or two. His twenty-ninth birthday was celebrated in a similar fashion. But for me these festivities entailed the drinking of too much hard liquor. I invited them all to Paultons Square after my return there, thinking I could keep control over the bottles, but my invitation was not accepted. In the end I had to beg off; and after that all I saw of Tony was *Hancock's Half Hour,* on the TV.

My limitations as a drinker had been brought to my notice by Alan Herbert, when I was leaving a riverside party at 12 Hammersmith Terrace, rather early. He reproached me for being a 'fair weather drinker'. He was no doubt right; and I certainly experienced nothing but fair weather at his home, which I had come to know well. After the war, when the theatres were beginning to open, I had sent his youngest daughter Lavender, whom I had met once, a telegram reading 'WILL YOU COME THIS WAY TO THE TOMB FRIDAY', and had received the reply 'CERTAINLY IS THIS MY END OR MY BEGINNING'. I referred to a play being put on at the Mercury Theatre. (The Post Office, in abolishing the telegram, has much to answer for: how could Herbertian wit travel by fax?) The Herberts were a family of exceptional warmth, vitality and generosity. Gwen, Lavender's mother, of a dark, Celtic beauty, was a painter when time permitted, and I once lent her my studio for two or three days. She had passed on her beauty to all her three daughters, her colouring to Lavender only. Crystal, tall and very blonde, was the wife of John Pudney, poet and novelist. Jocelyn, fair also, but more sturdily built, was married to Anthony Lousada, a City solicitor, who was a painter as well, and later Chairman of the Trustees of the Tate Gallery. Jocelyn had studied painting; and as soon as she had brought up her young children took up theatrical work. She has become, I suppose, London's best-known designer for the stage. The Lousadas lived just up the river in Chiswick Mall. Lavender, as well as enjoying the theatre, had studied the piano. She married Christopher Clarke, a City solicitor too, and they lived a few hundred yards down river. I became godfather to their first born, Diana. The riverside family (which included John, the youngest, in the navy during the war) made me feel one of themselves. I would spend the evening, occasionally the night, at one house or the other, playing the piano, or Alan would play – if he were not sitting quietly by the fire correcting proofs – and we would sing. Or Alan would take me to the Black Lion, to play skittles. Or there might be a trip in the *Water Gypsy.* This robust, second 'family life', with laughter all the time, did much to rid me of stiffness and timidity.

My work was now with the Commonwealth Relations Office. The Colonial Office was at a distance in Great Smith Street; the

'Colonial Service' was renamed 'Her Majesty's Overseas Service'; and – though the general rush into independence had not yet begun – Roberts-Wray and his assistants were hard at it drafting amendments to Constitutions to give more responsibility to the local political leaders. The Mau Mau in Kenya, and the Kabaka in Uganda, were amongst the worst of the Colonial Office's problems.

With the independence of India, Pakistan and Sri Lanka (Ceylon), the responsibilities of the Commonwealth Relations Office had increased, and I had as assistant Humphrey Oxley, a well-informed solicitor from the former India Office. Work involving independent rather than dependent countries suited my inclinations: I was never at heart a 'colonialist'. The Office was playing a rather curious part: it was attempting to fill the role of a Foreign Office towards countries which it must not on any account treat as 'foreign'. Protocol, precedent, constitutional usage, personal relations, were governing factors. On constitutional matters the supreme authority was Sir Charles Dixon, who had an incomparable memory. With a face as of white paper, a dark, wispy moustache, and narrow steel-framed spectacles, he looked like Rudyard Kipling. He lived in a residential hotel in Kensington, arrived at the office at 11 a.m., in his black overcoat and bowler, winter and summer, and scuttled quickly into a room on the ground floor. He was never known to eat lunch; and he had the misfortune to suffer from noisy emanations from his gullet which merged with his utterances. Hence the clerihew –

Sir Charles Dixon
Buzzes and fizzes
A peculiar manner
His is.

Perhaps aware of this, he had a habit of beginning every sentence twice, going back a few words and starting again, as if to make sure he was speaking. If one asked him what line had been taken with the Governor-General of Australia twelve years before, he did not have to send for the old files, he remembered. He wrote his minutes in a thin, spidery hand. They were brief. He hardly ever sent for a shorthand writer; if he did, the product was formidable.

The Secretary of State was Lord Swinton, and the Permanent Under-Secretary of State was Sir Percivale Liesching, who had been at the Board of Trade and Ministry of Food. Lord Swinton was a barrister, and knew when and when not to consult a lawyer. He held a meeting every Monday morning with senior officials to review current problems, which I was invited to attend. I did not often say anything, unless asked; but I began to feel firmer in my saddle. Swinton was able, forthright, and had the shrewd sense of a Yorkshire landowner, which he never ceased to be. One evening in the House of Lords, I heard him call out to another Yorkshire peer 'Are you lambing yet?'. At our meetings he was always down to earth. A question arose about the British Council. 'Is the British Council supposed to be taking our culture to other countries', he asked, 'or to be bringing their culture to ours? It's no good sending them to Paris and expecting the French to learn culture from *us*.'

Central and Southern Africa were beginning to present their insoluble problems. Southern Rhodesia had been a self-governing colony since 1923, and its affairs had always been handled by the Dominions Office, as had those of the three High Commission Territories as they were called, Basutoland (now Lesotho), Bechuanaland (Botswana), and Swaziland, which I had visited before going to Libya. The plans for federating the two Rhodesias and Nyasaland, which I had worked on earlier, had come to fruition, and the affairs of the new Federation were the responsibility of the Commonwealth Relations Office, though the Colonial Office retained responsibility for Northern Rhodesia and Nyasaland in non-federal matters. It was an awkward division, and became more awkward as time went on. The High Commission Territories, which adjoined the Union of South Africa, still within the Commonwealth, were an important factor in our relationship with the South African Government. South Africa had fought with us during both wars, and they were our friends. It was South African policy to take over the administration of the High Commission Territories, but apartheid had been introduced. 'Human Rights' were coming into vogue; and one day the High Commissioner, who had the double function of being a diplomat and a Governor, telephoned to me to say that he would like a Charter of Human Rights to be incorporated in the Constitutions of his three territories. I argued with him, and said that charters of human rights were no substitute for good government. He was offended, thinking that I was implying that his territories were not well governed. Of course I was not – rather the reverse. When the three territories eventually became independent, the Constitutions followed what had become the usual form, and included Bills of Rights. But Swaziland later dropped hers, and subsequent history has confirmed my view. Such 'Charters' are of no use in default of secure legal remedies to enforce them, which good government provides. Worse, they can serve as a cover for bad, inhuman government.

I had been at my desk in the Commonwealth Relations Office for no more than a few months when I was called down to see Sir Percivale Liesching. He told me that the Ministry of Education had invited me to go there as its Legal Adviser. It was a surprising invitation. A move of that sort amongst Whitehall Legal Advisers was rare, and I wondered how anyone at that Department, across the Park in Curzon Street, could ever have heard of me, let alone think I could add to its fund of legal knowledge in matters educational. Further, I suspected that life there would be dull. But I was flattered; I was being offered a new job, and a substantial increase in salary; and I accepted on the understanding that when Roberts-Wray retired I might expect to be asked back to fill his post. This was agreed, though I never had it in writing: Liesching was not the sort of Permanent Under-Secretary of State one asked to confirm such a thing in writing. Again I had to put up with surprised – not to say incredulous – looks from colleagues. I said goodbye to Swinton, with whom I had liked working.

I had not had a holiday that year, and I had to learn something about the law affecting education. I put *Wells and Taylor on the Education Acts* into the car, drove to Paris, and stayed a day or two with Tony and Honor Waterfield, whose house in Cheyne Row I had occupied during the war. Tony was now Scientific Attaché in the Embassy in Paris, and they had a flat on the Quai Montebello, overlooking the river and Nôtre Dame. I had become godfather to their second child, Cordelia. Parking the car was always a difficulty for me, as it had been unnecessary to learn how to park a car in Tripoli; and Honor would stand on her balcony and marvel at my struggles to satisfy the exacting demands of the bouquinistes with stalls on the quai below.

Amongst my notes on the Education Act 1944, I find the following:

> *October 4* I've loosed off from Paris and am on a wild dash through the French countryside, hood off and head down. Took my first lunch by the Loire yesterday, packed up by Honor's cook, with a half-bottle of Rosé d'Anjou, outside a café. The proprietress intrigued me greatly by trying to catch a grasshopper, which was hopping madly

but harmlessly about the pavement. Every time she stopped and showed her immense behind the grasshopper made another jump, and the one followed the other for five or ten minutes until eventually the insect was out-hopped. The woman explained it would amuse her canaries; but as soon as she put it in the cage it hopped out again. Then I joined in; but it hopped behind a machine for making mineral water, and we gave up.

Stayed the night at *La Charité*. The only apéritif was a half-bottle of Pouilly Fumé taken at such a temperature that the first glass frosts up to a toothpick's width above the wine line. It was pure heaven, light and airy and dryish but with a bouquet like primroses. The five-course dinner that followed was of no importance, nor was the Côte du Rhône with it, except for the steak, which cut like a ripe pear.

Today I crossed the river into Burgundy, through Nevers which has a double cathedral, the two built back to back as if propping one another up at a picnic, and Autun, with some lovely Roman remains. I came all the way along the wine list – Mersault, Montrachet, Volnay, Pommard, Beaune, and to Nuits St Georges. A noisy room, but a dinner which must be described in detail. All the waiting is done by a sort of Holy Family – Pa, Ma, and the Boy, all clothed in white, who gather round you at the beginning and at every course, and I must say I felt very like the holy ass. As soon as Pa has taken the initial steps in serving the course, with Ma's assistance, he hands over to the 'Christ-child', and withdraws to sanctify someone else's dish. At Nuits St Georges there is no such thing as a vin ordinaire. I had to have a bottle of Nuits St Georges 1943, which they poured into a brandy balloon, a little at a time. I ate mussels, each one done in a half-shell with a sort of stiff sauce, beef with olives etc, and grapes – they had a branch there and plucked the grapes from it. The other people were the sort one might find in the Moo Cow milk bar in Leicester Square, if one were lucky (I know, because I took the opera singer Nell Rankin there for supper after she had been Carmen in *Carmen* at Covent Garden – she would not go anywhere else). They were all building up dinners with as many storeys as the Empire State. No one smoked: one lighted cigarette, and the whole place would have exploded like a petrol dump.

Later I'm having three days on favourable terms at the Hotellerie du Moulin des Templiers, in the lovely valley of the *Cousin,* which runs from Avallon towards Vézelay. The idea was to do a little quiet preparation for the Ministry, and I've done a little each day before lunch. It is an enchanting little place on the river, millstream in full spate, no doubt built by the Templars, who built the church. The hotel is three sides of a square and I go up an outside stair to my room, which is next door to the smelliest lavatory yet encountered. Nor is the bed linen any too pure. But there is exactly the right sort of dog (called

> 'Bobbie', all white except for his brown collar and ears) who follows me about, or sits. I am the only guest, and have the meals brought to my own prescription. Madame fishes goujon out of the river for me, and snails are picked from the roadside. There is a grandfather clock which strikes everything twice. There is a print opposite me in the dining-room of a priest dashing drunkenly across the village street with a gun or a folded umbrella – I've always forgotten to look closely at the end of the meal. Monsieur has pruned his climbing rose to give it the shape of an exquisite but attenuated female skeleton, and is now 'flitting' it hard. OLK 72 (my car) is waiting in his kennel, clean. It is time to go. But I must stay for the postman's visit on his lightly motorised bicycle. When he leaves he mounts and then circles round the yard twice to achieve enough momentum to get up the slight slope and out. Perhaps I shall do the same . . .

I duly took my place at the Ministry of Education. Curzon Street was then virtually a high-class red light district; and my first act after sitting at my desk was to get up and look out of the window to see what was going on. The sight that met my eyes was that of my former wife Hetty, standing at the window across the way in a white jersey. She was standing sideways, then she turned and saw me; we waved, and in half a minute my telephone rang. 'A lady', said my secretary, entering precipitately on her new duties. 'What are you doing over there?' asked Hetty, and I told her. She was at the kitchen window of the flat at the end of Clarges Street where she and her husband lived, and practised jointly their profession of architect. Hetty was nicely settled in the Great Parallelogram, adding to its intelligence and beauty. We waved to one another for some years; and I often wondered what those of my colleagues in the adjoining and underlying rooms, who happened to be looking out of their windows, thought about the matter.

The Minister of Education was David Eccles, and the junior Minister Dennis Vosper. My new colleagues, from the Permanent Secretary down, gave me a most friendly welcome – all, that is, except the two lawyers immediately junior to me. These made their views clear: that they could not be expected to welcome a man who took away their chance of promotion. But it was done with good temper, I did not blame them for feeling like that, and we soon got along very well. But I found the work singularly devoid of interest. The Education Act 1944, the 'Butler Act', so much praised, seemed to me largely machinery for the distribution of money: voluntary schools, aided schools, maintained schools

– they did not mean much to me. My legal colleagues seemed to know all about them, actually visited them, were Governors of their old schools. Since I left Hull I had not been inside a school except once, to vote at a General Election. My senior assistant, Mervyn Longhurst, had been present at meetings on the 1944 Act, which had been drafted by the First Parliamentary Counsel, Sir Granville Ram. Whenever I discussed its provisions with Longhurst, he began by apologising for a cold in the head, and I could never tell whether he was saying it was RAB or RAM who had said this or that. One of the tasks he performed about 11 o'clock every morning, not to be disrupted on any account, was what I understood him to call the 'ceilig': this puzzled me, and it was some time before I discovered that he referred to the 'sealing' of the 'Instruments of Government' (a 'fine Cromwellian ring' about the term, Lord Goddard said in one of the cases) and the 'Articles of Government' of schools.

When the Government decided that every student having two 'A' levels should have the right to go to a university, we instructed Parliamentary Counsel to draw up a Bill. We received a draft of several pages in length. I had been brought up by Roberts-Wray to revere the Parliamentary draftsmen, and I felt unable to protest. But David Eccles refused to accept the draft, and eventually what became the Education Act 1962 went through. We had other Bills. One day Wilma Harte, a clever young woman, one of the best of the Assistant Secretaries, came into my room brandishing our latest Act. 'What I don't understand about *the law*', she began, pronouncing the words derisively, 'is this: we in Schools Branch decide we need some amendments to the Education Act, we instruct you, you instruct Parliamentary Counsel, he drafts a Bill, the Minister approves it, it passes, becomes an Act of Parliament, and lands on our desks. Then we have to come to you to ask what on earth it all means.' I could not do much about that. But I thought that the Minister's own regulations, drafted by the Department's lawyers, might be written in a simpler way. In 1947 the Government had set up a Foundation to secure the use of 'Basic English as a means of international communication, and a simple introduction to English'. C. K. Ogden, the philosopher, drew up a vocabulary of Basic English, limited to 850 words. I redrafted the Schools Regulations using no more than these words. The result was gibberish, and my draft went into the waste-paper basket. I returned to this problem in later years.

The Ministry of Education shared with the Charity Commission the function of making 'Schemes' to alter the objects of charitable trusts, the Ministry having jurisdiction over educational charities. In this work the Ministry's lawyers played an important part; and, on their advice, charitable trusts had been sanctioned for merely recreational purposes, such as sports clubs and playing fields. This rather shocked the Charity Commission: a dispute developed, and an informal enquiry was conducted by Harold Kent, a former Parliamentary Counsel, then the Treasury Solicitor. The Ministry was in the dock, and I had to defend it. In the end the reasonableness of its attitude was accepted, and the Recreational Charities Act 1958 was passed.

I gave evidence before the Franks Committee on Administrative Tribunals and Inquiries. The Committee was bound to be critical; and, called as the first witness, I nervously took my seat facing ten or so distinguished judges and other public figures ranged before me. But the Chairman, Oliver Franks, who was my old war-time colleague at the Ministry of Supply, and had then been its Permanent Secretary, and after that Ambassador at Washington, gave me a friendly welcome, and put me at my ease. The Committee's Report, advocating 'openness, fairness and impartiality' in the proceedings of administrative tribunals, resulted in the Tribunals and Inquiries Act 1958.

I began to see that I was fortunate in being able to serve for a time with a Home Department and gain some experience of the government of the United Kingdom, which was, after all, the source of our power abroad. I was being 'further educated', and had the thought of adding later, to my scanty entry in *Who's Who,* 'Educ: Ministry of Education'. At least I considered that, when the third edition of *The Law of the Parish Church* came out in 1957, my credibility as an authority on ecclesiastical law was marginally improved by the change from Commonwealth Affairs to Education.

The work was also less demanding; and I had more time, and more money, to devote to leisure pursuits. Chelsea was an agreeable place in which to live. It was still a village, served by its own bus, No 11. Chelsea was separated from the rest of London by the Parks, Eaton Square and Victoria Station, and had the river at its back. There was a Chelsea Society, and a Chelsea Music Society, of which Esther Darlington the singer, a friend from Whistler's House days, was secretary. Ladies and gentlemen lived in the village, in an easy-going, some in a Bohemian, fashion. There were writers such as the Sitwells, musicians such as Louis Kentner, artists such as Anthony Devas, actors such as Peter Ustinov and Alec Clunes, who was compère at the Players Theatre, where Jimmy Cyriax entertained his friends. One took an airing down the King's Road on Saturday mornings – Saturday was no longer a working day – to see who was afoot.

A restaurant opened opposite the end of Paultons Square called 'Le Rêve': it could be said perhaps to have been the first of the bistros, if one wished to compliment bistros. The owner and manager, Mr Bornemann, the brother of the tax silk, paid close attention to his customers. I was one of his first, and the restaurant became my dining-room. The food was good, and I introduced Mr Bornemann to the avocado, hitherto unknown to the King's Road. One took a bottle in if entertaining, but wine was not then a commonplace on every table. The service was in the hands of smiling, comely young women who lived in the village. One wished to invite them to sit down, in the seat opposite. In due time one of them did, but not at Le Rêve. Cynthia was a blonde girl from the Yorkshire Dales, resourceful, lively and amusing, who by then owned her own business, and a Triumph Convertible. Unfortunately she was by habit unpunctual. She would turn up at a dinner party an hour late, look round the table wonderingly at the seated guests, adjust her expression to one of determination, sit down quickly and fall to. This lateness of hers exasperated me so, that I had to abandon Cynthia. She was not, however, so extreme as an earlier friend, who was late naturally, by reason of a sort of entropy which overcame her as the hours advanced. One evening I was taking her to the Classic Cinema in Baker Street – she lived near the Marylebone Public Library and would never go further than a quarter of a mile from it – and she was so exorbitantly late that the Box office was closed when we arrived, and we saw the film for nothing.

I drafted a Bill for Alan Herbert, who was no longer, since the abolition of the University seats, a Member of Parliament. He was still bothered about the marriage laws. The Matrimonial Causes Act 1950 had left it to the parson to decide whether to marry in his church, or allow a brother clergyman to marry, a divorced person whose former spouse was still living. The bishops were putting pressure on the clergy to prevent their exercising a free discretion. Alan fought this, and wrote a novel *Made for Man,* to which I contributed a draft Bill. My draft was hailed as a 'seamanlike job' by the Admiral who was the father of the girl wanting to remarry, but the girl herself, on reading it, simply exclaimed 'What does it all mean?', like the girl at the Ministry of Education. Today I should have done it in plainer language. The point was dealt with by the Matrimonial Causes Act 1965.

The Herberts always gave a very large party for the Oxford and Cambridge Boat race, at which one would see Lord Attlee, Lord Montgomery, and other distinguished persons. Milling around with the numerous lesser figures, and not much caring which University won the race, I met on one occasion Constance Tomkinson, on the point of marrying Hugh Weeks, the economist, who had been at the Ministry of Supply. Constance, a Canadian girl, had danced with the Folies Bergères, and she wrote a book about her experiences called *Les Girls,* which was turned into a film. Constance and Hugh became very kind friends, and at their flat in Eaton Square I met Ann Appelbe, the wife of Ambrose, the solicitor in Lincoln's Inn. They had a beautiful Regency House, almost a stately home, on an estate – a small park – in Highgate, with a distant view of the heights of Hampstead. They, and their children Gabriel, Valentine, Robert and Felix, became very dear friends. Valentine (at school) and I adopted one another.

At Paultons Square I tried the experiment of having a maid who lived in, a French girl who had been a school teacher and wished, I gathered, for a richer personal life. This Jeanne did not achieve under my roof. I tried to get her out of her shabby old brown skirt and jumper, not very clean, and not suitable clothing to wear when waiting at table; and I sent her to Peter Jones, where I had an account. I wanted her in some sort of uniform, but she kicked hard at that: I said black and white anyway. She returned with a white frock split up the side, nearly to her ample behind, with one black button on one shoulder. She did not stay with me long: we parted by reason of mutual antipathy. Gwen Herbert found me Evelyn, who lived near Wandsworth Bridge, a first-class daily lady who stayed with me for some years.

I took piano lessons again, stimulated by Lavender Clarke, who told me I did not use my fingers properly. My teacher was an old friend from fish-pie days, Marguerite Wolff, now married to Derek Moss, a very successful estate agent, with (or about to be with) two young daughters, Crystal and Gloria. Those were still the days when a husband insisted that a wife brought up his family, and Marguerite postponed entry on a full-time career as a professional pianist. She was a better teacher than Franz had been, and converted me – for the time being – from Bach and Beethoven to the romantics: Field, Chopin, Brahms, Fauré. My upstairs neighbours were Edwina and Jim Reid, whom it would be right to call Bohemian, and their very young daughter Chloe. Edwina designed and made chic clothes, and Jim was a scientist and inventor. Neither they nor their Alsatian, Tom Pearse, who used to sit outside my door, ever took the slightest exception to my practising. Chloe I occasionally had in to breakfast.

I became close friends with Peter and Elizabeth Noble, who came to live next to me at No 12. Peter was the godson of the conductor Malcom Sargent, and very musical. He owned Christophers, the wine merchants in Jermyn Street, suppliers to some of the Inns of Court. Once or twice I went to an enormous, rich and alcoholic lunch in the firm's cellars, from which I would emerge, quivering with cold and inebriation, between 4 and 5 o'clock, and take a taxi home to bed. Elizabeth's elegant sister, Virginia Moffat, would turn up from Argentina from time to time. I amused them with stories from Sarawak not all entered up in my diary.

In France *Son et Lumière* had come into vogue, and I staged a parody of it against the high Tudor wall, originally the wall of Thomas More's house, which divided our gardens from that of the convent behind in Beaufort Street. For characters I already had the statue of a Victorian wood-nymph, and the bust of a balding Victorian worthy whom Peter, slipping one night over the low wall between our properties, had supplied with a couple of horns. I wrote a script, making an unorthodox use of the statute book for the purpose, which an unemployed actress and I recorded, with selections from Liszt on my Steinway. I was thus able to entertain my friends to Wine, Son et Lumière on fine summer evenings. The show disturbed the surrounding inhabitants, and angry shouts of protest, growing as one performance succeeded another, rather spoiled the effect. It is too late now to apologise to them all. I did throw in at the end one of the Liszt 'Consolations'.

XI

Diverse Pursuits

BOSWELL tells us that, conversing with Johnson about the education of children, he asked what he thought was best to teach them first. The doctor's answer was, 'Sir, it is no matter what you teach them first, any more than what leg you shall put into your breeches first. Sir, you may stand disputing which is best to put in first, but in the meantime your breech is bare. Sir, while you are considering which of two things you should teach your child first, another boy has learnt them both.' That robust view may be allowed to stand for mine: I think it is a question to which no general answer can be given. Fortunately no one at the Ministry of Education ever asked me for my opinion. I pursued my contacts with the wider educational world. I went to Oxford and Cambridge to give an occasional legal talk, and at Oxford was external examiner for two doctorates, with Harry Lawson, and with Rupert Cross. At Cambridge I helped Clive Parry with his comprehensive work on Nationality. In London Jock Logan, now Principal of the University, entertained distinguished lawyers at small dinner parties, and generously invited me. I could talk to Cyril Radcliffe, the intellectual amongst the judges; Raymond Evershed, handsome, witty, but of uncertain temperament; Norman Birkett, silver-tongued, the acknowledged successor to Edward Marshall Hall as an advocate; and, from overseas, Dean Griswold of Harvard. Every year Jock presided at a dinner for a few former colleagues from the Ministry of Supply: Robert Megarry, Victor Harries, Colin Pearson and others would come. There were also livery dinners at the Haberdashers' and the Drapers' Companies, notable for their schools, the tables gleaming with silver and crystal, with seven wine glasses at each place.

I drove to Reading to stay for weekends with my mother and sister. Hilda, with a Ph. D, and Licence és lettres from Lyon, was a Senior Lecturer in French at the University. She was at the same time looking after my mother, now in her eighties, but with faculties unimpaired. When nearing eighty she had bought the *Encyclopaedia Britannica.* She had lost none of her interests, nor her fondness for the young. I would often find someone's child or grandchild with her. I had long chats with her about the turns my life was taking; but we did not look into the future.

My car, with its name 'Le Sport', and its left-hand drive, called me to the continent. I had plenty of holidays; there was no need to plan, or book ahead; the limitation was the meagre allowance of foreign currency, but friends would help with that. I wanted to see more of France and Italy. I visited Tony and Honor Waterfield in Paris, and they introduced me to a remarkable young Australian woman, tall and straight, with violet eyes. With little experience, no French, no introductions, nothing to carry her along but a passion for clothes and a blind eye for obstacles, she had left Sydney with the ambition of becoming one of Christian Dior's models. After badgering one couturier after another she had been taken on by Balenciaga, and had now achieved her ambition to work with Dior.

Here was a diversion ... My intention had been to go to the Loire valley, and view the abbeys and chateaux. But I did what Tristram Shandy had done when he saw Janatone at Montreuil. I decided that the buildings could wait: they would remain as the masons and carpenters had left them, whereas the girl carried within her the very 'principles of change'. I took her out to dinner.

My Janatone, for such a stick of a girl, had a most hearty appetite. I asked in wonder whether she ate lunch. 'Good Lord, no! A cup of coffee round the corner, and an *oeuf* if I'm in funds. Anyone who takes me out to dinner gets stung, I'm afraid. But these places aren't *cher.*' About life as a model, she said: 'Glamour, but short on *salaire.* None of these girls can live on their pay. The best arrangement is to become the *maîtresse* of the couturier's financial backer.' It appeared to be an objective analysis. She had an elderly friend Henri, on the Bourse, who looked after her small investments.

She wrote to me. 'I have my flat until the *fin de mars*,' she said, 'but after that will have to look for another, financially a *besoin.*'

(As she picked up French words, these displaced the English; there seemed to be no room in her mind for both.) 'I hope you have some *joli* bulbs in your garden. *Gauloises* and *grenouilles* might improve your morale. Why not bring the car over for *Pâques*?'

I did that: we were to drive to the Loire. She had dressed in an old sweater and some pepper and salt trousers, and I thought this an error; we were destined for the Garden of France, not the Australian outbacks. Towards evening we stopped at the hotel at La Charité where I had stayed before, but they would not let us have two rooms. It was the same all the way along the valley. 'Of course they won't', I said, tired and exasperated. 'It is the Easter weekend. The Valley is filled with Parisians. The hotels can get four stomachs to feed.' But Jana's blind eye was working well. 'I'm sorry I didn't bring a tent,' I said. At Angers, practically on the Atlantic, we found a hotel where no one went except for family holidays in the summer; Jana had a room with two double beds in it, and mine had two doubles and a single. Next morning we turned round and drove back, stopping at Bourgueil for a wine tasting. I left Jana – now beginning to soften – outside her flat off the rue St Honoré, and hurried away. It was after midnight, and I had to find a hotel. Paris was full of English.

Next morning I set off again, for the Loire: Blois, Chambord, Chaumont, Amboise, Chenonceau (built across the river Cher), Azay-le-Rideau on the Indre, perhaps the most delightful of them all, and Chinon, on the Vienne; the guides with their gigantic keys, which they used to point with, while the groups of tourists swivelled their heads as if under remote control; the perfect manners of the Frenchman who, when the guide overturned a heavy table onto his foot and said *'Pardon'*, replied 'Je vous en prie'. I drank Chinon at Chinon, and Saumur at Saumur.

I left the Loire, and drove to Vézelay on its conical hill, with its superb, bare abbey church, and glorious view. From there I wrote to my adopted daughter Valentine, who was having difficulties with French pronunciation:

A certain young woman of Vézelay
Pronounced her words so nasally,
That even the French
Friends of the wench,
Could gather her meaning but hazily.

Afterwards there was Auxerre with its lovely cathedral, lunch including the famous *andouillettes* (pigs' guts in cases), Chablis (a beautiful church, an old man on crutches leaning against the wall and letting out a lyrical belch which echoed round the *Place* like a yodelling song), a glass of Chablis at 4 p.m., then Sens and another superb cathedral. At dinner in Sens I learned about eating snails. Monsieur, at the next table, was thin and had a half-dozen, Madame was enormous and had a dozen. The tweezers are not used to take up the snail, which can be harpooned by a good Burgundian with the small two-pronged fork; they may be used to help in the disposal of the residuary butter, bits of parsley and so on. Monsieur brought the shell and its inhabitant to his mouth, cornered and swallowed the snail, and drained off the rest by loud suction. Madame kept the shell on her plate, gripped it with the tweezers, and having harpooned and eaten the snail, shredded her bread and dipped it in, mopping up the liquid and eating the bread noiselessly.

This expertise I was able to pass on to Jana when I took her to dinner again some months later. Through her I came to know, as well as the bistros, something of the cultural life of Paris. She always went to the *vernissages* after work, and bought a small painting or two. We might go to a concert at the Salle de Pleyel or the Palais de Chaillot. Beyond all there was *couture,* so important on the right bank. I saw the *collections,* and Dior's models became familiar to me, as they twirled about. There was a Russian girl with slit eyes, an intellectual, with an American husband; Maria, Spanish, like a wooden puppet, with a perpendicular back to her head and a French boyfriend; a haughty, fair girl, twice divorced; a married woman with two children; a thin, pale girl living with a Count; a dancer, with an urchin cut and gold bracelet; Clothilde, 40, keeping her mother; Valla, Italian, living with her parents. Janatone was the majestic one, a little apart.

But the time came when Dior no longer had a place for her, and Janatone had to return to Australia. She departed in a gastronomic blaze. Henri, who was President of the *Société des Gastronomes de France*, or some such honourable institution, gave her a gargantuan luncheon, to which I was invited. I cannot be expected to remember the details. The colour of red remains in my mind: Henri's face; lobsters; a bizarre ham like a baby's bottom, as a run-up to the main course; and always a large carafe of Beaujolais to refresh us between the courses, pending the arrival of a wine of consequence.

In 1957 Lord Hailsham replaced David Eccles as Minister of Education, and legal questions at the Ministry, which I had always thought marginal, became more marginal still. He wrote his own letters and speeches, and hardly seemed to need civil servants, much less legal advisers. Our paths sometimes crossed in the corridor, and we exchanged greetings, but that was all.

Unexpectedly, my horizon at the Ministry of Education widened. The United Nations Educational, Scientific and Cultural Organisation had begun its existence after the war in London, with Julian Huxley as Director. The Government had not taken a great part in its activities. Margaret Herbison, the Labour Minister of Education, had emerged from a General Conference saying, for all to hear, 'Ay cann't abayde furriners'. The Organisation had early moved to Paris; and it had announced its intention of drawing up a Convention against Discrimination in Education. I was to take part in this as the Government's representative, with colleagues from the Ministry and the Foreign Office.

The Unesco Headquarters, in the Place de Fontenoy, occupied part of the former grounds of L'Ecole Militaire, and it was a pleasant, light, and airy building. The international atmosphere, with the many languages, was welcome to me. I at once took to Unesco's Legal Adviser Hanna Saba, an Egyptian with green eyes, who sat like a cat on the right of the Conference Chairman, and pounced at once on anyone he thought to be making an unsuitable suggestion. With his hands on his papers, he would raise his forefinger and wag it from side to side; and that was enough to stop the speaker in his tracks. I marvelled at the skills of the interpreters. There was simultaneous translation into English, French, Russian and Chinese; and the interpreters' voices could be heard trailing along in their respective tongues two or three sentences behind the speaker. I talked to the Soviet representatives. The head of the Russian delegation, an educational expert, liked to discuss Dickens. White-haired, with a rubicund face and steel spectacles, he looked like Mr Pickwick, of which he was aware. But he could be quite unPickwickian.

There were two matters particularly arousing controversy. One was the position of the English public schools, whose independent character had to be preserved. I quoted the saying that the battle of Waterloo had been won on the playing fields of Eton; and I told the Conference that I did not want to return home to be told that I had lost the battle of Eton on the playing fields of L'Ecole Militaire. On the second matter a fiercer controversy arose, of which I was at the centre. This concerned the 'Colonial application clause'. The Colonial Office never imposed an international Convention on the Colonies; it was left to the Government of each territory to decide whether to adopt it; and the wording of the Colonial application clause, which achieved this result, was sacrosanct. The Russians would not have this; they said our attitude was a pretext for maintaining colonial discrimination. I had arguments with Mr Pickwick and his team, but they would not be convinced of our good faith. They thought that if a country expanded over *land,* as did Russia, it was blameless, whereas if it did it over the *sea*, this was 'Imperialism' (what we called the 'Salt Water Fallacy'). The whole Convention was in danger of foundering on this point, on which I had specific instructions. Ultimately, at 4 o'clock in the morning, in the flat of a friend, I drafted on the back of a letter a clause under which the Convention would apply in principle to colonies, but preserve their choice. Next morning I put my new clause to the Conference, and it was accepted unanimously except, curiously, by the Australians. Article 15 of the United Kingdom Treaty Series No 44 (1962) retains for me a whiff of perfume.

The drawing up of the Convention, and after that the Protocol providing for its enforcement, then later a Report – entrusted to me by Saba – on its working, took a few weeks of every year for five or six years. I became a member of the standing Legal Committee of Unesco. At one meeting of a drafting Committee a problem arose, and the great French jurist René Cassin, who had been de Gaulle's legal adviser in London during the war, and I, were invited to produce a solution during the tea break. Saba came back to the meeting with a look of mischievous pleasure, announcing that Prof. Cassin's draft was in the English style, and mine in the French. My draft was adopted.

David Eccles was again Minister of Education, and came to the meetings of the General Conference with Lady Eccles. We sometimes travelled together by boat and train; and Sybil, who was the daughter of Lord Dawson of Penn, King George V's physician, would pass over to me advice given by her father to patients with phlebitis, from which I suffered at the time. On one occasion, on the ferry boat, Gerald Lascelles, George V's grandson, sat down opposite us, removed his bowler hat, wrapped it up in his *Times,* and took from his pocket a cloth cap. Then, apparently satisfied that he had changed his identity, he disappeared below deck.

I went much to Rome. I stayed at the Albergo Nazionale, in the centre near the via del Corso. I had an attic bedroom from which there was a view over the red roofs of Trastevere to St Peter's (with dome), and the Janiculum hill beyond. The moment I found myself walking in the sun along the Corso I felt an unmistakable lifting of the spirit, a sense of arriving at my destination. In a day or two I should make contact with friends. Meanwhile I breathed the intoxicating air, basked in the sun, listened to the Italian, observed some shapely young woman walking up the via Veneto. In the ruins of the Forum I dreamed of the great figures of classical Rome. Mussolini's maps of Empire still showed there on the wall.

A waiter at the restaurant in the piazza Navona, where I usually had lunch in the sun, would greet me. One day he said to me: 'You always come back – and you're always alone'. He was quite right, on both points. My Roman friends did not eat in restaurants, they entertained me in their homes. About the third day I began to do some telephoning, enquiring for the resident signorina. An undertaking of this kind would require half the morning, and for it I used the bars. There was a narrow street near the Corso, one side of it consisting almost entirely of bars. Every morning (except Sunday) one would see young men trying to telephone, running from door to door like priests distributing tracts against *l'alcoolismo.* Entering one of these bars, I would dial a number, and receive the whine of the *occupato.* Someone would leave his station at the bar for my station at the telephone, and I would go to the bar. After more attempts I would get through, to be told *'La signorina sta a letto'*. I would order a *cappuccino.* I drank it slowly, to give the signorina plenty of time to wake up. Then I would go again to the phone, to find I had no *gettone.* Obtaining a supply from the *cassetta,* I returned to the phone, but someone else was there. The bar was filling up. I went next door but one, and started again. I got through, but the signorina was still in bed. I drank another *cappuccino;* then I dialled again, and the voice said *'La signorina è in bagno'*. Changing to an *espresso,* I imagined the girl in the bath. To drink an *espresso* at a Roman pace is the work of a moment. Nevertheless, the signorina was quicker, for to my next call the reply was *'è fuori'*. It didn't much matter. I would walk up to the Campidoglio, view Marcus Aurelius on his horse, saunter about the Palatine, try to identify the Seven Hills of ancient Rome. Towards lunch time, the moment came for a *campari,* and I would enter a bar again. Told that the girl was still out, I asked for her mother; we would have a chat; and that ended in an invitation to lunch.

Mario Conti, who had been Italian ambassador to Libya, was back in Rome as head of the Cultural Affairs Department at the Foreign Ministry. Lunch with the Contis was a great pleasure; Mario, beaming and polished, Marisa, welcoming and a little teasing, Valeria, intelligent and enquiring (and not a late sleeper), and Giulio, serving in white gloves – the elegant table of a senior diplomat. Mario was later ambassador in Athens, and I stayed with them there.

Valeria, in her mid-twenties, was my friend, teacher, and benefactress. Her English was excellent, accurate, and at the same time up to date; Agatha Christie was one of her favourite writers. After she had married Ippolito Nievo, descendant of the distinguished writer of the same name, she acted as simultaneous translator at international conferences. She gave me lessons in Italian conversation: I remember her being unable to suppress her laughter only once, when I told her I had had 'boiled porter' for lunch, confusing *tacchino* (turkey) with *facchino.* She once asked me as a conversational gambit, and perhaps also because she really wanted to know, what I would do if I found myself walking along Piccadilly behind two beautiful girls. I replied that I would get in front of them, and try to improve my Italian. And Valeria, though she did not come to London herself, became my benefactress in this respect. Every summer she wrote to tell me that some friend was coming to London for a week or two: would I look after her?

The first of the summer swallows was Giovanna, who lived in the via Archimede, as did the Contis. Her father, il Conte Ancilotto, was at heart an agriculturist, and spent most of his time on his estate in the Veneto. We became great friends; and when he was in Rome for Easter I used to go shopping with him, usually for razors. Giovanna had an uncle in Kenya, and two brothers. Her mother seemed never to leave the via Archimede; and she was as exquisite, as white and fragile, as her collection of delicate porcelain snuff boxes on the glass shelves surrounding her. Giovanna, amusing and delightful, was betrothed to Nicola Manfredi, making his name at the Bar as a *penalista.* I later attended their wedding at the lovely church of Santa Maria in Cosmedin, and Nicola and Giovanna – a lively and entertaining, if scarcely decipherable, correspondent – remained close friends.

Then there was Francesca, who startled my neighbours in Paultons Square one July evening by suddenly flying through the door of a taxi in a brilliant red dress, her blonde hair streaming. She moved in a whirlwind, was always late, and was always amusing. I could never believe that she was a school teacher, but I was assured by her grandmother, with whom she lived in Rome, that she had her serious moments. *La nonna* was a sweet lady, the perfect grandmother; and I had long chats with her while waiting for the arrival, released from school, of Francesca, by then boisterous.

There came others also: Grazia, literary, named after her grandmother, the Sardinian writer Grazia Deledda; and Manuela, determined to pass the stiff State examination for *notaio,* and to succeed her father Guglielmo, in one of the best practices in Rome.

All these were amongst my friends. At the end of my Easter season in Rome I would entertain them to an apéritif – usually nominal in the case of the women; then we would all go off, men and women, to dinner at some *trattoria* in Trastevere, vouched for by *notaio* Guglielmo. Next morning, sick at heart at having to leave, I would delay my departure from the Nazionale until the last possible moment for catching the plane.

I moved from Chelsea. The move resulted from chance, from a dinner party, which is another way of saying the same thing. Eric and Peggy Sachs, who had been friends since the war, were entertaining Hubert Parker and his wife Loren, and invited me. Eric was now a High Court judge, and Hubert Parker was a Lord Justice of Appeal. The Parkers had no children, and were forever on the move. After Hubert had become Lord Chief Justice he was said to have told a young barrister, driving him home one night after a public dinner (in those days a Lord Chief Justice was not provided with a car), that he and Loren had moved house thirty-three times. They had now acquired a flat in Lincoln's Inn, but did not want it. Loren, with an American woman's zest for interior alterations and decoration, had spent a great deal of money on this flat. But she was in a fix, as she could only dispose of it to someone approved by the Inn, preferably a member (which I was not) or at least a barrister. She set about persuading me that it was the perfect home for me, telling me tales about Nell Gwynn's living there, and a priest's hole. I went to see the flat. It was at 20 and 21 Old Buildings, dated from 1525, and was one of the most spacious in the Inn, with three large, elegant living-rooms. It was a beautiful flat, and would have been more beautiful had Loren Parker let it alone. But she had covered the fine wood-block flooring with thick carpeting, sawn off the bottoms of the doors in consequence, converted a fourth room, with the best view in the flat, into a second bathroom, and installed wooden wall-racks in a fifth, windowless room, from floor to ceiling, as if intending to keep battery hens or possibly rabbits. In the magnificent bow window overlooking what was called the Kitchen Garden, in the full view of everyone passing beneath, was stationed a three-quarter double bed (frame only), also for disposal.

To Lady Parker the move would mean nothing more than a change of milkman, but for me it would be a dislocation. I enjoyed living in Chelsea: the freedom and amenities of life there, and the society of my friends and neighbours. I should exchange these for the confines of an Inn of Court, and the cold touch of the lawyers. My friends viewed the idea with surprise, or alarm, depending on the intimacy between us. I took a referendum on the question: I gave lunch-time picnics in the sun, on the soft turf of the pile carpet, round the bed. I consulted Ann and Ambrose Appelbe, who had lived in the Inn: they spoke of the tranquillity, the curfew bell at 9 p.m., the gates locked at 11 p.m. That was what I feared. But it would be a privilege to live in Lincoln's Inn, and a confirmation of my seriousness as a lawyer. My mother helped me with the outlay; I bargained with Loren; and Hubert persuaded his fellow Benchers to let me have the flat.

I set out to furnish it in period; and advised by Olwen and Jasper Peck, both experts, I attended Christies. I bought Charles II and William and Mary walnut chairs, an oak refectory table, six Sheraton dining chairs of fruitwood, and a splendid 17th century oak sideboard 8 feet long. These pieces furnished the dining-room, a room which had retained something of a medieval simplicity, and silence. In the panelled drawing-room the Steinway

Grand, having mounted the winding stairs with some difficulty, justified itself by its inherent beauty. Looking down on it all from the top shelf of the 18th-century niche was the 12th-century Tang priest or teacher, sceptically asking 'Well, now you have all this elegance, what are you going to do with it?'

I offered sherry. It was all I could offer, to propitiate the Tang dynasty or my occasional visitor. It was essentially the Inn drink; and as one American visitor said, she would expect it to be 'piped in'. It was a wet July evening, and looking out of the window she also said 'Lincoln's Inn is beautiful even in the rain'. None of my neighbours called on me. On my staircase, in the two smaller flats above me, lived two bachelors; but neither made any contact. I learned to put up with the Inn stare, which said: 'Do I know you, or don't I? In any case I needn't recognise you.' Signs rising out of the ground said 'KEEP OFF THE GRASS': they seemed to express the spirit of the place, the *genius loci.* To stave off claustrophobia, I installed a tank of tropical fish in my hall, and they fought one another. On Saturday morning I walked over to Gamages, to replenish my stock. They served to get me out for a walk, like a dog.

The cloistered atmosphere of the Inn lent itself to further study of Italian. In a 'reader' containing extracts from Italian literature I came across a short story called 'A Tour of the World'. The narrator had signed a promissory note, for a small sum, but as the due date approached he became so worried that he had a nervous breakdown, and was ordered to take a world tour. The story is almost entirely about what takes place in the station waiting-room while he is waiting for the train, and it delighted me: ironic, mocking, debunking, very amusing, the perfect 'throw away'. It was by Massimo Bontempelli, of whom I had not heard. I enquired about him in Rome the next Easter. My friends were vague: 'Oh yes,' everyone said, 'Bontempelli? Yes – certainly I know of him'. 'Is he still writing?' 'I haven't heard of anything lately.' 'Is he still alive?' 'I'm not sure.' 'Have you read anything of his?' 'Not lately'. Even Valeria was uncertain, non-committal. In the bookshops they shook their heads. There seemed to be almost a conspiracy of silence.

I spent the following August searching for traces of him. Descending from a flat in Parioli where I lodged, a little cooler than in the centre of Rome, I worked the bookshops. At last, in an obscure street not far from the Street of the Bars, I found a second-hand copy of *Primi Racconti.* I asked the proprietor of the shop, an oldish man who had developed the indifference to the wants of his customers usual in the sellers of second-hand books, whether Signor Bontempelli was still living. He seemed reluctant to answer, and busied himself with someone else, hoping no doubt that I should go away. But I stood there; and at length taking me aside, he put the back of his hand in front of his mouth, and half-whispered in his guttural Roman tones: *'Bon-tem-pel-li a-ve-va un'a-man-te ... la scri-tri-ce Pa-o-la Ma-si-no'*. He would say no more.

Possessed of this clue to the author, and his first book of short stories, I sat down at the nearest café table. I spent most of August in this way, sweltering in the cafés, reading happily. These stories had been written before the First World War, twenty years before 'A Tour of the World', and their style was a straightforward narrative; but they were full of original characters and satirical humour. *Il Collezionista* – 'The Collectionist' rather than 'The Collector' – relates how the Baron Raimondo, whose sole object in life is to build up collections, progresses from the mundane to a loftier plane, and finally drives himself to disaster. When I translated this story later, and Harry Leon sent it to the *Atlantic Monthly,* the reply came: 'This is a very fine translation but the story itself would be impossible to sell here. It is a remarkable *tour de force* but just not an American magazine possibility. I should be very happy to see other stories that are a little bit closer to the norm.'

But nothing Bontempelli wrote was 'close to the norm'. I had found at the Italian Institute in London an article about him in *Smith's Dictionary of Modern Literature.* Born in 1878, he was described as an 'odd combination of the scholar and the advance guard experimentalist', this giving his writings 'their peculiar charm and vitality'; his style was 'natural, effortless'; and his topics or plots 'the most bizarre imaginable'. Learning that Bontempelli was still alive, I wrote to Mondadori, his publisher, and they gave me an address in the viale Liegi in Rome. I wrote expressing my admiration for his stories, and asked permission to translate them. I received an encouraging reply from Paola Masino, who said that Bontempelli, because of age and health, was not able to attend to work. I obtained an option on thirty-seven of the stories, signed by Bontempelli. Next time I was in Rome I went to the flat in viale Liegi, excited, and nervous about my

Italian. I felt I knew the author well in spirit already. Especially in my mind was *Un'anima in un Bar,* where the writer enters a bar behind a soul, the soul of a civil servant wearing a bowler hat. I was entering a garden, full of shrubs and trees. Imagine the *frisson* when, through the trees, I saw the sitting figure of a man, white as death. I stopped, near to terror, and then made out that the figure was of stone. I went up in a clanking lift, was welcomed by Paola Masino, and was flabbergasted by the state of the upholstery, which had been torn to shreds. I understood Paola, who spoke very quickly, to apologise for their four cats. On a later occasion she said that she had 'one cat', but preferred my version as *'più divertente'*. Behind a communicating door was Bontempelli, but I was not allowed to go in. He died two or three months later.

He had never been translated into English, except for one story, and a play *La Piccola,* performed at the Arts Theatre in 1930, though he had been translated into fifteen other languages. This neglect was perhaps partly due to the growing divide between the two countries caused by Fascism – yet Pirandello, whose friend Bontempelli was, transplanted very successfully. I felt I had 'discovered' him, and I wished to share my discovery with my fellow countrymen. To some extent I did. I read some of the translations to friends; and Ann Appelbe had a soirée at the Elms, at which I read and Marguerite played the piano. In June 1961 my translations of *A World Tour* and another story I called *Dining Out* were read on the BBC's Home Service programme. Five others were published by John Murray in *Cornhill.* But, notwithstanding an enthusiastic letter from the Director of the Italian Institute, Gabriele Baldini, Murray was unwilling to risk publishing a book of stories by an author unknown here and now dead. Paola Masino did all she could to encourage me. She introduced me to literary friends, including Mario Praz, and Natalia Ginsberg, who was Gabriele Baldini's wife. For a brief hour I became almost one of the Rome literary circle. Paola thought that Bontempelli was an '*autore estremamente difficile*', but I did not think that. He led the movement for magical realism, and was, it seems to me, in the direct line from *Tristram Shandy* to postmodernism. The fact was that, as he himself put it, he did not 'write for the porter.'

XII

Commonwealth Relations

AT THE Ministry of Education I resolved to take a step which probably remains unique in the history of government service. I declared my post as Legal Adviser to the Ministry to be semi-redundant, on the ground that there was only half a day's work there; and I suggested that I should spend the remaining half of the day with some other Department where there was a shortage of legal advisers. In Whitehall the effect of this announcement was similar to that of the dropping of his rifle on parade by the guardsman, in the H. M. Bateman cartoon. There were murmurs of 'letting the side down'. Harold Kent, the Treasury Solicitor, said 'You must be a glutton for work'. I happened to know that they needed help at the Foreign Office; and for a period I formed one of the small band of legal advisers there, for half of the day. I had become a member of the Travellers Club, at 106 Pall Mall, a ten-minute walk from Curzon Street; and it was quite convenient for me to have lunch there and then walk on to the Foreign Office. At the top of the Duke of York's Steps men coming out of the various clubs would converge. I once heard the word actually used: 'Edward, my dear fellow, how are you?' one clubman exclaimed to the other. 'Shall we converge?'

In any case the time was coming for me to return to Downing Street and to succeed Kenneth Roberts-Wray as Legal Adviser to the Commonwealth Relations Office on his retirement. They had promised me that. But to my surprise I was told it would not be possible. The Treasury objected, just as it had objected after the war to my return to the Colonial Office, but this time more strongly. The Commonwealth side of the work had, in my absence, been in the hands of Sir Ralph Hone, a competent and experienced lawyer, with many years' service behind him in the Colonial Legal Service. Since he had been – at least nominally – working under Roberts-Wray, his salary was less than mine would be at the grade of Legal Adviser. The Treasury saw that it could economise on a top post, and I suppose have some of the Foreign Office work done for nothing. The Commonwealth Relations Office did not think the matter important enough to justify a dispute with the Treasury. But it was important to me: I regarded my return as a plain matter of justice to myself; and I was dismayed that the Department I expected to advise on matters of good faith and fair dealing should pay such scant regard to honouring its word. Affairs remained in this state for some time, until Peter Hampshire, the Director of Establishments, whom I had known since the war years, told Savile Garner, who had become Permanent Under-Secretary of State, that I was not being fairly treated. The Treasury was prevailed upon to give way. I said goodbye to my colleagues in Curzon Street with personal feelings of regret. They had been very pleasant to work with; and they had treated me with kindness and deference, though I had been something of an intruder into their world. At least I had kept them out of the courts.

At the Commonwealth Relations Office I now had to assist me, besides Humphrey Oxley, Sir Orby Mootham, who had been Chief Justice of Allahabad. It had become a different office, in size and outlook, from the one I had joined in 1936. The Dominions Office then had five departments and three or four overseas posts; by now there were twenty-three departments in the Office and ten or more overseas posts. The Commonwealth Relations Office continued to grow, so that eventually there were twenty-seven departments and thirty overseas posts. The Secretary of State for Commonwealth Relations was in 1961 Duncan Sandys, and for the Colonies Ian Macleod. The Duke of Devonshire was Minister of State.

Harold Macmillan had succeeded Anthony Eden as Prime Minister in 1957, and he was more sympathetic than his predecessors to the Commonwealth association. He made a number of tours of Commonwealth countries as part of his effort to restore Britain's relations with its friends abroad after the Suez disaster; and these tours both increased his understanding of the value of the Commonwealth association to Britain, and demonstrated to its other members that Britain continued to take an interest in them. He also saw that 'decolonisation' was inevitable, and in 1960 he told the South African Parliament, in a speech which had been drafted by a Commonwealth Relations Office diplomat stationed in Pretoria, Arthur Clark, that the 'wind of change' was blowing through Africa, 'whether we like it or not.' Ghana, Malaya, Cyprus and Nigeria had become independent while I had been away, and so passed from the control of the Colonial Office to full statehood within the 'Family' – if one could still call it that – of Nations. At any rate they were members of the United Nations with the benefits and obligations of members, like other nations of the world. The Commonwealth Relations Office now handled our relations with them; hence the increase in its staff and work. The independence of Sierra Leone was to follow almost at once, and in 1962 came that of Jamaica, Trinidad and Tobago, and Uganda.

One of the most difficult problems facing the Macmillan Government was that of Central Africa. In 1953 I had had a share in the creation of the Central African Federation, and I now became involved in its dissolution. The trouble was that Northern Rhodesia and Nyasaland, with African populations which were not in an advanced stage of self-government, had been joined together in a Federation with Southern Rhodesia, a country which since 1923 had been governed by white settlers, elected, and largely independent of British control. Federation had promised economic advantages for all three territories, and it had resulted in considerable development. But economic considerations did not come first with African politicians. The enthusiasts for federation were the educated and more realistic white leaders in Southern Rhodesia, backed by Tory stalwarts at home such as Lord Salisbury, who had been Dominions Secretary earlier, and Oliver Lyttleton, who had been Colonial Secretary. Northern Rhodesia and Nyasaland had been reluctant partners from the beginning. There had been unrest in both territories, with riots in Nyasaland, and Hastings Banda, the political leader in Nyasaland, had been put in prison. The Africans saw independence coming all around them. Nyasaland was now pressing to be given the right to secede from the Federation, which would mean its breaking up.

In London the problem was bedevilled by a divided control: the affairs of the Federation and of Southern Rhodesia were handled by the Commonwealth Relations Office, whereas Northern Rhodesia and Nyasaland, except in federal matters, were in the care of the Colonial Office, whose policy was to bring them to self-government. There was so much dissension between the two Departments that in 1962 Macmillan, unable to bear the disputes any longer, set up a new, small Department to deal with all matters concerning the three territories. He called it the Central Africa Office, and put R.A. Butler in charge of it, making him also, in some compensation, First Secretary of State, and Deputy Prime Minister. Butler had the most persuasive and subtle mind in the Government, and was in the competition for becoming Prime Minister. Mark Tennant from the Ministry of Labour became the Permanent Secretary, and Duncan Watson, from the Colonial Office, Under-Secretary. I was the legal adviser. We worked in a little 18th-century building, a cottage amongst the edifices of Whitehall, nearly opposite the Horseguards Parade, called Gwydyr House.

Butler began by inviting Dr Banda to discussions, and these were followed by his announcement in the House of Commons that the Government acknowledged the right of Nyasaland to withdraw from the Federation. This created a storm amongst the Tory stalwarts, and in Salisbury, the Federal capital. The Prime Minister of the Federation was Roy Welensky. Butler, who had not much respect for the quality of the Salisbury politicians, observed that Huggins (now Viscount Malvern), the Federation's first Prime Minister, was what he thought was meant by a 'buffer' ('old buffer'). But he had a regard for Welensky – of 'Prime Minister material', he said, knowing we would get the reference to himself. Welensky asserted that at the time of federation a pledge had been given by the British Government that there would be no right to secede from it. There was no evidence of such a pledge, and no one had any recollection of one. But Butler, who had a strong conscience, was worried. As the question involved the good faith of the Government, it was placed in the hands of the Lord Chancellor. Since Macmillan's 'night of the long knives', he had been Lord Dilhorne, formerly Reginald Manningham-Buller, or 'Bullying-Manner', as he was often called. This soubriquet did indeed describe him, though it fitted him no more accurately than a number of Tory Ministers, who – unlike Labour Ministers – tended to bully one. I had had an unpleasant discussion with Reggie (as he was called) over some matter; and after it was over

George Dudman, who had been his Legal Secretary when he was Attorney-General, asked me how I had got on. 'Not very well', I replied; 'he never let me finish a sentence'. 'Now you know what my life was like', said Dudman; 'never finished a sentence for ten years.'

Reggie called a meeting. His usual manner in the cold weather was to tell us that he had set the thermostat at 70 degrees: 'A good, healthy, temperature, and if anyone feels cold he can get his overcoat.' On this occasion he did not say this. The meeting was of Ministers, and very extraordinary it was. Besides Butler there was the Home Secretary, Henry Brooke, and the Minister of Health, Enoch Powell, and perhaps others; and none of them had anything to do with the matter. A White Paper was to be drafted, and the job was assigned to Enoch Powell, as the stylist of the Cabinet. (Many years later I reminded him of this, but it had entirely passed from his memory.) The White Paper was issued, showing there were no pledges, but containing the not very reassuring phrase used by Lord Swinton at the time of federation: 'You cannot legislate against the United Kingdom Parliament going off its head.' Still Butler was uneasy. He had a meeting with officials. He was full of self-pity. 'You are my only friends', he said. He considered it a moral issue. 'I think I ought to offer my resignation to the Prime Minister, but I don't want to put ideas into his head.' A little later: 'The Prime Minister is the most worldly man I know.' The Ministers from Salisbury were summoned to London, headed by Julian Greenfield, a local lawyer from Bulawayo, who was Minister of Justice. The Lord Chancellor again presided, and Butler sat at the other end of the table, saying nothing, paring his nails. Not a flicker came into his face as Reggie proceeded to put his foot into it. The argument about the legal position became warm: 'No lawyer would say that, Mr Greenfield.' 'But I *am* a lawyer, Lord Chancellor.' At six o'clock Dilhorne said: 'I think we had better have a drink. Let us have some sherry in.' He rang his bell. 'I'm a teetotaller, Lord Chancellor', said Greenfield, who was also a local preacher. The order for sherry was countermanded.

There was another debate in Parliament, and it was acknowledged that all the Governments had the right to secede. This of course included the Southern Rhodesia Government; and Winston Field, the Southern Rhodesia Prime Minister, said his Government would not take part in the arrangements for dissolution of the

Federation unless Southern Rhodesia was promised its independence. Nevertheless we went ahead with the proposed Conference at the Victoria Falls Hotel to plan the arrangements for the dissolution. Butler was far from happy. He had already been to Salisbury to prepare the ground for the Conference. 'Why am I in this awful place?' he murmured. But he persuaded Winston Field that it would be irresponsible of him to obstruct the Conference, and we went on to the Victoria Falls. In that splendid hotel, within a short distance of the Zambesi and those stupendous Falls, the delegations of the five Governments – 60 or more people I think – faced all the issues raised by the impending dissolution of the central Government. That was in June and July; a timetable was agreed – the Federation was to disappear on 31 December – matters of principle were settled, and committees set up. Butler was at his best: cool, courteous, the statesman, carrying his cross with irony. Security measures had been taken by the Southern Rhodesia Government which, for those days, were tight. Butler was faintly amused. His sense of humour was always there. At a meeting of the British delegation in one of the small rooms, he became irritated by the rattling of the door caused by the high wind. At length someone got up and wedged it with a piece of paper. Not long afterwards the door was suddenly thrown open and a security guard burst in. 'Excuse me, sir', he said, 'there is an object outside your window.' Butler, who was sitting with his back to the window, and all of us turned to look. Something was hanging there: it might have been a small bomb, but it looked rather like a lavatory pull and chain. 'What are you going to do about it?' asked Butler. 'We shall investigate at once, sir, and report to you'. 'Thank you.' We were expected to vacate the room, but Butler made no move. The guard began to hurry away. 'Don't forget to replace the piece of paper in the door, will you', Butler called after him.

After the Conference I remained in Salisbury for some time, and spent three months of 1963 there altogether. In providing for the transfer of responsibility back to the three territorial Governments, the transfer of assets and liabilities, and legal continuity generally, I had the friendly help of the Minister of Justice, Julian Greenfield (who once remarked to me, 'I don't liken myself in all respects to the Lord Chancellor, but we have one thing in common – we are responsible for the judges'), and 'Polly' Yates, the Attorney General. In addition, Stanley and Bambi Weinberg, my old friends from Libyan days, were living there. Stanley was working in the Attorney General's office, and would be without a job at the end of the year. He had valuable knowledge of local matters. The Conference had set up two Committees, one for working out the detailed arrangements generally, the second to settle financial matters. The latter was under the chairmanship of Sir Algernon Rumbold, an Under-Secretary from the Commonwealth Relations Office; and I was soon asked to take over the chairmanship of the former, in addition to carrying on my functions as legal adviser. As we settled the substance of one provision after another to be embodied in the legislation, I sent instructions home to David Gordon Smith, one of my assistants, and an able draftsman; and he drafted the required Order in Council, piece by piece.

I was admitted to temporary membership of the Salisbury club, the only place I could afford to stay on my daily allowance. The weather was hot and there was no one much there except at lunch time, when the farmers would come in, just as they would in an English town congregate in the hotel on market days. There was a slump in prices – I was offered a fine house in the best suburban area, freehold, for £250 – and a general air of depression. At the club, the two or three members there for tea took off the lids of their teapots as soon as they were brought, to cool the liquid. I don't know what my Yorkshire aunts would have said at this disrespectful treatment of the cup that cheers.

On the whole I enjoyed my time in Salisbury. The city had some beauty, though in the distance it looked like Croydon. Every time I arrived there it seemed to smell of horse urine – I did not discover why, as I never saw a horse. I came to know the politicians well, and one evening I was asked by Ian Smith, then Financial Secretary to the Southern Rhodesia Government, to join him for a drink. I was busy, and I declined. I have often wondered if, had I been on drinking terms with him, I could have convinced him later on that he was on a hopeless quest. I visited some of the magnificent country; also the 'antiquities', the ruins at Zimbabwe, which I realised dated from a century later than my flat in Lincoln's Inn. One weekend I went with Algie Rumbold to see the Kariba Dam, one of the great achievements of Federation, and we stayed in the rest-house. We breakfasted looking over the Dam. Algie had brought his pocket radio. De Gaulle had turned down Harold Macmillan's application to join the Common Market, and Algie enlarged on the disadvantages membership would bring to us, regarding the Market as a scheme for boosting French and German agriculture. Then, as we gazed over the great waters, we heard the news of the assassination of President Kennedy.

When I eventually left Salisbury in December, the work done, I returned home by way of Cape Town, determined to see its scenic beauties. I had time to spend three or four nights in the Mount Nelson Hotel, on the side of the hill overlooking the town, of all the hotels I have stayed in my favourite. I sampled some of the excellent white wines. Napoleon, when on St Helena, had provided himself with wine by importing it from the Cape, transplanting vines from French vineyards, and they had escaped the phylloxera. I was presented with a bottle of brandy, some of which I drank on the flight back, to avoid customs duty. It was of top quality, worthy of Table Mountain. But Verwoerd had made apartheid the policy of his Government, and I found some of its results repulsive. In 1961 the country had left the Commonwealth; South Africa was no longer a 'relation'.

No sooner was I back than I became involved in the dispute over the return of Chief Enahoro to Nigeria, for trial on charges of conspiracy to overthrow the Government. The Opposition lawyers became very heated, particularly because Dingle Foot, one of their number, and Noel Gratiaen, who was in his chambers, were not to be allowed by Nigeria to defend him. They accused both the Home Secretary, Henry Brooke, and the Attorney General, John Hobson, of bad faith, and pursued charges of misconduct against the latter. The Benchers of the Inner Temple declared them unfounded, as indeed they were. John Hobson was a man of complete rectitude, who sadly died early. Macmillan had himself to justify the Government's position before Enahoro was sent back, defended by a third counsel from Foot's chambers, and convicted.

The year 1963 was a bad one for the Macmillan Government. Early in the year the Profumo scandal broke. John Profumo was the Secretary of State for War, and he was reported by the press to be sharing the favours of a 'model', Christine Keeler, with the military attaché at the Soviet Embassy. If this were true, our military intelligence and security were at risk. To reassure the country, Profumo made a personal statement in the House of Commons with Macmillan sitting by his side. He declared there was no truth in the stories, and this was accepted as concluding the matter. But the stories persisted. A little later while Macmillan, who was unwell with prostate trouble, was in Scotland, and Butler was acting Prime Minister, I was at a meeting with him in his room at the Cabinet Office, when he was interrupted by a call to the telephone. We waited while he had a long conversation, obviously confidential. When he returned to us he could not keep it to himself. 'A very serious matter,' he said. 'I ought not to tell you . . . you will hear soon enough . . . the Secretary of State . . . for War . . . not the truth . . . The Prime Minister can handle this.' In a day or two it all came out. Profumo had abused the trust placed by the House of Commons in the personal statement of a member, and he had to resign. More scandal followed. Stephen Ward, a doctor, who was closely involved in it all, was convicted of the offence of living on immoral earnings, and other offences, and committed suicide.

1963 was also the year in which Kim Philby, serving in the embassy in Beirut, failed to join his wife at a dinner party, and subsequently surfaced in Moscow, the third man with Burgess and Maclean. Harold Macmillan felt too ill to continue, and resigned. I met him only once. An important figure from a Commonwealth country had arrived, and nothing had been done to entertain him. A late evening party was suddenly called at Number 10. In the time available few people were able to gather, and I was the only one there from the Commonwealth Relations Office, except for Duncan Sandys. Macmillan himself was continually disappearing and reappearing, as if taking advantage of some hiding-place. When I did talk to him, it was his hooded eyes that made an indelible impression on me. There was an unearthly light in them under the heavy drooping eyelids, and it hardly seemed a human face: it was like that of an old reynard looking out of his lair in the undergrowth.

Alec Douglas-Home succeeded him as Prime Minister. I had had contact with him at the Ministry of Education, when he took a Bill for us through the House of Lords, making a light task of it. Butler went to the Foreign Office. Disappointed of the Premiership, he enjoyed himself there. 'I'm loving my new job', he would say, as I occasionally met him in or about Downing Street, in his brown, pork-pie hat. I always found him a pleasure to work with – unlike Mark Tennant, the head of the Central Africa Office, who thought him flabby. Butler would telephone to Mark at his home every Saturday morning, and a plaintive voice would ask 'Mark, what am I to do with my weekend?' A most skilful politician, he exercised his skill without one being aware of it. He liked to shock us, or perhaps embarrass us, with his indiscretions, and to amuse us with his wit. 'He wears remarkably clean linen,' he said, after his first meeting with Kenneth Kaunda. After the Government changed, he retired to Cambridge as Master of Trinity College, where his father's uncle, Montague Butler, had been Master. The stories travelled from there. We heard how, when Butler ultimately left the place, one of his boxes was found to contain some of the College's valuable plate. He had understandably assumed that it was family silver.

Something else happened, during that eventful year 1963, which affected me personally and deeply. During the preparatory period for the Victoria Falls Conference my mother died. She was 93, and suffered no illness. Firm of purpose, but gentle always, kind, generous, thoughtful for others, she knew that her end was coming when I was so much required in London. But I was able to travel to Reading every night, until the day came when the doctor told me I had better stay. My sister and I buried her in Garton churchyard next to my father, who had lain there for nearly thirty years. There were few relations or family friends left to attend the funeral.

My sister resumed her teaching career at Reading. I had left almost at once for Victoria Falls. When I once more settled down in Lincoln's Inn I felt my social life to be stagnant. As a bachelor I received invitations to dinner, but I was not able to give dinner parties in return. I decided to end this state of affairs by employing a cook, and to give a dinner party regularly every month. A young woman bought the food, arrived at 6.30 p.m., cooked it to what I was told was a *cordon bleu* standard, served us, washed up, and went, having apparently enjoyed her evening, and the richer by £5. These dinner parties, for eight, established for me a social springboard. I was able to entertain old friends and new: amongst the latter were young Libyan diplomats, including Omar Muntasser, much intrigued by my evanescent household. My dinners began with oysters, supplied by a 'Mishter Shmith', as he pronounced his name, from a stall in Leather Lane. I used to stop and talk to him on my Saturday morning walks to Gamages to buy my Siamese fighters, and occasionally bought a lobster from him. His general appearance was watery. He wore a cloth cap which dripped in the rain onto his soiled white coat, he had watery eyes, and a red nose with its independent supply of moisture. It seemed that he had a kind of hay fever in the months with an 'r' in them. On the evening of a dinner party I would hear him trudging up my wooden staircase, and there he would be at the door, with a small sack over his shoulder. He would sit down in the kitchen and open the oysters; and over a glass of sherry we had a good, cockney conversation, and he would tell me how 'Mishish Shmith' cooked scallops. I paid him five shillings a dozen for the oysters. He never removed his cap; and when he was late – as he often was – it was a business getting him out of the flat before the first guest arrived.

After a time I replaced my visiting cooks by a resident housekeeper. Lidia, Italian, small and hunched, was a reliable cook, and looked after me well. But she liked to stand over me and talk while I, sitting in the bow window overlooking the garden, ate breakfast. I wished to read my *Times*. It was too late for me to pretend that I did not speak Italian. One day I opened the paper at a picture of Archbishop Makarios, by then President of Cyprus, sitting on his balcony having breakfast, and reading the newspaper – the *Times* of course. I asked myself 'Have I to become a turbulent priest, or an Archbishop, or President of a Republic, to be able to eat breakfast in silence?' I resolved to make a change. Lidia easily found another place, and I interviewed a number of applicants, including, to my surprise, Blanche Patch, who had been Bernard Shaw's housekeeper for thirty years, until his death. We talked about his vegetarian dishes, and the steaks she had cooked for T. E. Lawrence on his visits. But we should not have suited one another, and I took on a Spanish girl whom Omar Muntasser found for me. She did not last long. She wept over the washing up, and told me she wanted to be a 'thale thlady'.

On New Year's Day 1964, a late breakfast was interrupted by a telephone call from my new assistant, Julian Larby, a Cambridge graduate in international law who had been recommended to me by Clive Parry. He told me to go to the office at once. Makarios had run amok, and the Secretary of State had summoned an urgent meeting. This was my first serious encounter with Duncan Sandys, and I was not well prepared for it. I had been at the Ministry of Education when, on Cyprus becoming independent in 1960, we had entered into treaties of guarantee and alliance, involving Greece and Turkey. Then I learned that Duncan Sandys had himself, characteristically, flown to Cyprus over Christmas, in the small hours, on reports of serious rioting. Now Makarios had, on account of the movement of Turkish forces, purported to abrogate the treaties. I expected a close cross-examination about our legal obligations; but instead of that Sandys left me to consult the Foreign Office lawyers, which I was glad to do. I talked to Henry Darwin, who was the great-grandson of Charles Darwin himself, and of formidable brain power. This was made more commanding by what George Eliot called a 'superfluous height', but I could get round that by telephoning. It seemed to me the treaties put us under a legal obligation to intervene, whereas he argued against. But Sandys was off in a day or two again, persuaded Makarios to substitute 'secure termination by appropriate means' for 'abrogate', and then arranged a conference in London between all the Governments concerned. Things went from bad to worse, there was fighting, troops were sent, and a United Nations force. Eventually there was a Turkish invasion, and in 1975 complete separation of the Turkish northern part of the island.

Duncan Sandys had been Commonwealth Secretary since 1960, and Colonial Secretary since 1962. He had also taken over the Central Africa Office for its short life after Butler went to the Foreign Office. He had the reputation, particularly with officials abroad, of being yet another 'problem area'. 'A very difficult year', one of them had said to me in Salisbury. 'We had first Sandys, then the Congo.' Then his wife added: 'Sandys is more difficult. We cannot partition *him*.' He was determined to get to the bottom of everything, partly to test the knowledge and skill of his officials, partly to be able to understand the matter fully himself. He also had a passion for altering wording; and if a Minister indulges in that, he wastes a great deal of time. He was at his most difficult over drafts of Acts of Parliament, and he would not accept, as most Ministers would, the legal-technical language in which the Parliamentary draftsmen draft our legislation. I had sympathy with him, because, in Libya especially, I had become acquainted with the much simpler style in which the continental draftsmen draft their legislation. Duncan Sandys told us of his experience, when Minister for Housing and Local Government, with the 'Derequisitioning' Bill. The Government was proud of this measure, which freed thousands of properties from war-time requisitioning; but on going through the Bill, he said, he had found that neither requisitioning nor derequisitioning were mentioned. (It became the Requisitioned Houses and Housing (Amendment) Act 1955.) It was my duty to pass his strictures on any of my Bills to Parliamentary Counsel, of whom the chief at this time was Noel Hutton. He had gained a double First at Oxford, and was a rowing blue as well, and had a formidable intellect, like most of his fellow draftsmen. Happily I had formed a friendship with Noel, who would drive me in the evening, in his open racing car, to his large house and garden in Dulwich. We bought a bottle of wine on the way, in a pub, and his wife Virginia gave us dinner. Mr Secretary Sandys was recognised in Noel's office as a maverick.

Certainly working with Duncan Sandys did not leave me much time for translating. There were long meetings at which every word was examined, every document rewritten. He seemed to be constantly seeking to justify himself. He began one meeting about Southern Rhodesia by telling us that the Lord Chancellor 'agreed with my view that independence meant recognition', though we were well aware that the Lord Chancellor was strongly against Sandys's policy. He seemed a curiously disordered worker. He was often late, at times very late, and in spite of his strong character did not seem to be in control of his arrangements. In the middle of a meeting he would be reminded of an appointment in the House of Commons, and would dash off, apologising. I made a note of the dialogue at one of his meetings, which should have begun at 5.30 but instead started at 7 o'clock.

S of S (rings for Freda, his personal Private Secretary, before we begin):
Have I a pair tonight? (Pulls out some cards like football fixture cards)
Freda: Yes
S of S: You should let me know if I have a pair. You never let me know last night.
Freda: No, John Osborne didn't phone up till late. But it was all right.
S of S: At what time were you going to let me know tonight that I had a pair?
Freda: You can take it you have a pair unless I tell you to the contrary.
S of S (pause): Oh! (exit Freda)
S of S (looks at document): Let us have a typist (rings . . . a miserable little dark, half-beatnik girl comes in and sits a foot away from him)
S of S (proceeds to go through document, alters nearly every word, sense exactly the same. Has to go back and re-alter to the original. Keeps saying to the girl):

Say 'Yes' when you have it.
Typist: Yes, thank you.
S of S: You needn't say 'thank you'.
(later)
Now read it . . . Louder . . . Louder . . . Louder . . . really loud, can't you, as if you were calling for help (rings bell again . . . Freda appears).
Ring up my home and tell them I'll be late.
Freda: You're dining with Mrs X.
S of S: Yes, I know. That's why I want them told.
(We are not half way through, everyone is stealing out, or getting up to cancel engagements . . . Ten minute interruption on Zanzibar)
S of S (dictates telegram to someone): He is probably drunk by now.
Mark Tennant (whispering to me): I wish I was.

After an hour and a half we all emerge, with one and a half pages done. As we go through the door the Duke of Devonshire says to me: 'Extraordinary man, the Secretary of State: I've never known anyone before who could pack four hours work into twenty-four.'

There would be the meetings after dinner in Duncan Sandys's house in Vincent Square. He began by offering us brandy, which I declined. He put this down to abstemiousness, but that was wrong; before leaving home I had drunk some whisky to fortify myself for the night's work. The room was hung with the Secretary of State's abstract paintings. He was indeed an extraordinary man. He was a member of the Magic Circle, and that certainly mystified us. He was a complete contrast to Butler, whose father had been a distinguished member of the Indian Civil Service. Butler had lived in India when young, and seemed to have inherited some of the subtle and sinuous qualities of the Indian. But Duncan Sandys had the aggressive and forceful characteristics of the rufous. He was a man of great courage and tenacity. Injured in a motor crash during the war, and with a slight limp, he often suffered from severe pain. It was typical of him, nevertheless, to fly to Ghana lying flat in the bomb rack of an RAF plane because that was the only way to get there quickly, and to make President Nkrumah, whose life had just been attempted, drive with him in an open car through the streets of Accra, to test whether the Queen could safely go; to visit British Guiana at the height of communal disturbances; and to fly to the Far East to prevent the President of Indonesia from hindering the conclusion of the agreement between Malaya, Singapore and the Borneo Territories for the creation of Malaysia.

If one can imagine these two Secretaries of State in a political drama to be played out beyond the Styx, one would cast R. A. Butler as the magician, and Duncan Sandys as a pugilist.

XIII

An Unexpected Announcement

A LABOUR Government was returned to power in 1964, after thirteen years of Conservative rule. Harold Wilson went to No 10, with a majority of only four in the House of Commons, and Arthur Bottomley came to the Commonwealth Relations Office. As it happened, this was the only time in my life I had voted Labour. I can no longer remember exactly why – it cannot have been that I wanted to be rid of Duncan Sandys. I never gave Ministers any indication of what my politics were, and they never asked me. They would no doubt think of me vaguely as belonging to the 'establishment', a conception of ill-defined meaning then in vogue; whatever else it signified, it certainly did not include the Labour Party. One of the advantages of being in Government service was, I always thought, that one was expected to be indifferent to party politics. Certainly what interested me was good government.

Harold Macmillan had had to face the very difficult problem of federal government in Central Africa; and he had solved it by dissolving the Federation, with the result of independence for Nyasaland and Northern Rhodesia. But this left Harold Wilson with the intractable issue of Southern Rhodesia; and while the first was largely a local problem, the second was on a global scale. There were two political, ideological, forces opposing one another across the world, and one of the battlegrounds was Southern Rhodesia. Ian Smith had succeeded the gentlemanly Winston Field as Prime Minister, and he was the leader of the Rhodesian Front. The party's policy was independence for Rhodesia, and it felt amply justified in claiming it. On the other side was the opinion of black Africa, and of opponents generally of racial discrimination. Rhodesia had a Land Apportionment Act under which the Europeans had secured the best farming land, and a Detention Act under which obstinate black politicians, such as Sithole and Nkomo, were shut up. The Africans had no vote. They classed Rhodesia with South Africa and upholders of apartheid. This was not a fair view. Southern Rhodesia was not governed by Boers, but largely by Englishmen, who were moderate in their policies. But one of the points the white Rhodesians had made when resisting the breaking up of the Federation was that it would inevitably force them into closer dependence on South Africa. The African cause was taken up by the United Nations and other international bodies. It was also supported by the Labour party here; and the change of government was unwelcome to Ian Smith.

Conditions for independence had been formulated by Butler before he left the Central Africa Office, and these included progress towards majority rule and the ending of racial discrimination, with the addition of guarantees to the minorities after majority rule had come. These conditions were adopted by the Wilson government. In an attempt to see what progress could be made, the Prime Minister sent Lord Gardiner, the Lord Chancellor, and Arthur Bottomley to visit the country and discuss matters with the Rhodesian Ministers. I went with them, with Derek Oulton, the Lord Chancellor's Private Secretary, and I renewed my contacts with the judges and lawyers. But we returned from this mission empty-handed. In May the Security Council passed a resolution calling on the British Government to take action to prevent a declaration of independence. But the very next day Ian Smith and his Rhodesian Front won a sweeping victory at a general election. The opposing forces were lining up, with ourselves in the middle.

Other memorable events took place in 1965. In January Winston Churchill died. On the day of his funeral I walked, in morning dress and top hat, from Lincoln's Inn to St Paul's Cathedral. In Chancery Lane I met Lord Denning on the way back from buying his morning paper. He gave me one of his smiling, quizzical looks, as if to ask 'Are *you* invited?' Early as it was, it was difficult to push a way through the crowds filling Fleet Street. On arrival at the cathedral I joined the group of ushers, some of them Under-

Secretaries from the Commonwealth Relations Office, surprised to find me there. They seemed not to know that I was of the same rank as they. My station was at the intersection of the south transept and the nave, and some of those who came up I knew. Amongst these were Alan and Gwen Herbert. Alan was apprehensive about his capacity to remain in his seat for two or three hours, and I ushered him to one of the unpublicised features of the cathedral. Later Michael Ramsey, Archbishop of Canterbury, hurried past, his hair dishevelled, his face that of a medieval scholar. The organ began to play. From 'the round earth's imagin'd corners,' as John Donne, a former Dean, had put it, the great men arrived. I had a good view of them all: Kings and Queens, Presidents, General Eisenhower, Robert Menzies, Ian Smith, and towering above all the figure of General de Gaulle (I couldn't help remembering Harold Macmillan: 'He used to look like a bottle of claret, now he's like a bottle of burgundy'). When all was still, the coffin was borne up the nave, and laid on the bier in front of me. As it reposed there, tender music came from the organ loft – Parry's Elegy – and when it was finished the service began.

It was growing dark when I returned to the Inn, feeling exalted by that remarkable ceremony, at which many war-time memories had crystallised. Twenty years had passed, and I had been living in the Inn for nearly seven years. My flat had been for me a place of quiet and retreat, even something of an ivory tower. I still had not met one of my two neighbours up the stairs, and I took no part in the activities of the Inn. I could have eaten dinner in Hall, but never thought of doing so, except as an occasional guest. I did not even go to the Chapel on Sunday mornings. The service was followed by lunch for the Chapel-goers in the Benchers' rooms, but Sunday lunch had for me a different connotation. I preferred to take it in Soho, in the company of someone I had myself chosen. I was told later that – though I did not intend it – I exuded a general air of bachelor self-sufficiency. I had freed myself from the constraints imposed by a resident housekeeper; and a woman came every morning after I had left, and we communicated by scribbled minute. But I continued to give dinner parties with the help of Mr Smith and a visiting cook. I gave an occasional lunch party as well, for official guests.

I ate experimental breakfasts, the easiest being nothing but a raw egg in port wine, but I found that after that I never completely woke up all day. If exceptionally hungry I breakfasted at Fortnum's Fountain Bar. At lunch time there was no difficulty: the Travellers Club met my need for a quick, simple lunch, a glass of water, and a place to clean my shoes – and no *camaraderie*. In the Inner Morning Room there was a meat dish, on Fridays fish, two vegetables and a pudding, for five shillings. Men from the Foreign Office frequently lunched there – they would not have to talk to one another – and this room was known as the Foreign Office Canteen. One day I was sharing my table with a stranger, military-looking. It was shortly after the introduction of decimal coinage. He seemed to want to say something, but we maintained the customary silence. When he had finished his meal, he indignantly jerked his shoulders round at me, and flung onto the tablecloth a 50p coin. 'Can you tell me,' he spluttered, 'is that *ten bob?'*

There seemed to be something about the Inner Morning Room that imposed a veil of invisibility as well as of silence. One evening I was asked to dinner, in the 'Coffee Room' upstairs, by Ian Maclennan, an old schoolfellow and friend, who was High Commissioner in New Zealand. He had also asked Romney Sedgwick, a colleague from the Office, and a distinguished historian. Sedgwick and I often saw one another in the Foreign Office Canteen. On my way up to dinner I went into the lavatory, and there was Sedgwick standing, with his back to me as might be supposed. He had an unusually large, pear-shaped head, set on a thin, small back, and I gave him a friendly slap. 'Hallo, Sedgwick!' I cried, 'I hear we're dining together.' He kept his balance, and looked round. 'Oh! Are we . . . are we?', he said. I followed up my advantage. 'I didn't know you were a member of this club, Sedgwick,' I said. He turned again. 'I've been a member for twenty years,' he said. 'I didn't know you were a member.' The dinner was reasonably convivial. The next day we both lunched in the Inner Morning Room, but Sedgwick gave no sign of seeing me.

The services of a barber were available. He had not heard of the silence rule, and I kept away from him. At the time of the Korean war I had formed a resolution that I must go at least to Dieppe for a haircut. I had been in Paris, when the strategic question was whether the American forces should advance beyond the 38th parallel. My hair was rather long and I apologised to the barber. 'Oui, monsieur,' he said regretfully. 'Il a passé le parallel.' Such wit, I thought, would be worth the fare.

I had a piano lesson every fortnight from Marguerite Wolff. She was an excellent teacher, and I played Field, Chopin, Brahms, Fauré and Debussy. But I was arriving at a stage when advance in technique seemed to be blocked by a poor ability to memorise; I could not read the page quickly enough. I never mastered Chopin's piano sonatas.

I had reached a point of happiness in my life which I had not before attained. But a cloud was beginning to appear – the next year I was due to retire. There would be no escaping from it. The Diplomatic Service had been formed at the beginning of the year, and when I was given the choice of joining it or remaining in the Home Civil Office, I had chosen unhesitatingly, but perhaps foolishly, the Diplomatic. If I had chosen the Home Service, there would have been a chance of staying on for a year or two. But in the Diplomatic Service, I was told, I could expect to see the Establishment Officer in my chair, about the time of my birthday, reminding me of my obligations. I was to be 'superannuated' – an ugly word, and the fact was even uglier. What was I going to do? I had no intention of joining the 'returned empties', as we disrespectfully called retired members of the Colonial Service wanting jobs in Whitehall. Nor did I want to become one of the elderly gentlemen in the Inn, slowly decaying, and awaiting the passing bell (if they were Benchers).

I began to think about Italy. I had given up Bontempelli, but not Rome at Easter. At other times I had gone elsewhere: Florence of course, and Venice, and Assisi, Ravello, Ravenna, and the Ligurian Coast. I had been tackling the stories of Carlo Emilio Gadda, more 'normal' than those of Bontempelli, but not written in his limpid prose, and more difficult to translate. I made a translation of one of his best known stories *L'incendio di via Keplero* and wrote to the author; but he would only give permission for the translation of the whole of the book, and I could not undertake that. I had thoughts of settling in Venice – it was almost a duty to live in that lovely but apparently doomed city if one could; and supplementing my pension by teaching English to select pupils. Perhaps I might obtain permission to play the organ at that great basilica of St Mark.

The prospect of retirement was the more unwelcome since the scope of my legal work was broadening. The Empire was dissolving at a rapid rate. There were now twenty independent States within the Commonwealth, and many more were to come.

The newly independent countries had before relied on the Colonial Legal Service – in India and Pakistan the Indian Civil Service – to staff the Governments' legal services; but now the men of these services were returning home. The new Governments were losing expertise, at the very moment when they most needed it. I was instrumental in forming the Commonwealth Legal Advisory Service, which received the approval of Macmillan himself. We gave this into the charge of the British Institute of International and Comparative Law, of which Lord Denning was the Chairman. I was a member of the Managing Board of the Institute, and with the support of Andrew Cohen, an old friend from Colonial Office days, who became Governor of Uganda, then the Permanent Secretary of the Ministry of Overseas Development, I obtained an annual grant for the Institute towards running the service. Advice was given by correspondence to all Governments asking for it. But it soon became clear that this was not enough to meet their needs. What they lacked was trained staff to cope with the everyday work, particularly in the fields of legislation and international law. Again with the support of Andrew Cohen and others, especially George Coldstream, the Permanent Secretary to the Lord Chancellor, Noel Hutton, First Parliamentary Counsel, Gerald Fitzmaurice and Francis Vallat, successive Legal Advisers to the Foreign Office, and the Treasury Solicitor, who all promised lectures by their staffs, I initiated the Government Legal Advisers Course. The Professors of International Law at Oxford, Humphrey Waldock, and at Cambridge, Robert Jennings, with Clive Parry and others, collaborated with enthusiasm. The Course was entirely financed by the Government, the British Council looked after the housing and welfare of the students, and we had twenty of them for a five-month course every year. It was perhaps a unique example of co-operation in Whitehall, amongst individuals, for altruistic purposes, and the Treasury must be included. The Course, reduced to three months, is still running, and the Commonwealth Legal Advisory Service flourishing.

There was another development. The English common law was the basis of the legal systems in nearly all Commonwealth countries. It could be a potent source of Commonwealth solidarity, and Lord Gardiner and I conceived the idea of a Commonwealth Law Institute, or Common Law Institute, in London, which would be a centre for all Commonwealth lawyers and a support for the rule of law. But funds were not forthcoming for the project – it was no doubt too imaginative.

In the summer, in Sydney, the Commonwealth and Empire Law Conference took place. A periodical gathering of practitioners and judges, it had not up to then had much support from Government quarters, but this time things were to be different. Lord Gardiner had brought to fruition his plans for creating English and Scottish Law Commissions, and the value of the law as a social force was being recognised. A Commonwealth Secretariat had been set up, with Arnold Smith, a vigorous Canadian diplomat, as Secretary-General. As a result nearly all the top figures in the legal world of the Commonwealth went to Sydney; and they included Lord Gardiner, Hubert Parker, now Lord Chief Justice, and Elwyn Jones, the Attorney General.

The Conference opened with a service in the cathedral, followed by an enormous gathering in the Town Hall addressed by Robert Menzies, the Prime Minister, who had once been Attorney General. His style was Churchillian. Apologising for his arrival at the cathedral only just in time to greet the judges as they came out, he said that he had been hoping to breathe the odour of sanctity, but all that he could detect was the smell of moth-balls. This notwithstanding, he came to many of our gatherings. At one of them a proposal was made for the creation of a Legal Division at the Commonwealth Secretariat; I supported it; and Tom Kellock, an English barrister who had been at the meeting, became the first Head of the Division.

I enjoyed Sydney. The weather was warm and sunny; and I often escaped from Conference circles at lunch time to Fisherman's Quay, where I furthered local contacts. When Elwyn Jones remarked on it, I said he could see how seriously I took my duties to the Commonwealth; but he thought I was not taking them seriously enough. I saw Joan Sutherland in *Lucia di Lammermoor* at the old opera house – the new one in the harbour was being built – deputising for Gerald Gardiner, in company with his delightful wife and daughter. And I walked up Main Street on the last afternoon arm in arm with Polly Elwyn Jones, in her strange 'ethnic' clothes, discussing my future. 'All you have to do to provide for your retirement', she advised me, 'is to buy a few extra shirts.'

After Sydney we went to Canberra for separate meetings of Chief Justices and Law Ministers. I liked the flat landscape of

Canberra with its rim of distant hills, and the old 'colonial' hotel came up to the standard of the Mount Nelson at Cape Town. From there I went to Melbourne for a few days, to see an old friend and that gracious city, with its fine Art Gallery and park.

Then it was Hong Kong, and a week with Michael and Patricia Hogan. Since the time Michael had been with me in the Colonial Office, clearing up after Palestine, he had been Attorney General of Kenya, and was now Chief Justice of Hong Kong. I would go down with Michael to his chambers, look at the work of the court, and Patricia would come later and show me the town. I did not fall in love with this flourishing colony of ours; I felt crushed by the skyscrapers.

Then on to Japan, ten days of the unknown. I was entirely by myself, knew not a word of Japanese, and all signs, including the names of the streets, were written in Japanese characters. But I got about without much difficulty, saw all I wanted to see – the parks, the enchanting gardens, the temples – travelled by underground, found my way to restaurants, all by means of a match box. In my bedroom at the hotel was a box of matches with on the obverse the name and address of the hotel in Japanese, and on the reverse in English. On setting out, I told the hotel porter where I wanted to go in English, he told the taxi driver in Japanese, I had a street map, and when I wanted to return to the hotel I showed the box, Japanese side, to the taxi driver. Or to a passer-by. People in the street, especially the young, were friendly and helpful. They were pleased to be able to practise their English, which they learned at school, or in evening classes, but had no opportunity to speak. They would go out of their way to walk with me, and on one occasion a young man accompanied me in the Underground to make sure I got out at the right station. I particularly enjoyed the delicate food, the saki (the perfect drink to accompany it), the night I spent in one of the old 'inns', and the gardens, which were to me ideal: plants, rocks, pools, and one flower.

I took a specially fast train to Beppu. It did not arrive at the promised time, and with other passengers I went to the ticket office on arrival to collect my refund. From Beppu I travelled by night across the Inland Sea to Hiroshima. A most friendly man stood by my side as we watched the lovely landscape glide by, and in response to his interested enquiries I talked a good deal about myself. When darkness fell, and I said I intended to spend the night on deck, he protested, and insisted that I should occupy his cabin. After breakfasting together, we said warm goodbyes, and he gave me his card, in case I ran into difficulties: on it was printed after his name 'Criminal Investigation Department, Hiroshima'. I didn't see him again.

During my two or three days in Hiroshima I forced myself to visit the museum of horrors; and I drank much saki. The saki there was said to be the best in Japan, and it was not served in less than 75cl bottles. I flew back to Tokyo, and had an enchanting view of Mount Fuji, blue with a white hood.

My flight back to England took me over Italy, and I spent the last day or two of my holiday as the guest of an American lady. She had a house in Sermoneta, a hill-top village in the Castelli Romani, and I had met her the previous year in London at the house of an Italian friend. In America she had been making and exhibiting rugs, to the designs of Milton Avery, Stamos, and other painters. She had now established an *artigionato* at Sermoneta, and she taught sixteen girls there, who would otherwise have been unemployed, to make hand-hooked rugs. These original and beautiful rugs were now designed by Severini, Gio Ponti, and other Italian artists, and exhibited in Rome. We ate on her cobbled patio under a vine, and went to Felice Circeo and Gaeta to swim.

So ended my Tour of the World.

In London there was growing consternation over Rhodesia. In October Ian Smith came to London with some of his Ministers to discuss the principles on which independence might be agreed, but no progress was made. The General Assembly of the United Nations passed a resolution demanding that we should use all means, including force if necessary, to prevent a unilateral declaration of independence. In a desperate effort to stave off disaster, Harold Wilson, Arthur Bottomley and Elwyn Jones went to Salisbury, and I was there once more. This visit was a mistake on the Prime Minister's part. He had little authority, involved himself too much in racial politics ('You must get your facts right Prime Minister', I heard the Chief Justice say to him on one stormy occasion), and left having achieved nothing. On 11 November Rhodesia issued its Unilateral Declaration of Independence. It came as no surprise to me. I had grown to know the Rhodesians, and had found in Salisbury a tendency to think as if the world below them – Salisbury was nearly 5,000 ft above sea level – did not exist; or at any rate that they could exist without it. I had formed the same view about Jerusalem, at an altitude of less than half that, it is true, but then there was the drop of over 3,000 ft to the Dead Sea. Could it be that living at certain altitudes – connected perhaps with the oxygen supply – was conducive to a blinkered attitude? My sketch of a theory was confirmed when I read some years later that Hillary would never pitch a camp at an altitude which was exactly that of Salisbury.

However that may be, each side had misjudged the other. When Ian Smith had been in London with his Ministers, I could see from the exchanges of glances between them that they were determined to go their own way. They probably underestimated the support which Wilson had on this issue from the Conservatives, as well as from his own party. But the Commonwealth Relations Office had been misled by the views of the older political figures in Salisbury, Malvern and Welensky, and Tredgold, a former Chief Justice, who thought the regime would collapse.

Sanctions followed, an embargo on the supply of oil was imposed, and later a complete ban on trade. A Commonwealth conference took place in Lagos, in which Australia under Robert Menzies refused to take part; it stopped short of requesting the use of force, but that was demanded at a meeting of the Organisation of African Unity. It was out of the question for us to send an army to fight the Rhodesians. The battle was fought on the economic and, for what it was worth, the legal front. The startling doctrine was put forward that under the Roman-Dutch law, which was the foundation of the law of Rhodesia as of South Africa, legislation had no effect unless officially 'promulgated'; and that, as the Smith Government had not promulgated the United Kingdom's Southern Rhodesia Act of 1965 and the Order in Council under it, invalidating the acts of the rebel regime, they had no effect. It was necessary to scotch this doctrine promptly, and I sent a Memorandum to the Lord Chancellor showing that, whatever the effect of Roman-Dutch law, it could not prevail over the clear intention of an Act of Parliament.

The judges in Rhodesia were in a growing quandary: loyal to the Queen, bound by their judicial oaths to uphold the law, they nevertheless had to administer justice under a Government which, though illegal, was well in control of the country, and seeking to maintain law and order through the regular judicial machinery. Hugh Beadle, the Chief Justice, came over to see us, and we did what we could to stiffen him. He by no means lacked courage. The issue was coming to a head in the case of an African called Madzimbamuto, who was in detention in Rhodesia under the rebel regime's legislation; and I had to arrange a conference in the Temple at twelve noon on my sixtieth birthday, with Louis Blom-Cooper, Noel Gratiaen and Eugene Cotran, in Dingle Foot's chambers. I had better things in view for celebrating the day, but these three seemed to want to go on for ever discussing the law. At last, well past the time one could obtain lunch, I said 'Will you forgive me, I must go. I'm getting married at four'. This unexpected announcement galvanized them, as I intended it to do. My learned friends jumped out of their seats, uttering exclamations of incredulity; they all regarded me as an irredeemable bachelor. It was a vivid example of a consensus proving itself wrong.

The lady I was to marry was Gloria Finn, lately resident in Sermoneta, and now moved to London, becoming colour consultant to ICI. I was on time at the Chelsea Registry Office, and we followed up with a service of dedication at St Saviour's, Walton Street. For my birthday Gloria had arranged a surprise dinner party at her flat, and this turned into a wedding breakfast. The guest-list remained the same: my sister, my two nephews, and a few close friends. I had acquired three splendid American stepsons, Peter, Michael and Jeffrey Finn; but they were unable to appear at short notice, and were a joy to come. On account of my work our honeymoon had to be taken in instalments, and we flew to Edinburgh and spent the weekend at Gleneagles. To greet us on our return there came from the Temple trio a jeroboam of champagne.

My quick jump into matrimony sent a wave of agitation through the Commonwealth Relations Office. It appeared that there was a rule in the Diplomatic Service that before marrying a foreigner one must obtain the permission of the Secretary of State. Even if I had known about the rule I should have ignored it, as I had not thought of my wife as a 'foreigner', and I was in any case soon to retire. But the Office took the matter so seriously that I began to wonder whether I should not deal with the question in the next edition of *The Law of the Parish Church.* If the marriage had been in church, by banns, would Arthur Bottemley have had the right to rise from the pews and forbid it? After submission to him of my wife's credentials Mr Bottomley, who was a good sort, retrospectively gave me his permission to marry Gloria Spellman Finn, of Westchester County and Washington DC, a citizen of the United States of America.

Next there arose the issue of my retirement itself. There was probably no precedent in the Diplomatic Service, in the Foreign Service before it – or, I should not wonder, in the Home Civil Service either – for a man's contracting the obligations of marriage on the very day he is due to retire from the service. That would seem to contradict the whole philosophy of superannuation. The Establishment Officer soon appeared, took the comfortable chair next to my desk, and with a solemn face enquired about my intentions. His were plain enough – he wanted a date. We settled on 31 December.

There was also disturbance at Lincoln's Inn. My daily woman, as soon as she learned my intention to marry, said indignantly 'I'm not stopping you know', and promptly abandoned me. As she had just returned from a fortnight's paid holiday, I took a poor view of her behaviour. The Inn's surveyor, Mr Clapham, was also much perturbed. The Inn had a plan to pull down the part of my flat facing West over the Kitchen Garden, and the chambers beneath it, and to erect a large new building on the site. Mr Clapham came to see me, almost to protest. He had expected to have a compliant bachelor to deal with, but now I had spoilt his plans; would there, he asked helplessly, be a family? I said I would not rule it out.

As if to confound the surveyor further, Gloria received a remarkable letter of good wishes from an Italian friend, 'telling her a few fatherly things in consideration of the fact that marriages are made but also unmade'. As this letter was so wise, and the writer's 'few items' have perhaps some general application, I reproduce it here, with permission:

'a. Don't be a baby ("You promised to take me to the theatre," etc).
b. Don't be too possessive or obsessive (when a man *is there* as a husband there is not much more he can do and he should not be pestered).
c. For the same reason leave him his freedom of mind and movements and keep some for yourself (a complete jam is hard to bear, after all partners still remain two separate individuals).
d. Having the feeling of freedom is often as good as being totally free. One does not want more than the feeling.
e. Keep your private relations as something intimate and confidential. Distrust friends especially society people.

f. Remember that USA women are often too matriarcal (I don't know how to spell it). In Europe the man still wants to be the boss even if only by 51%.
Now bless you and live happily ever after.'

Lincoln's Inn in summertime, with its ancient brick buildings, spreading green trees and lawns, and rose beds, can smile at its residents. When the Crystal Palace had sold off its statues and vases, I had bought six vases for distribution amongst friends with gardens, and given one to the Inn; and the gardener had filled it with geraniums and placed it under our bow window. Inside the room, with its Adam ornamentation, stood the enormous, Leonard family, four-poster bed, conferred on the newly-wed couple by my cousins Judith and Dinah. The summer social round took on a new colour for me, now that there were two of us. There were the Garden Party at the Palace, the Garden Party at the Inn, the Lord Mayor's Dinner for the Judges at the Mansion House, and the Grotius Dinner held in Hall by the British Institute of International and Comparative Law.

I had a close connection with the Institute, and Lord Denning had the year before asked me to go there as Director, but I had not wished to leave my Government post prematurely. Now I was sorry to have missed the chance of an interesting job and a good income for some years. But we managed well enough. Robin Bridges, the Under Treasurer of the Inn, helped us to find a good daily woman at four or five shillings an hour; and dinner for two in a first-class restaurant would cost no more than £5. In September we went to Spain for the second instalment of our honeymoon: first to that very fine hotel with its spacious gardens, the Reina Christina at Algeciras, then along the coast to Marbella.

From my youth up I had suffered occasionally from an intense pain in my stomach, especially when empty. We saw two or three doctors, and were persuaded by a surgeon that he should operate; he likened my condition to having a time bomb at the bottom of my garden. I was in St George's Hospital therefore when Harold Wilson had his unfruitful talks with Ian Smith on the *Tiger*. The Commonwealth Relations Office, renamed the Commonwealth Office, had absorbed the Colonial Office; there was a single legal staff; and an able assistant, Henry Steel, went in my place. The operation did nothing for me, and I continued to have severe stomach aches at times of tension, particularly when, later, Gloria went into hospital with her birth pangs. But Elwyn Jones had telephoned me at St George's; and when he told me he would have to find an assistant in international matters, and accepted the offer of my services, I left hospital rejuvenated.

At the end of the year Saville Garner gave a small cocktail party for me in his room at the Office. There were no speeches, and the function concluded my thirty-two years of pensionable service as a legal adviser. One of my friends in the Office, Bill Hamilton, made a surprising remark to me in farewell: 'You are one of the best administrators I know', he said.

However that may have been, it was not administration but legal acumen that the Law Officers wanted out of me, and I enjoyed my time with them. It was almost like being back in the Temple. We were housed in the Law Courts; Elwyn, and Dingle Foot, the Solicitor General, were most agreeable to work with; the professional staff of four, of which Tony Hetherington was the head, and a secretary or two, constituted their Department. Requests for the Law Officers' opinion came usually from the Legal Advisers to the Government Departments, and concerned difficult questions of law, or a mixture of law and political wisdom. If the papers were not complete, or we thought the Department had not thought out the matter, we sent the papers back. Work was very select. There was no lack of international and Commonwealth problems: the agreement with France for the building of Concorde; the foundering, and subsequent sinking, of the *Torrey Canyon,* and the legal problems to which the oil spill gave rise; Biafra's attempted secession from Nigeria, and the civil war there; the dispute with Spain over Gibraltar, and Spain's closure of the frontier; the offshore radio pirates, and the Marine Broadcasting (Offences) Act. There was the unhappy affair of the Kenya Asians, whose right of entry into Britain, as holders of British passports, had to be restricted by legislation. I went with Elwyn to see James Callaghan, who had just been moved by Harold Wilson from being Chancellor of the Exchequer to being Home Secretary. He was cross and edgy, and objected to my presence. This was the time of the Race Relations Act, the occasion of Enoch Powell's much misquoted speech at Birmingham: what he said was that the Bill would 'risk throwing a match into gunpowder . . . Like the Roman, I seem to see the river Tiber "foaming with much blood".'

Rhodesia continued to plague us. In the Madzimabuto case the trial judge had decided that the courts should give effect to measures that could lawfully have been taken before UDI for the maintenance of law and order, and his decision was upheld by the Rhodesia Appeal Court. Five African nationalists, notwithstanding reprieves by the Queen, were executed, the requests for reprieve having been rejected by the Rhodesian Chief Justice. Harold Wilson again had talks with Ian Smith, on the *Fearless,* again without success. Madzimbamuto went to the Judicial Committee of the Privy Council, and I was much involved, though we were not direct parties to the case. Sydney Kentridge, from South Africa, and Louis Blom-Cooper were briefed, and the Privy Council decided that the measures of the Rhodesian Government had no legal effect. But the judgment was ignored by the Rhodesian Appellate Division, who ruled afterwards that the regime had acquired the status of a lawful government. Rhodesia settled down to being a long-term problem.

On the island in the Strand opposite the Law Courts is the church of St Clement Dane's, the RAF church. In memory of my brother Reggie, who is on the Roll of Honour there, my mother had woven a tapestry cover for a kneeler. I was allowed to practise on the organ, and if I was not in my room at the Law Courts when I should have been, Tony Hetherington knew where to find me.

Our baby daughter, Rosemary Lincoln, was christened in the crypt of the church. It was remarked by those present that she, rather than the rector, presided at the ceremony. She breathed in the atmosphere of the law. She slept in her pram in the Kitchen Garden; was wheeled under our Law Courts windows by her mother, when Elwyn and Dingle would put out their heads and call a greeting; and by myself down Middle Temple Lane one Sunday, when I let the pram free-wheel down the slope, it overturned, and a bleeding little face was soon back in the Inn.

I wheeled my daughter about on other occasions, more smoothly. We twice had to evacuate our flat: first when the bedroom ceiling fell in, bringing the Adam centre-piece with it, and the cowdung had to be replaced by hardboard; secondly when the 'priest's hole' and room above it were demolished as planned, to build Hale Court. Each time we rented a flat in Chelsea; and I took the pram round the borough to show off my new family. I had a most enjoyable time. Rosemary was a delight to me; and I could see that with her to my credit I had taken on a new dimension in the minds of my friends.

It was about this time that the Japanese artist and showperson Yoko Ono was producing a film to be called 'Bottoms'. That was the era of the sensational film, and this was to be no exception. Yoko Ono felt short of exhibitors of class, people who were in *Who's Who;* and a friend of Gloria's, an art critic, asked us if Gloria and I were willing to contribute our mite, as it were. The project seemed rather out of the way for a Government lawyer, but we said we would consider it. On the next Sunday evening Yoko Ono was round with a crew and a great deal of apparatus. She was to show us clippings from the film so far as she had got. We entertained her to cups of Earl Grey, while the crew were occupied with their paraphernalia. They took a long time over fixing it up; and the flat was reduced to complete disorder, with the furniture moved and cables trailing from room to room. After well over an hour Yoko Ono's then husband, who was one of the crew, came to say he was very sorry, but they had forgotten to bring the plug. All was dismantled and carried away. Before leaving Yoko Ono told us that the bottoms were to be bare, which we had not realised. We went to a special showing of the embryo film, to help us to reach a decision. I had become most amused, and should not have minded, nor I think would Elwyn. But Gloria was adamant: 'Special Assistant to the Law Officers of the Crown' in the list of Credits? No!

At Lincoln's Inn we were too cramped. Rosemary's bedroom was a walk-in cupboard containing the gasmeter. Elwyn too began to prod me: he wanted to see me working in some more independent position. I had a surprise telephone call from Vincent Evans, Legal Adviser to what had become the Foreign *and* Commonwealth Office: would I consider going to Beirut as General Counsel to the United Nations Relief and Works Agency for Palestine Refugees? For answer I paid a short visit to Beirut; Gloria and I went to New York for some indoctrination; we packed up; gave a farewell dinner party; danced round the table; and were off.

XIV

Beirut

FOR the third time I was to live on the shores of the Mediterranean. But on this occasion I was able to present to the immigration officer a beautiful wife, who dazzled him with her clear blue eyes, a daughter, perhaps of trifling age but no less beautiful, and a blonde young nanny, Christine. We were greeted at the airport by the French lawyer on my staff, Philippe Giblain, and Raja Shehab, a Palestinian, UNRWA's outdoor man. It had been difficult to find us accommodation, as the town was crowded. In the summer Beirut, hot as it was, was nevertheless cool compared with the countries of the Persian Gulf; and the flat Shehab had found for us, on the sea above the Pigeon Rocks, had just been vacated by a Saudi Princess. It was filthy, and we refused to unpack. Philippe was possessed of sorrowful eyes, and he and Shehab persuaded us that it would be impossible to find another flat then. Philippe distributed sheets of *Le Figaro* over the chairs and table, Christine washed some plates and glasses, and we settled down to supper. Shehab had brought us a bottle of Lebanese wine, but had forgotten to bring a corkscrew. The flat, intended for Moslems, did not include one amongst its appointments; and Shehab got round the difficulty by violently shaking the bottle up and down for some minutes, until the cork blew out. At the sight of the frothing red liquid, Philippe's eyes grew even more sorrowful.

Next morning Shehab found us a refugee woman to clean the flat to Palestinian standards, and he and my wife set off to hunt for a better place. I announced myself to the Commissioner-General of UNRWA, 'Mich' (Michelmore), but he told me to help in the search for a place to live. We turned down an old house, with a garden, in the Ashrafieh – the Christian – quarter of Beirut; and after a few days chose a flat in a block scarcely completed, in the Ramlet al Beida in the Arab quarter. The flat was on the fifth floor, with balconies overlooking the sea. The rooms were light, larger than anything to be found in London outside Belgravia, the floors were of marble, and overhead was what a Japanese had once called 'the honourable air conditioning'. We had brought no furniture from England, and we moved into a flat empty except for beds, and a garden table and four chairs bought on the wing from a migrating banker (there were ninety banks in Beirut). At this table we ate our meals; and at this table we found Christine sitting, on our return from our first evening out, weeping tears of homesickness (we came to expect this from a new nanny about the seventh day).

Gloria was introduced to the antique markets by Laurence Giblain and Afif Boulos, a musician and a Palestinian. She came home with three blue Islamic tiles – the beautiful being preferred to the useful – difficult to hang on the plaster walls. But she soon furnished the flat, chiefly from Basta, the Beirut equivalent of the Portobello Road; a dining-table with three leaves, apples carved on the legs, and twelve dining-chairs; two arm-chairs in the style of Louis Seize; a fancy dressing-table; lamps; and a Hi-Fi set (not from Basta). Later some of her furniture came from America. From time to time she bought a rug from an itinerant seller, who always said: 'If you take it, Madam, you will be pleased; if you don't take it, I will be pleased'. We obtained a resident maid, Nanette, a solid girl from the mountain, and a non-resident Lebanese cook, Georges, who had unfortunately learned his trade in the British army.

Under a brilliant sun I walked to the office, a few minutes away, past the army barracks. The Headquarters of UNRWA were in what was called the Unesco building, owned by the Government. It was a shabby building, in keeping with the somewhat shabby nature of the Agency's mission. This was to soothe the world's conscience about the million refugees resulting from the creation of the State of Israel. They were to be provided with 'relief and works'; but the idea of 'works' had had to be dropped, and since the Arab-Israel war of 1967, the 'six-day war', the number to be relieved stood at a million-and-a-half. A third of these lived in the Agency's 'camps', a misnomer, since much of the housing was in solid buildings of wood and cement. In addition to housing, the

Agency provided medical care and education, and a food ration: flour and oil (as supplied to the prophet Elijah) with the addition of pulses, sugar and rice. The ration did not meet the minimum standard of the Food and Agriculture Organisation, which required some animal protein. The Agency suffered from a chronic shortage of funds, which were in part raised by more or less passing the hat round at the annual meetings of the United Nations General Assembly in New York. The Headquarters building was furnished to a minimum degree of comfort; there was no honourable air conditioning to help us through the hot, humid summers, and no heating during the winter, which could be cold and very wet. Working hours were from 7.30 a.m. to 2 p.m., and Beirut was excessively noisy. We had to keep our windows wide open in the summer; and when an aeroplane descended overhead to the airport a mile or two away – as one did every minute – talking had to stop until it had passed. I ordered a pair of ear muffs, as used for road drilling. The *Daily Star,* interviewing me soon after arrival, told its readers that, as a contribution to solving the Beirut noise problem, I had 'had all the telephones in my room fixed so they won't ring there, but in the office of my secretary'. This was Mimi Asseily, an excellent woman, a Palestinian like most of the locally engaged, as opposed to the 'international' staff. The Agency's 'charity' began in the next room. But there was more to it than charity. In all the professions in Beirut (as opposed to the merchants and business men), and amongst the best of the workers, we found Palestinians – no longer refugees, but Lebanese citizens, like Mimi herself. This was due in part to their stalwart character and innate worth, and in part to their British schooling during the Mandate, and effortless English.

The refugees were spread over Lebanon, Syria, Jordan, the Israeli-occupied West Bank of the Jordan and the Gaza strip, with a few in Egypt. This meant a good deal of travel. My first trip was to Syria, where there were 170,000 refugees, with an UNRWA Field Office in Damascus. The journey lay over good mountain roads, and Gloria and I had our first sight of the wonderful Lebanese scenery which we were to come to love so well. Damascus was 140 kms from Beirut, and it was a quiet place, originally built in an oasis. A tranquil stream, shining in the morning sun, ran between grassy slopes into the ancient city. Damascus delighted us: the narrow streets of the Moslem quarter, with their overhanging houses, the sūqs filled with vendors bargaining over their wares, the bright colours illuminated by shafts of sunlight, and the silent Great Mosque, with its exquisite mosaics, and where the faithful were always to be seen bowing down in prayer. The Syrian Government, a Baathist dictatorship, was not easy to deal with, and the official attitude was one of unfriendliness. Our local legal adviser was Fred Arslanian. Fred and his wife were generous and hospitable, and we saw much of them. They introduced us to the only passable restaurant. The difficulty with Fred, who was an Armenian, was his poor English. I pleaded with him, as my predecessor Derek Bowett had done, to communicate with us in French, but he would not do so. We had to make the best of statements of the law such as 'Rents are fetchable, not portable', and similar pieces of advice.

I was beginning to grasp my functions as General Counsel, or chief Legal Adviser, to UNRWA. They involved international law, and the internal law of the countries in which we were operating. I had on my staff, as well as Philippe Giblain, an Austrian lawyer, Peter Polletin, and Pascal Karmy, a Palestinian. There was in addition a local practitioner to advise the Field Office in each country.

The Agency's international relations were important, and often delicate. Its activities involved it in making deep inroads into what would normally have been the functions of the State Governments, and as a subsidiary organ of the United Nations it had the right to ask them for their assistance. Apart from this general and vague right, it had made particular agreements with the Governments for the provision of free services such as transport and storage, sites for the camps, and similar matters. Under the general Convention on the Privileges and Immunities of the United Nations, the Agency's premises, property and staff were supposed to be free from interference, but there were plenty of instances of unauthorised entry, by civil and even military forces, into our offices and other buildings. The Agency and its staff were exempt from direct taxes, customs duties, and restrictions on imports, and the Governments were required to recognise the validity of the United Nations *laissez-passer*. Syria declined to do this in regard to local staff, and half-way through my time with UNRWA Syria suddenly refused to recognise *my laissez-passer.* Even Fred could not discover what they had against me, and I was unable to enter the country.

The Agency made thousands of contracts every year, for the purchase of commodities, supplies, equipment and vehicles, transport, insurance, the construction and maintenance of buildings, the provision of services, and the sale of articles no longer serviceable – and in all parts of the world. A Contracts Committee, of which I was Chairman, had to approve the award of all but the smallest contracts. (A good safeguard against corrupt inducements: it was not long before I was made an offer.) The Agency was immune from court proceedings, and the contracts usually contained an arbitration clause. Some of the policies of insurance, particularly marine insurance, had been made completely unintelligible by many amendments, and the legal advisers were engaged in a perpetual struggle to have them redrafted. Another side of the work involved questions between the Agency and its staff: matters of discipline (there was a Code of Conduct) and claims for benefits under the Provident Fund Rules. These last I did redraft.

Towards the end of the first year we went to Jerusalem. Our way lay due south down the coastal road, past the banana groves, through Sidon and Tyre, and across the frontier. I was back in 'Palestine', and it was difficult to recognise the fact. Haifa had spread enormously, but what mainly struck the eye was the spread of small houses over the countryside. Parts of it were now cultivated, but the houses were ugly, of cement block, each carrying a solar heating installation on its roof. The general effect was of a suburban rash, until one began the ascent to Jerusalem – and then the effect became even more distressing. The view of Jerusalem, once an entrancing sight, had become a vision of ugliness. What the eye saw was a parade of concrete skyscrapers built on the hills, having the appearance of fortresses rather than dwelling-places. There was of course a reason. The Arab countries were still in a state of war with Israel, and a part of Jerusalem itself had been fought over in the six-day war, and annexed by Israel. The Arabs had begun that war.

Inside the city the impression was better. The Holy Places remained, and the places sacred to Islam, the golden Dome of the Rock and the Mosque of Omar. The splendid YMCA building was there, the organ still without its missing stops; and it and the King David Hotel had the mixture as before of Solomon's Temple and the Tottenham Court Road. More welcome than the restoration of the King David was the continued existence of the American Colony Hotel, with its garden (now supplemented by a Souvenir shop). It was still owned by the Vester family, and that was where we stayed.

I had business with the Israeli Foreign Ministry. The Government tolerated UNRWA, but did not love it, considering the 'camps' nurseries of disorder. We were provided with an army officer as guide, and he took us to one of our camps, near Jericho. We saw rows of well built wooden hutments, painted green, all empty. We asked the officer why. He shrugged: 'We won ze war', he said. We paid our first visit to Jordan, crossing by the Allenby Bridge, then back, and on to Gaza.

At home again, George cooked for Christmas what he called a 'turko'; but when he presented us with unbelievable bills for his expenditure while we had been away, insisting that Rosemary and Christine had consumed 10 kilos of bananas, we decided he must go. Marie replaced him: she was an Armenian, tall, thin, an excellent cook, and she became a part of our family. But just after Christmas we had a sharp reminder of where we were: Israeli helicopters wrecked the aircraft of Arab lines standing at Beirut airport, in retaliation for mortar attacks across the Lebanese border.

Through John and Josie Brinton, and Peter and Rosey Joy, who early became special friends, we made an increasing number of acquaintances in Beirut; and such was the warmth and hospitality of the Lebanese that acquaintances quickly became friends. John Brinton's father had been American Judge of the Mixed Courts in Egypt, and John had been in the American Embassy in Cairo. The Brintons had a house outside Beirut in Chemlan, to which they often invited us. Peter Joy was the regional Information Officer at the British Embassy in Beirut, and the Joys lived in a house similar to that offered to us on our arrival. These two houses, and others in the leafy Ashrafieh quarter, belonged to the Sursock family, whom we met through the Joys. The finest house belonged to Linda Sursock. To call on her was to enter a cool mansion, with marble floors, a fountain, arched colonnades, windows in red, green and blue glass, and panelled rooms filled with mother of pearl furniture. This remarkable lady had red hair like Queen Elizabeth, and her memories went back to the Turkish pashas. Of the next generation was Yvonne, married to Desmond Cochrane, the Irish Honorary Consul, and Yvonne had founded a Society for the Preservation of Ancient Buildings. There was no town planning in Lebanon, or social planning either; decorative old houses were being pulled down, and concrete blocks going up. Henri Pharaon, the antiquarian and collector, clung to a beautiful old house in the quarter, where he could display his antiquities. Anna Tabet, of another old family, was a shade younger than Linda; she was at all the large parties, and swam every day, winter and summer, in the pool belonging to the St Georges Hotel. In the more modern part of Beirut Rosemary and Christine, through other children and other nannies, were increasing our circle of friends.

Gloria took up archaeology, went to Professor Baramki's lectures at the American University, and catalogued the Roman glass for Jim Pritchard, of Pennsylvania University, who was excavating at Sarafand. She began to collect ancient beads, glass and pottery, became adept at detecting fakes, and was before long a match for even the Lebanese dealers, who had been at the business for hundreds of years. There were expert craftsmen in the town. We had a 'butler's tray' table made, much admired. In Damascus Gloria bought a pair of carved and painted cupboard doors out of an old house; and these, when built up by the superb Lebanese craftsmen, gave us a cupboard as beautiful as an Italian Renaissance *armadio*.

Always present were tensions, breaking out into strife. The Lebanese State was built on a delicate balance of power between Christians and Moslems, and between the different sects: the President must be a Maronite Christian, the Prime Minister a Sunni Moslem, and so on, down to the Museum staff. At the last census the Moslems had not been far behind the Christians in number, and as their birthrate was higher, another census was delayed for fear of what it might reveal. The Palestinians in the camps aggravated the population problem, besides being a potential for disquiet and disorder. Yasser Arafat's Palestine Liberation Organisation was finding a footing there, and commandos were being trained. Palestinian attacks increased across the frontier, the Israelis bombed the villages, and 50,000 angry people, deprived of their homes, marched on Beirut. Agitation increased when King Hussein rounded up the guerillas in Jordan. The volatile temper of the Lebanese was always ready to show itself. A young official at the British Embassy was driving home for lunch along the Corniche when a car driven by a Lebanese man, related to the Minister of Justice, started hooting behind him, and ramming his rear bumper. The British official stopped and got out of his car. The Lebanese did the same, and straightaway shot him in the head. He died shortly afterwards. This driver may have been taking drugs. But the Lebanese were in any case wild drivers (though not so wild, as we later discovered, as the Iranians); and certainly one of the joys of Beirut was to drive down a one-way street in the wrong direction. No one took any notice of traffic lights; and – perhaps as a result – we saw few accidents.

Every Sunday we drove out for a picnic, found some new Roman temple, and in the Spring gathered armfuls of anemones and what Rosemary called 'sicklemens'. For local holidays we drove up to Lakluk, where there was snow and skiing in the winter, past the famous cedars, now threadbare, or we went to Syria (until I was stopped). We could, if we wished, drive north up the coastal road past Byblos, where we would stop to buy beads picked up on the shore by Michel Lahoud – a young teacher earning 200 Lebanese pounds (£25) a month – and across the Syrian frontier at Latakia. Standing on its crag was the magnificent Crusader Castle of the Crac des Chevaliers; and there was the surprising great Gothic cathedral built by the Crusaders at Tartus. There was the old city of Hama where the giant water-wheels, built by the Romans, creaked all night, still lifting the water from the stream to ducts supplying the town; and where giant cockroaches frequented our pillows. Further north were broad agricultural lands, then Aleppo, with its citadel, and the Baron Hotel, well known to travellers, and managed by Crikor ('Coco') Mazloumian, and his English wife Sally. After Aleppo came the 'dead cities', ruined churches and mansions built in Byzantine times.

Gloria, a collector by nature, was then collecting, besides ancient beads, Roman glass, ancient pottery, and Palestinian and Syrian costumes, which could be found of a high quality. Driving to Aleppo on one occasion, she saw walking along the road a woman wearing a Syrian costume heavily embroidered, fetching the water. Gloria stopped, and through her driver asked if she could buy the dress. They went into the village, and several women brought out their dresses. The commotion attracted a small crowd of men, children and dogs, and Gloria bought a dress. One of the men asked Gloria if she were married, and then how many children she had. She told him four. He looked at her admiringly, and asked how much her husband had paid for her. 'Nothing', she said; and he became very angry. 'For my wife', he said, 'I pay four camels; and she have not one child'.

We never grew tired of Syria, and Damascus became Gloria's market town. She was indifferent to Israeli air raids, and other threats of danger. On an expedition there with American friends, she was out and about, and dismayed to find them cowering in the doorway of the Museum. 'What are you doing there?' she cried. 'Come along, there's an air raid on – prices will be down'.

In Jordan, Amman was struggling to recover from the six-day war. A very large club and games complex had been built. They were proud of the restaurant, very large too, but empty. We cast eager eyes over the vast menu. We asked for one dish after another, but it was not available. Finally we fell back on the *plat du jour*. 'Sorry, no *plat du jour*', said the waiter. 'But you have it here'. 'Every menu has to have a *plat du jour*', he replied. The volume was not there as an indication of the cuisine, but as an artifact. On the way to Amman, we had visited Palmyra with its streets of Roman ruins. Beyond Amman, the dramatic landscape presented us with stupendous views: Petra, its buildings mere facades in the pink rocks, peopled by ghosts, and where we slept in a tomb; Madaba and its mosaics, with a 6th century mosaic map of Palestine; the Crusader fortress at Kerak; and the Wadi Rum, at the far end of which our jeep broke down, and we had to be rescued by the army.

In Gaza, Gloria found some talented girls in the camps and set them to work on embroidery. Dresses, cushions and waistcoats, of remarkably fine quality, were the result. Gaza was a sad area, isolated between the desert and the sea. It contained some brave people, who stood up for their rights: the mayor, the stalwart lady who owned the hotel, and the UNRWA lawyer, Abdul Rahman.

My contract had been to go to Beirut for two years, but it was renewed; and after a summer holiday in England we returned virtually as citizens. There was a brilliant sun again in a cloudless sky, the summer winds were gone, and the temperature and humidity were moderate. The Lebanese were back from Europe, or down again from the mountain. The streets were full of women shopping: new clothes had come from Paris, and furniture from Italy. Mothers were hustling their children from shop to shop to buy new outfits for school; and just when they needed larger shoes, there was not a size 6 or 7 to be found.

Outdoor life – breakfast and lunch on the balcony, swimming in the late afternoons at the beach club, Sunday picnics in the mountains – continued until nearly Christmas. Then came the carol concert, attended by all English-speaking Beirut as a matter of honour. It was conducted by Afif Boulos. I had hired a grand piano, and he sometimes came to us to sing. (On one celebratory occasion Afif, who was rehearsing for *La Belle Hélène*, and had come to the party in his powder-blue costume, was seized by the guests and rolled up in a rug.) The tone of home music-making was raised when the direct descendant of one of Franz Schubert's brothers suddenly arrived at the Austrian Embassy. George Schubert was an accomplished pianist, with the family reputation to keep up; and he brought with him a magnificent Bösendorfer built to his specification.

The social life of Beirut was formidable, and sometimes overwhelming. At a Lebanese cocktail party, a request for 'sherry' was interpreted as for cherry brandy, and we took a small flask of sherry with us, filling our glasses when no one was looking. There were many dinner parties. Ambassadorial dinners, being disciplined ('thrifty' would perhaps be the right word sometimes), were manageable. The invitation would announce '*diner assis* – black tie', timed for a European hour; and as soon as the guests had risen from the table and downed their coffee, they would leave. A Lebanese dinner party was not like that. The invitation would be for 8.30, you would be a fool if you got there before 9.30, and eating might begin at 10.30, *provided* important guests had arrived. If not, we had to wait. For me, the hour was past my bedtime, and all appetite had gone. The large tables would be loaded with Lucullan foods: up to fifty different dishes of *mezze* – 'hors d'oeuvres' would be a poor description of them – to begin with, whole fishes, a smoked salmon (flown from Paris our hostess would tell us), huge joints of meat, salads, French cheeses, Baklawa and other pastries, and – the best of all – apricots, peaches, figs and dates preserved in syrup. There was an air of Imperial Rome about these feasts, which extended to some of the ladies, one of whom, we knew, had a make-up at the French hairdresser's every evening, and another had a masseuse in to perfume her whenever she took a bath. We ate our food standing, or seated about the rooms in small groups, the Lebanese men not talking to the women, but amongst themselves. Our own dinner parties came halfway between the European and the Lebanese. Marie would do the shopping, going to the French sūq for fruit and flowers; our table from Basta seated twelve; guests were invited for '8.30 for 9', and soon found that we meant it; on the other hand we did not expect them to leave at the drop of a *demi-tasse*.

In few Lebanese houses or flats did one see a book. Culture was almost absent from the country, with one exception, the International Festival at Baalbek; and this was so striking an exception that it almost overturned the rule. The Festival was due to the influence and energy of Rose Kettaneh and Salwa es-Said. It had been founded in 1955, and lasted from mid-July to the end of August. Baalbek was 85 kms distant from Beirut, and one either stopped at Zahleh for frogs' legs at the restaurant, or took a picnic supper and a bottle of champagne. The entrance was through a long, vaulted passage, leading to the Temple of Bacchus, which appeared to have been miraculously preserved, wholly intact, through eighteen centuries. The Amadeus Quartet played, and the audience sat, inside the Temple. But performances of ballets, operas and concerts were usually on the steps of the Temple, or in front of the vast Temple of Jupiter, its six surviving columns soaring into the night sky. Performances were timed for 8 p.m. An hour late bugles sounded, the steps were flooded with light, and the performers appeared out of the mysteries of the Temple itself. We saw the Bolshoi Ballet, heard the Chamber Orchestras of Stuttgart, Warsaw and Prague, the Budapest Opera, and Ella Fitzgerald. One unforgettable evening in our first summer we heard both Richter and Rostropovich, with the Leipzig Symphony Orchestra, Rostropovich playing the solo cello part in the second Brahms Piano Concerto. During the interval Salwa es-Said introduced us to Rostropovich, and I had the great pleasure of a short talk with him. When we went to our seats again it was turning cold. We always huddled under a blanket for the second half of those magical evenings.

But after our second holiday in England our return to Beirut coincided with the killing at the Olympic Games at Munich, by the 'Black September' group of terrorists, of two members of the Israeli team, and the seizure and subsequent murder of nine hostages. There were air strikes by Israel against Palestinian bases in Lebanon, and to within thirty miles of Beirut, and raids on camps near Tripoli, in which thirty people were killed. In April, on Gloria's birthday, we had arranged to go to the St Georges for dinner, and see a famous belly-dancer from Cairo, but we had had a party, and decided to stay at home. We should not have got there. Israeli commandos landed from a boat, not far from us, went up the road, killed three Palestinian leaders in their flat, and returned to their boat – unnoticed by the security forces. This gave rise to demonstrations, and accusations of collusion against the Government. Constantly changing as it was, it changed again.

On a morning in May I was at my office desk, and glanced out of the window. A man was running across a wide, open road below me. As I looked he fell to the ground, and remained where he fell. I was puzzled – why should he do that? A moment later my telephone rang – it was Gloria, telling me to go home at once, as fighting had started. Then I understood, and said it was too late. But the office was emptying, and I made a dash for home. The Lebanese army was attacking the armed Palestinians in some of the camps, and a civil war was developing round us. The first objective of each side was to take possession of the roof tops. Palestinian forces had taken over ours, and Lebanese soldiers were on a neighbouring roof, and from time to time they fired at one another. The cook in one of the flats in our block was standing on the balcony watching, and was killed. For a period of forty-eight hours there was fighting all over Beirut, and bombing by Lebanese planes. Then there was a lull for a day or so. Rosemary had already gone to stay outside Beirut with her friends the Kashoggis, and we went into the hills to the Brintons at Chemlan. The fighting and bombing broke out again for a further forty-eight hours, after which the Lebanese army withdrew to barracks. It had made no impact on the Palestinians.

Not long afterwards the time came for us to pack up and leave. There were several parties: our Austrian friends, Elmar and Ingmar Schneider, gave a lunch party for us, but lunch did not start until 5 p.m., as they had to wait for someone; the Joys gave a dinner party, at which, for our benefit, the fare was almost exclusively caviare; and we had eighty or ninety people for cocktails. My colleagues gave me a Melchite icon; we said a tearful goodbye to the Palestinian staff; and left in our white Mercedes.

We drove up the coast through Syria – I had no difficulty in obtaining a visa at the border as a 'tourist' – then along the southern coast of Turkey where, in desolate country, the car broke down, and we were rescued by a kind Turk; and we took ship at Izmir. I thought I had done well for the family by reserving a 'state room' for us; but it turned out to be in the hold, and Gloria refused to go down there. She persuaded the captain that it would be wise – psychologically speaking – to find her a cabin on the upper deck, and she shared this with Rosemary, while I shared my state room for two nights with the cockroaches. Driving up the coast from Brindisi to Rome the ladies thought they would like a swim at Gaeta, and while they were in the water the car was broken into, and every single thing taken except suitcases in the boot: passports, travellers cheques, wallets, watches, brief case, Rosemary's clothes, were all gone. After many hours delay waiting for the police, we reached Rome, with a few thousand lire generously lent to us by a passing German, and Rosemary still in her swimming suit. The Albergo Nazionale insisted that as an old customer I should have the pent-house suite, at a special rate, unaware that I had no money to pay for it. Giovanna Manfredi lent Rosemary some of her daughter's clothes and me some money; and we had a happy holiday while waiting for temporary passports, and replacements for our travellers cheques.

So ended an unforgettable five years: the sun, the sea, the clear air, and the mountain were in our blood, and the hospitable people of the Lebanon in our minds. Rosemary, after two years at the Collège Protestant, left with a perfect French accent, Gloria left with an expert knowledge of the antiquities and crafts of the Middle East, and a number of examples, and I with a broadened legal experience. But the Israel-Palestine problem seemed no nearer to a solution.

XV

Time Present

I HAD thought that on my return from Beirut I should 'retire', as the expression is, and live in the country. That surely was what one did at sixty-seven, without the income to support life in London? We had bought a house with a large garden, amongst trees and fields – strong in the azones one associates with Haywards Heath. But I quickly realised that a life of that sort was not for me: the first bill for the oil-fired central heating convinced me of that. It happened that soon after we had moved in the vicar called, and asked me to deputise for his organist whilst on holiday. How he had learned that I played the instrument I do not know. I put in some daily practice, and earned £6 by playing at a couple of funerals.

I consulted Elwyn Jones and Dingle Foot about my financial plight. Dingle said 'While there's death there's hope'. Elwyn found a seat for me in his chambers in Lamb Building, of which Sam Silkin was the head. Life seemed to be repeating itself, time past to have become time present, and likely to be time future: my earnings coming from playing the organ, and I was trying again to practise in the Temple, this time with a family to support. Lord Denning raised his eyebrows when I told him. After the winter miseries of the three-day week, for which I stayed at the Travellers Club, the Government changed: Elwyn became the Lord Chancellor, and Sam Silkin the Attorney General. It seemed unlikely that I should pick up much, if any, chambers work.

Kenneth Jones, the Legal Adviser to the Home Office, invited me to help there with the cases going before the European Court of Human Rights at Strasbourg. This was the sixth Government Department I had served; and now I found myself 'commuting' for the first time in my life. It was eight miles to Haywards Heath station, and I had to learn to drive a car again. Gloria undertook to give me a refresher course; but it is well known that any attempt by husband and wife to drive a car jointly is bound to break down. A professional was called in; and he would say to me, as I painstakingly followed a milk-float, 'You know, sir, it is not *absolutely essential* to drive in bottom gear.' The important thing at the time was to be able to drop Rosemary at her school in Cuckfield rather than to get myself onto the train. I did both. The only near-disaster occurred when I was sitting on the train. Just as it was starting someone got in, and the proofsheets of the fifth edition of *The Law of the Parish Church*, leaning against the door in a Harrods bag, fell out onto the line. I did not think the emergency justified resort to the thin red chain; and in the evening the station master handed me the bag. I was luckier than T.E. Lawrence, who lost the manuscript of *The Seven Pillars* at Reading Station, and had to write it all out again.

Kenneth Jones was very good to me, but I never came to know him well enough to ask why Clive Parry called him 'Jackety Jones'; or why he kept an encyclopaedic range of footwear on the bottom shelf of his bookcase. There were brogues, Oxfords, shoes with elastic sides, pumps, goloshes and, as bookends as it were, a pair of dwarf Wellingtons – all in black. It was possible, I thought, that the Legal Adviser to the Home Office had duties that took him out in all weathers: to the cenotaph, for example, or to the burial of a Privy Councillor, or even to an open prison. A predecessor of his, Leslie Brass, the Legal Adviser when I was at the Colonial Office, had always worn buttoned boots. I did not much care for the Human Rights work, and felt so lukewarm about one of the cases that Kenneth had to threaten – in the nicest possible way – to lock me in my room until I had drafted the Government's Memorial to the court. Roy Jenkins was the Home Secretary, but I never met him. I heard he struck out sentences beginning with 'And'; I concluded that he had not read the best authors. I spent some days in Strasbourg on two of the cases, and we lost both.

I wrote to the head of the Legal Division at the Commonwealth Secretariat, who was by then Kutlu Fuad; his father had been a judge in West Africa, and Kutlu himself later became a Judge of Appeal in Hong Kong. He asked me for my *curriculum vitae*. I thought this an unnecessary piece of research, and referred him to *Who's Who*. That work may not have been on the shelves of the Commonwealth Secretariat, for Kutlu insisted; and ended by inviting me to start a *Commonwealth Law Bulletin*, to contain information on statutes, cases, and other legal developments in all Commonwealth countries, contributed by the countries themselves. It was an excellent idea. The first issue of the Bulletin contained 50 pages; it appears quarterly, and now, for long under other editorship, it runs to 600-700 pages.

The next thing Kutlu did was to summon a small conference of lawyers to consider ways of training legislative draftsmen in the developing countries. There was a serious shortage, only partly met by the course I had started when at the Commonwealth Relations Office. I asked what sort of legislative drafting would be taught; there were simpler styles than ours. A comparative study was needed. Kutlu obtained a generous grant to enable me to undertake this; and after visiting New York and Ottawa I spent two months in Paris, two weeks in Stockholm, and two in Bonn. Gloria came to Paris with me. We have always been ready to revive our honeymoon on propitious occasions, and this was one of them. I had my work during the day, whether in the library at the Conseil d'Etat, or in conversation with the distinguished lawyers there or in other institutions, all of whom put up with my inadequate French. I formed valued friendships, particularly with Bernard Ducamin, now President of the *Section des Finances*, then the Secretary General of the Conseil. In the evenings I met Gloria for dinner, and we had some memorable meals. Most of us have our recollections of remarkable French meals; but the most remarkable to me was the one I never had. We were looking for a small flat, and were told of one behind the Palais Bourbon. There was a notice displayed, and Gloria left me to investigate. A woman with greying hair, dressed in black, answered my ring. I enquired about the flat; and she led me into a large room, which was an empty restaurant. The tables were laid, with yellow cloths, yellow napkins, cutlery and wine-glasses. There was no sign of any food, or of a customer. But in the far corner was a coat-stand, with a man's coat hanging on it – I think two, an overcoat and a raincoat – and a hat and umbrella. The woman talked – gently, nostalgically, regretfully: she talked only of her dead husband. I made attempts to lead her to the subject of the flat, but to no avail. We stood against one of the tables, as if I were waiting to sit down.

Everything, she assured me, was as he had left it, they were his last *couverts*. She had, *en souvenir*, hung up his outdoor clothes there, when they had been to the dry-cleaners. The restaurant was his memorial. After a short pause she asked if I would sit down, and permit her to prepare a meal for me . . . that was the meal I never had.

In Stockholm I had been recommended to Judge Anders Linquist, the nephew by marriage of Joyce Gutteridge, a Foreign Office lawyer and daughter of Harold Gutteridge, one of our few comparative lawyers. Judge Linquist was waiting for me wearing a 'boater', as he called it, and a red beard; and we immediately struck up a warm friendship. He has been my constant guide to Swedish law, speaking perfect English, and in manner an Edwardian gentleman. At appropriate times he wears a cape or cloak. I told him that I had never seen anyone before who looked like *both* Sherlock Holmes *and* Dr Watson.

The result of all this was *Legislative Drafting: A New Approach*, a comparison of the legislative styles of France, Germany and Sweden with our own, very unfavourable to the last. I had naturally thought of Butterworths as publishers; but Clive Parry reminded me that I had hungry mouths to feed, and thought I should do better with Oceana Publications, of Dobbs Ferry, New York. He gave me an introduction to the proprietor, who happened to be in London for a few days. I went to see him in his bedroom at the Savoy, where he was dressing for dinner, and waiting for his trousers to be pressed. He was not very polite, and did not offer me a good standard of production. I took the typescript to Neville Cusworth at Butterworths, who I knew would produce a handsome volume. They did it in a hurry, as it was needed for a meeting of Commonwealth Law Ministers shortly to take place. To save time I spent a few days at Fakenham in Norfolk, where the printers were, to correct the proofs. The next thing was a telephone call from Kutlu, when we were having tea on the lawn, to congratulate me on the excellent review in that day's *Times*, which – due to gardening – I had not yet read. I had other very favourable reviews. I sent a copy of a summary to Mrs Thatcher, then leader of the Opposition, and to Geoffrey Howe; the latter said he was 'in total sympathy with your approach', and the former was approving, sending a copy to Michael Havers, Lord Chancellor in waiting. None of them, when in power later, did anything to improve our drafting processes and style. Elwyn Jones tried to persuade James

Callaghan, when Prime Minister, to take the matter up, but he was defeated by Michael Foot and Tony Benn, apprehensive about their own legislation. Gerald Gardiner wrote to me to say the book was 'the only serious and comparative study we have ever really had of legislative drafting methods . . . an invaluable contribution to the problem'. Kutlu said it would take twenty years for the book to have effect here. I hope he was right, as time is getting on. The book, now out of print, is well known in many other countries, and has had some effect in Canada and Australia.

Gloria and I had the pleasure of paying a visit to Hull and its University, from which I received, at the hands of Lord Wilberforce the Chancellor, the honorary degree of Doctor of Laws. About the same time, Ian Sinclair, then Legal Adviser to the Foreign and Commonwealth Office, asked me to take over, as Director of Studies, the Government Legal Advisers Course, which I had started in 1964. After a little hesitation I agreed, and I am its Director still.

We decided to return to London, and bought a house in De Beauvoir Square in Islington (Hackney, strictly). The square was built about 1830, and the delicate pseudo-Gothic lineaments of the houses showed gracefully through the general decline. Central heating had to be installed. While this and other work was being done, Franz Osborn's widow June, now married to Jeremy Hutchinson QC, with great kindness let us have the studio cottage behind her house in St John's Wood. It was where Franz had last given me piano lessons. I walked across Regent's Park to my Course, then held in York Terrace, and I received the prettiest compliment I have ever had. One morning calling on June on the way, to pay our modest rent, I trapped my finger in her front door, and was delayed. Apologising to my students for being late, I explained that I had injured my hand when paying the rent. Later, the Indian students came to my secretary to express their concern. 'We did not think,' they said, 'that Sir William' – I had been knighted, at the time the four Beatles received their MBE – 'that Sir William would pay rent; we would have thought he would receive it.'

Now we could send Rosemary to Wycombe Abbey, and off she went, with *her* boater and cloak. We could be sure that she would have as sound an education, and as charming a Headmistress, as it was possible to find. At the school's speech day of 1980 Miss Lancaster began her address by saying, rather coyly, like a small girl announcing the title of a poem she was about to recite, 'I should like to begin by congratulating two of our Governors, one on becoming Archbishop of Canterbury, and the other the Foreign Secretary' (Runcie and Carrington).

Kutlu Fuad wanted me to write a definitive book on the Commonwealth. I was not keen, but I agreed to do so. It was not the fun to write that *Legislative Drafting* had been, and the part I enjoyed best was the first, in which I summarised the constitutional history of the Empire and Commonwealth in 27 pages. I regarded my book as the successor to Roberts-Wray's *Commonwealth and Colonial Law. The Modern Commonwealth* – like my previous book – had to be completed in a hurry, as it was required in time for a meeting of the Commonwealth Law Conference, and some kind friends assisted me at the end. Butterworths again took on the publication, and again responded to the urgency. They invited me, and Gloria as well, to Hong Kong, where the Conference was. On our way home we spent a fortnight in Kashmir, a country of dreamy loveliness. We were the guests of the Governor, B.K. Nehru and his wife Fiori, who kept up Raj standards: the flag was run up by the guard at sunrise, and run down at sunset. We went to Ladakh for a few days, on the edge of Tibet, at an altitude of 15,000 feet. In Kashmir a retired Indian judge told me of the three outstanding benefits the British had brought to India: the English language, the Indian Civil Service, and the Railways. I asked about the Law; but he would not put that above these three.

We had already been to India and Pakistan, and to Nepal, Singapore and Malaysia, as emissaries of the British Council. We had arrived in Kuala Lumpur on a Saturday afternoon, and in our air-conditioned bedroom unpacked our suitcases to loud noises from a racecourse under our windows. It sounded as if we were at Epsom: galloping hooves, excited comments from the loud speakers, and the roaring cheers of a large crowd. We looked out of the window, and down at the extensive racecourse, and the roofs of the grandstands. But the racecourse was empty: there were no horses, no riders, and no spectators, if we believed our eyes and not our ears. We found out later that the racing that Saturday was in Singapore – where they took turns with Kuala Lumpur and I think Bangkok, relaying it by television to the other racecourses, in case anyone wished to take a seat there for the afternoon.

Our move to Islington was ill-judged. Since the war it had been spoken of as an 'up and coming' area – but most of it had not made the grade. There were many newcomers, and there seemed to be no stable population. Young people came, then went. Couples, married or not, were perpetually splitting. We owed our house to the early breakdown of the matrimonial life of the vendors; and next door to us three couples disintegrated and left in a period of three or four years. One of the advantages of the neighbourhood was that it brought us Elsie Welch, who lived nearby, and proved a staunch friend and helper. But it had a growing number of unpleasant features. We could put up with the inquisitive workers looking out of the windows of the factory behind us; the front gardens an eyesore; the Turkish Cypriot a few doors away, who slaughtered his animals in his backyard, and sold the pieces out of his front door. It was the advancing tide of disorderly youth that drove us out. We had no idea what we had done to attract their hostile attentions. We were friendly and generous when they made noisy calls at our front door. First, an impromptu 'pop group' of three, armed with the most persistent of all instruments, the guitar, took its station at bed-time on the kerb opposite our bedroom window. Nothing we could say would move them. A little later on a number of youths took to gathering round the house; and when one evening they appeared with staves I called the police. Finally, one Sunday morning, the *Sunday Times* came through the letter box edged with black. When I opened the door I found it, the porch, and the steps, covered in tar; and there in the street was the barrel, and tar-brush, kindly left by the borough council.

On the occasions when after our return from Beirut we had been to Lincoln's Inn, we had looked longingly up at the windows of our old flat. It had been let by the Inn to a banking organisation, and there seemed no chance of our getting back there. One or two other flats became available, but they went to Benchers. We looked in Chelsea and Kensington, but there was nothing there we could afford. One morning Robin Bridges, still the Under Treasurer of the Inn, telephoned to say that the bank was giving up our old flat, and there was a chance that we might get it back. George Carman, a Bencher, wanted it; one or two friends who were Benchers knew our situation and pressed our needs – especially (I guess) David Renton, who had been Treasurer, and Mervyn Davies; George Carman most generously withdrew; and we were given back our old home.

We were very happy with the exchange of our roomy house in Islington, with central heating, for the circumscribed and draughty accommodation, but the tranquillity, of Lincoln's Inn. Rosemary, who was still at Wycombe Abbey, put up with the small windowless room at the back as a 'bedsitter'. For her 'year off' she went to Washington, and after that to Manchester University. Gloria had just enough room for her collections. Elsie continued to come, and still does, though she and her husband Bob have moved to Potters Bar. I disposed of my grand piano to George Malcolm the harpsichordist, who had by a happy coincidence lived for many years in my studio cottage in Cheyne Walk. I changed to the harpsichord, as more conformable to the environment.

At the conclusion of my recollections do I wish to try to sum up? I do not think so, as that would lead me into a discourse upon present times, which would mean Book II. Rather I have in my mind feelings of thankfulness: that my life is full of years, thanks to the excellent genes of my parents; and, thanks to my wife, family and friends, full of happiness as well.

My sister Hilda is still there in Reading; and has recently translated into blank verse, and published, the long and difficult poem of Marguerite of Navarre called *The Prisons*. Gloria's sons, though in America, remain a strong support to us: Peter is a civil engineer in Houston, Texas; Michael a cardiologist in New Orleans; Jeffrey a journalist in Washington. They come over to see us; and Jeffrey even came to be married in the Chapel of the Inn, by Archbishop's licence, to Carol Adair, while I played the organ. Gloria and I, on the twenty-fifth anniversary of our wedding, gave a dinner party for nineteen in our flat: the company included, besides Hilda and my cousin Dinah, our American family with wives and children, and my nephew Reggie with his wife Susan. Rosemary, who had taken up a career in advertising, was accompanied by her friend Simon Hallgarten. They married; and they too – alas! – are living in America.

It is a benefit to belong to one or two sound institutions; and a little work also helps. The Institute of Advanced Legal Studies in Russell Square, which owes its origin to the foresight of Lord Atkin, my godfather in the law, provides me with a base for work. It is housed now in one of the ugliest buildings in London, and even taximen baulk at it. But one does not notice that from the inside, and it has one of the best law libraries in the country. Research, writing and teaching are open to me; and every year colourful characters from all parts of the world come for tuition and guidance, many of them to my three months course. If I lose patience from time to time, I remind myself that I am a life member of the Polite Society; and of the words in its Code of Courtesy which require me to 'exercise the maximum self-control in all situations likely to test my patience and temper.'

I am a life member of the Travellers Club. The Inner Morning Room – the 'Foreign Office Canteen' – is now out of bounds unless one is accompanied by a lady, like the bar in the Chateau Laurier in Ottawa fifty years ago. Lunch is upstairs in the elegant 'Coffee Room', where coffee is not served. The Duke of Wellington, a foundation member, still presents his iron nose to us from the direction of the fireplace. The room is full of talk and laughter; but anyone wishing to maintain his right to apartness may – politely – do so. The Club's servants are the members' friends; and downstairs in the hall Grafton, the porter, sings gaily behind his window as he marks me out.

Nearby in St James's Square is another institution, the London Library, to which too I belong for life. I drop in there, to take out a book or two, or to join the non-sleeping fraternity in the Reading Room. The silence is ecclesiastical; and the rich store of works of reference is invaluable to anybody who happens to be writing his autobiography.

So home to Lincoln's Inn, of which also I am a life member (we are all members for life). I pass through the narrow gateway, to nods of greeting from Leslie the Chief Porter, and the gatemen. They are harassed at this time of the afternoon by the press of traffic: solicitors in limousines, clients in taxis, dispatch-riders with urgent papers on motor cycles, pedestrians enquiring the way. Gloria slips by on her bicycle. Barristers are coming back to chambers from the courts, through Wildy's entrance into New Square, some still wearing their gowns and wigs (depending on the weather). There is a party of tourists near New Hall; and I hear their guide telling them that 'It looks like a church, really it's the Hall.' The tourists look about them, bewildered. In *A Short History of Lincoln's Inn* Gerald Hurst said that the lay-out of the Inn had altered so little that 'a ghost returning from any year after 1500 would be able to find his way about.'

I see no likely ghost amongst the tourists, and no wonder they appear bewildered. It is not only the lay-out of the Inn that has altered little – little else has altered either – and that constitutes one of its charms. It is governed, as always, by a Council of Benchers, self-electing, composed in the main of judges of High Court rank and Queen's – or King's – Counsel. The numbers of the judges and 'silks' have increased vastly in recent years, so that there is now not room for them all on the Bench; and the Bar presses for yet more of both. The Inn needs a new Constitution, better administration, and a more regular source of funding, perhaps from its members. But I leave these matters on one side.

The Inn shows best as a dwelling-place during the vacations, and at weekends. A stillness descends, and the Inn can have the atmosphere of a medieval college. Gloria and I have the gardens almost to ourselves. Two mallards have arrived, at the right time, in the octagonal basin in New Square. There is croquet on the lawn near Cherry Tree Walk; or we can sit reading in the sun in the Kitchen Garden, where Rosemary once slept in her pram. The beds of red and white roses, and the wide border running the length of New Hall, are brilliant with colour; and the perfect lawns stretch as far as the eye can travel. The Head Gardener, Reg Bennett, is the author of all this beauty, but he is usually invisible. He has a black hat, and may be mistaken for a Bencher. The walnut tree planted by Queen Mary was blown down in the great storm of 1987, and some of the ancient trees as well. The ladies resident in the Inn, on Gloria's initiative, subscribed funds to buy another walnut tree, ceremoniously planted in New Square by Princess Margaret, our Royal Bencher.

On Sunday mornings during term the bell rings us to morning service in the Chapel, built to the design of Inigo Jones in 1623. John Donne, who had been Reader of Divinity, or Preacher, to the Inn, preached the dedication sermon. 'The bell doth toll for him that thinks it doth,' he told us in his much quoted *Devotion*. He meant the passing bell. But we have only one bell (captured at Cadiz in 1596), and if I think it is ringing for me I go to the service. The Prayer Book is virtually the one John Donne used, and the lessons are read from the Bible of James I. The ear thrills to the sonorous language, and to the stirring music from the choir and organist.

On Saturday mornings I go into the Chapel and climb the steep stairs to the organ gallery. After all the years of wandering I have again been granted an organ to play, and it is on my doorstep. For an hour or two I pour out my soul to the music of J.S. Bach. Then, as I descend the worn staircase, dark and narrow as a tomb, I am confronted by a digital clock fixed to the wall. The minutes flash by in red: 12.01 . . . 12.02 . . . 12.03 . . . Pinned up is a scrap of paper, probably the work of my friend Alf, the Verger, bearing a pencilled communication:

'WHEN A BENCHER DIES
1. TURN KEY TO MANUAL
2. PRESS FUNERAL BUTTON
3. TURN KEY TO AUTO
BELL RINGS FOR 30 MINS'

A rite of passage, exclusive to Benchers, on auto.

As I lock the Chapel door behind me I think of that other line of our poet's: 'No man is an island, entire of itself'. No, indeed. But Lincoln's Inn, for century after century maintaining within its walls its forms and customs, and its charms, perhaps is.

Index

Aleppo, 194
Alice, 21-23
Altitude, effect on politics, 179
Appelbe, Ambrose and Ann, 141, 152, 155
Appelbe, Valentine (Thomas), 141, 145
Archbishops, 12, 14, 23, 59, 63, 166, 173, 205, 207
Archer, J. B., 89, 92, 93
Articles, service under, 15-20, 22, 23
Ascent of F6, The, 72
Atkin, Lord, 26, 29, 207
Avory, Mr Justice, 32

Baalbek, 197
Ballistics, experiments in, 7, 10
Bar, English, 24-35
Bar, Palestine, 43-55
Beadle, Hugh, 180
Beckett, Eric, 61, 121
Beirut, 187-199
Bentwich, Norman, 46
Bevir, Anthony, 60
Bicycling, 3, 9, 13, 21, 34, 35, 69, 208
Birkenhead, Lord, 18, 26
Blom-Cooper, Louis, 181, 185
'Blue Cockatoo', 78
Bombs, 70, 71, 76, 77, 79
Bontempelli, Massimo, 153-155
Boothby, E. B., 128
Bottomley, Arthur, 171, 172, 179, 181, 182
Boulos, Afif, 188, 196
Brinton, John and Josie, 192, 198
British Institute of International and Comparative Law, 176, 183
Brooke, Anthony, 82, 87, 93
Brooke, Bertram, 82, 91, 93
Brooke, Charles, 82, 95
Brooke, Charles Vyner (Rajah), 82-95
Brooke, James, 81, 82, 84, 95
Brooke, 'Princesses', 84, 94
Brooke, Sylvia (Ranee), 83-87, 89, 90, 92-95
Bryant, Arthur, 82
Bundy, Leslie and Eve, 41, 51
Burns, Alan, 97, 102
Bushe, Grattan, 57, 60, 61, 63, 65, 79
Butler, R. A., 137, 159, 160, 161, 164, 165, 169, 170, 172
Butterworths, 29, 203, 205

Canada, 98, 99, 202
Canberra, 177
Carman, George, 206
Cassim, 37, 38, 41, 54
Cassin, René, 148
Cecilia, 28, 29, 31, 33
Central African Federation, 158-163
Chamberlain, Neville, 66, 67, 68
Chelsea, 139-142
Chinese, 85, 87, 89, 90, 91
Christine (Chapman), 187, 188, 193
Church-going, 4-6, 209
Churchill, Winston, funeral, 172
Clarke, Christopher and Lavender (Herbert), 132, 141
Clergy, 'unusual', 4, 12

Cockin, Charles Irwin, 16, 17
Cohen, Andrew, 60, 176
Colonies, difficult geography of, 57-59, 105
  Indian verdict on, 109
  law in, 58, 60, 205
  standing up for, 102-109
Colonial office, 55, 56-67, 68, 80, 89, 93, 96-98, 100, 102, 103, 111, 112, 130, 132-134, 158, 159
Commonwealth Law Bulletin, 202
Commonwealth (and Empire) Law Conference, 177, 205
Commonwealth Legal Advisory Service, 176
Commonwealth (Relations) Office, 98, 132, 133-135, 157-170, 171, 172, 179-181, 184
Commonwealth Secretariat, 201
Conti, Mario and Marisa, 126, 150
Conti, Valeria (Nievo), 150, 153
Cooper, John Spyvee, 16, 19
Cooper, Priestley, 16, 17, 23
Copland, Judge, 40, 41, 42, 52
Corderoy, George, 70
Costley-White, Cyril and Elizabeth, 71, 72, 100
Cotran, Eugene, 181
Country life, 200
Creech Jones, Arthur, 97, 98, 100
Cusworth, Neville, 203
Cynthia, 140
Cyprus, 50, 166, 167
Cyrene, 124
Cyriax, James, 69, 72, 140

Dale, Emily Hilda, 4, 7, 11, 35, 79, 144, 165, 181, 207
Dale, Gloria, 179, 181-183, 185-188, 193, 194, 198, 199, 201, 202, 205, 207
Dale, H. J. (Jim), 71, 181
Dale, H. R. (brother 'Reggie') and Pauline, 2, 10, 14, 35, 43, 56, 64, 68, 71, 185
Dale, M. R. (nephew 'Reggie') and Susan, 71, 181, 207
Dale, Rose, 1, 2, 4, 5, 35, 71, 79, 144, 152, 165, 185
Dale, Rosemary, 185, 187, 193, 199, 201, 204, 207
Dale, Rev. William, 1, 4, 10, 15, 23, 35, 55, 56
Damascus, 189, 193, 194
Dancing, efforts at, 33, 43, 53, 89, 186
Darwin, Henry, 167
Davies, Mervyn, 206
Dawson, Christopher, 85-87, 91-93
'Decolonisation' 111, 158
de Gaulle, General, 173
Denning, Lord, 172, 176, 183, 200
Devas, Anthony and Nicolette, 78, 140
Devlin, Patrick, 70
Devonshire, Duke of, 157, 169
Diacono, Ronald, 126
Dior, Christian, 144
  his models, 146
Divorce, 72, 74, 118
Dixon, Charles, 133
Dominions Office, 63, 80, 134, 157
Donne, John , 173, 209, 210
Drafting, 117, 123, 138, 202, 203
Ducamin, Bernard, 202
Duncan, Harold, 57, 58, 79
Dunn, Arthur, 20, 71
  Emily, 1, 9, 20, 66, 71
Dyaks, Land, 85
  Sea, 85, 90, 91

Eastwood, Christopher, 60, 71
Eccles, David and Sybil, 137, 138, 147, 148
Education, Ministry of, 135, 137-139, 147, 148, 156, 157
Emma, 64, 68, 72, 74
Enahoro, Chief, 163
English, Basic, 138
English, Philip and Pat, 126
Evans, Vincent, 186

Fair weather drinking, 132
Farwell, Mr Justice, 32
Felici, Mario, 126
Field, Winston, 160, 171
Files, treatment of, 76, 97
Finn, Gloria. *See* Dale
Finn, Jeffrey and Carol, 181, 207
Finn, Michael, 181, 207
Finn, Peter, 181, 207
Foot, Dingle, 163, 181, 184, 185, 200
Foreign (and Commonwealth) Office, 121, 156, 167, 174, 186
Franks, Oliver, 71, 139
Fuad, Kutlu, 201, 202, 204

Gadda, Carlo Emilo, 175
Gahan, Frank, 31, 33-35, 54
Gambia and Rio Pongas, Bishop of The, 58
Gammans, David, MP, 91-93

Gardens, demands of, 6, 7, 11, 56, 203
enemies in, 7, 13
Gardiner, Gerald, 172, 176, 177, 204
Garner, Savile, 157, 184
Garton-on-the-Wolds, 12, 56, 165
Gaselee, Stephen, 59, 60
Gaza, 41, 62, 192, 195
Giblain, Philippe and Laurence, 187, 188
Gibraltar, 111
Gold Coast ritual murders, 97
Gordon Smith, David, 162
Gore, C. H., 9
Government Legal Advisers Course, 176, 204, 208
Graham, Kathleen, 106
Grand Jury, 30
Gratiaen, Noel, 163, 181
Gray's Inn, 23, 29, 64
Hall, dinner in, 24-29
H. C. Richards Essay Prize, 29
Holt Scholarship, 23
spendthrift – tipping, 24, 26
Great Parallelogram, The, 131, 137
Great War, The, 8
Greenfield, Julian, 160, 161

Haircuts, 174
Haley, Tim and Dorothy, 115, 120
Halifax, Lord, 30
Hall, George, 83, 93, 97
Hama, 194
Hancock, Tony and Cicely, 125, 131
Harpsichord, 207
Harries, V. P., 69, 143
Healy, Tim, 26
Herbert, Alan and Gwen, 80, 98, 132, 140, 141, 173
Hewart, Lord, 32
High Commission Territories, 134
High Commissioner, Palestine, 41, 51
Hiroshima, 178
Hobson, John, 163
Hogan, Michael and Patricia, 98, 178
Hogg, Quintin (Lord Hailsham), 34, 147
Home Office, 76, 200
Hone, Ralph, 157
Hong Kong, 178, 205
Hooper, C. N., 115, 116
Horses, unruly, 62, 65, 82
Hudson, J. W., 14
Hull, practice in , 30, 31
Human Rights, 134, 201
Hutchinson, Jeremy and June (Osborn), 204
Hutton, Noel and Virginia, 168, 176
Hymers College, 9

Illustrated London News, 74, 82
In Defence of Colonies, 102
Inns of Court lecturers, 27
Institute of Advanced Legal Studies, 207
Islington, 204-206
Israel, 188, 192, 197
Italy, 175, 179. *See also* Rome

Jaffa, 36-55
Janatone (Jana), 144-147
Japan, 178, 179
Jean, 74
Jerusalem, 38, 42, 43, 46, 191
YMCA, 43, 46, 191
Johnson, Dr, on Education, 143
Jones, Elwyn and Polly, 177, 179, 184-186, 200
Jones, Kenneth, 200, 201
Jordan, 192, 195
Joy, Peter and Rosey, 192, 198

Kantlin, Hetty, 98-103, 110, 122, 137
Kent, Harold, 139, 156
Kentridge, Sydney, 185
King David Hotel, 39, 98, 191
King Edward VIII, abdication, 63
King Idris al Sanussi, 115
Kirkbride, Sir Alec and Lady, 120
Kuala Lumpur, racing in, 205

Lascelles, Gerald, 149
Law Officers Department, 184, 185
Law of the Parish Church, The 29, 69, 139, 181, 201
Lawrence, D. H., 28
Lawrence, T. E., 166, 201
Lawson, Harry, 23, 76, 143
Lebanon, 187-199
Legislative Drafting: A New Approach, 203
Leon, Harry, 31-33, 35, 52, 63, 79, 154
letters to, 40, 44-49
Leonard, Dinah, 207
Leonard, T. H., 2, 9
Le Quesne, C. T., 31
Libya, 112-129, 130
elections, 119
Ministers, 114, 115, 117-119, 123, 127
Treaty with, 126
Lili, 72, 73
Liesching, Percivale, 133, 135

Lincoln's Inn, 151, 152, 153, 165, 173, 182, 183, 206, 208-210
Linquist, Anders, 203
Listowel, Lord, 111
Logan, Douglas, 69, 78, 143
Loire Valley, 144, 145
London, a British capital, 131
London Library, 208
Longhurst, Mervyn, 138
Lousada, Anthony and Jocelyn (Herbert), 132

MacBryan, G. T. M., 83, 89
Macmillan, Harold, 157-159, 163, 164, 176
Madzimbamuto, 184
Mahony, W. F., 14
Makarios, President, 166
Malays, 85, 87, 93
Malta, 111, 124
Manfredi, Nicola and Giovanna, 150, 151, 199
Manningham-Buller, Reginald, 159, 160
Marie, 192
Masino, Paola, 154, 155
McNulty, Anthony, 96, 110
Meals, memorable, 39, 91, 126, 136, 146, 202
Megarry, Robert and Iris, 69, 71, 78, 143
Menzies, Robert, 177, 180
Modern Commonwealth, The, 205
Moffat, Virginia, 142
Montrose, J. L., 23
Mootham, Orby, 157
Morle, P. B., 29, 30
Morrison, Herbert, 70, 121
Moss, Derek and Marguerite (Wolff), 141, 155, 175
Motoring, 2, 3, 121, 135-137, 144-146, 201
Mouflet, Gem, 33, 35
Munich Pact, 67
Muntasser, Mahmoud, 114, 116, 119, 120, 126, 127, 128
Muntasser, Omar, 128, 165, 166

Napier, Albert, 126
Nehru, B. K. and Fiori, 205
Newfoundland, 98
Noble, Peter and Elizabeth, 142
North-Eastern Circuit, 30, 31
Northern Rhodesia, 134, 158. *See also* Central African Federation
Nyasaland (Malawi), 112, 134, 158. *See also* Central African Federation

Orange cricket, 104
Organ, blowing, 5, 27, 32
  playing, 5, 6, 10, 13, 14, 18, 20, 23, 27, 32, 41, 62, 185, 200, 209
Osborn, Franz and June, 78, 79, 94, 204
Oulton, Derek, 172
Outdoor exercise, eschewed, 15, 18
Oxley, Humphrey, 133, 157

Palestine, 36-55, 60, 97, 191
Palestinian refugees, 188, 189
Papo, J, 37, 41, 42, 45, 49, 50
Pardi, Francesca, 151
Parker, Hubert and Loren, 151, 152, 177
Parliamentary draftsmen, 138, 167
Parry, Clive, 143, 166, 176, 201, 203
Patch, Blanche, 166
Payne, Harold, 15
Pearson, Colin, 70, 76, 78, 143
Peck, Jasper and Olwen, 96, 100, 118, 152
Piano, playing, 5, 9, 71, 78, 79, 120, 122, 123, 126, 141
  tuners, 122
PLO, 193
Polite Society, The, 208
Pollock, Mr and Mrs, 43, 51, 53
Powell, Enoch, 160, 184
Preston-in-Holderness, 1
Profumo, John, 163, 164
'Public interest', 75, 113

Qasem, Anis, 123, 124, 128

Ramadan, 41, 43, 123
Red hair, 3, 21
Rees-Williams, David, MP, 91-93
Reid, Jim and Edwina, 142
Renton, David, 206
Richardson, 'Richie' and Doreen, 35, 37-39, 45, 49, 52-54
Roberts-Wray, Kenneth, 57, 58, 79, 80, 112, 128, 133, 156, 157, 205
Rogers, Philip and Heather, 60, 79
Rome, 65, 149-151, 153-155, 199
Rumbold, Algie, 162
Russell, Alison, 62

Saba, Hanna, 147, 148
Sachs, Eric and Peggy, 151
Salisbury, 62
Salisbury (Harare), 161-163
Salter, Clive, 30, 31
Sandys, Duncan, 157, 164, 166-170
Sarawak, 81-95, 103

Sarawak (*contd.*)
  Astana, 85, 87
  breakfast, 89
  Cession Bill, 89, 92, 93
  Council Negri, 89, 92, 93
  Governor, assassination of, 93
  healing properties of, 92
  Rajah. *See* Brooke
  Ranne. *See* Brooke
  Supreme Council, 89, 93
Saunders, J. V., 9-11
Sciatica, cure for, 70, 71
Scott, Frederick Arthur, 16
Sedgwick, Romney, 174
Sheep, speech-eating, 124
Shehab, Raja, 187
Shuckburgh, John, 62, 94
Simpson, Rev. C.E., 28
Smith, George H., 16, 17, 20
Smith, Ian, 162, 171-173, 179, 180, 183
Snowdon (Mount), 28
Solicitor's bill, 101
South Africa, 163
Southern Rhodesia (Zimbabwe), 134, 158, 171, 172, 179-181. *See also* Central African Federation
Steel, Henry, 183
Stewart-Jones, Diana, 72
Stewart-Jones, Richard, 71
Stickling, 70, 76
Stock, Capt. Reginald, R. N., 14
Storrs, Ronald, 38
Subhi, 38, 50, 53
Superannuation, 175, 182
Supply, Ministry of, 69, 70, 74-76, 80, 143
Sursock, Linda, 192
Sursock, Yvonne (Cochrane), 192
Swazliland, 113, 134
Swift, Mr Justice, 29, 32
Swinton, Lord, 133, 135, 160
Sydney, 177
Syria, 189, 190, 194, 198

Tabet, Anna, 193
Taormina, 66
Tel Aviv, 42, 47, 53, 54
Tennant, Mark, 159, 164
Territorial Army, 18
Toulouse-Lautrec, Countess, 78
Travellers Club, 156, 174, 200, 208
Tristram Shandy, 88, 144, 155
Trust accounts and bookkeeping, 19, 20
Trusted, Harry, 46, 113-115
Tunisia, 127
Turtledove, S., 37, 41, 49, 53

UDI, 179
Unesco, 126, 147, 148
United Nations, 112, 114-116, 126, 179
United Nations Relief and Works Agency for Palestine Refugees (UNRWA), 186, 192
United States, 99, 100
  lecture tour, 102-109

Vézelay, 145
Victoria Falls, 161

Wallace, Miss, 10
Wartime, 68-80
  rations, 71
  walkings, compulsory, 76, 80
Waterfield, Tony and Honor, 71, 135, 144
Watson, Duncan, 159
Weeks, Hugh and Constance, 141
Weinberg, Stanley and Bambi, 115, 116, 161
Welch, Elsie and Bob, 206, 207
Welensky, Roy, 159
Wharram-le-street, 10-12
Wharram Percy, 10-12
Whistler's House, 71, 74
White, Dennis, 93
Wife, Italian advice to, 182
Wilson, Harold, 171, 172, 179, 183
Witch of Dorking, 34
Wyndham, John, 74, 75

Yoko Ono, 186